ROUND AND ABOUT IN GIPPSLAND

Other books by Jim Connelly

Tom and Anna on the Trail: the Case of the Missing Schoolgirl (2014)

Tom and Anna in Danger: the Case of the Disappearing Dogs (2014)

Tom and Anna take a Chance: the Case of the Bungling Bird Bandits (2015)

My Folk: Four Hundred Years of Hazards, Tooths, and Connellys (2015)

Mountain Boy (2016)

Talk of the Town: Warragul/Drouin (2017)

Talk of the Town (2): Warragul/Drouin (2018)

Pickled Pieces and Rollicking Rhymes (2019)

Wild Beauty (2019)

ROUND AND ABOUT IN GIPPSLAND

Jim Connelly

Copyright

Copyright Jim Connelly 2020

Paperback ISBN: 978-0-6486658-1-6

All rights reserved.

No part of this publication may be reproduced or transmitted in any form or by any means, electronic or mechanical, including photocopying, recording, or any information storage and retrieval system, without prior permission in writing of the copyright owner.

A CIP catalogue record for this book is available from the National Library of Australia.

First published in Australia 2020 by

James Timothy Connelly

12 Craig Street,

Warragul, Victoria, 3820

AUSTRALIA

ajcon@dcsi.net.au

Oh, I love to be by Bindi, where the fragrant pastures are,
And the Tambo to his bosom takes the trembling Evening Star,
Just to hear the magpie's warble in the blue gums on the hill,
When the frail green flower of twilight in the sky is lingering still,
Calling, calling, calling to the abdicating day:
Oh, it fills my heart with music as I loiter on my way!

Frank S Williamson, 1912

Book Cover

Fabric art: Anne Connelly

Production: Craig Braithwaite, aussiepics.

Contents

Bairnsdale	11	Morwell and Churchill	171
Bruthen, Buchan, Nowa Nowa	21	Nar Nar Goon, Tynong, Garfield	181
Bunyip and Longwarry	31	Neerim South	191
Cann River	41	Omeo	201
Corner Inlet	51	Orbost	211
Drouin	61	Phillip Island	221
Hayfield	71	Rosedale	231
Koo Wee Rup	81	Sale	241
Korumburra	91	Stratford	251
Lakes Entrance	101	Trafalgar and Yarragon	261
Lang Lang	111	Traralgon	271
Leongatha	121	Walhalla	281
Maffra	131	Warragul	291
Mallacoota	141	Wilson's Promontory	301
Mirboo North	151	Wonthaggi and Inverloch	311
Moe and Newborough	161	Yarram	321

Round and About in Gippsland

FOREWORD

The title of this book indicates that it is to be taken as a free-wheeling personal account of Gippsland.

It is not a historical work. It is not a travel journal. It is not a gazetteer. It is simply what is in my mind as I reflect on people and places I know intimately.

I ask that readers might read the whole work, and not merely the chapter that deals with their own town and district. Any one chapter is necessarily somewhat 'bits and pieces', but a consistent perception of Gippsland as a whole will emerge from the book taken in its entirety. Or so is my belief.

My hope is that readers will be interested in my comments and will set their own thoughts against mine. Those who disagree with me may be challenged to write their own book!

This book went to press before the coronavirus pandemic had fully gripped our land. I'm sure that Gippsland will never be the same in the post-pandemic world. This may be a last glimpse of Gippsland in the sweet times that preceded the new age.

Jim Connelly,
April, 2020.

Bairnsdale

"Its inhabitants are among the nicest and most hospitable people whom you could possibly meet". So says Mrs John Forrester in her novel, *Myrtle*. The poet, EJ Brady, claims that "Bairnsdale is to East Gippsland what Mecca might be to the pious Arabian". Hal Porter, on returning to the place of his childhood, writes, "My first sight of Bairnsdale strikes me breathless and still and smaller'. Marie Pitt wrote an ode to Bairnsdale:

> *Bairnsdale by the Mitchell side!*
> *A city still you are to me*
> *When night brings peace that day denied,*
> *And dreaming sets my spirits free ...*

All over Gippsland I find there's great warmth towards Bairnsdale. Earth has many a noble city; Bairnsdale, thou dost all excel!

Maybe, however, we're turning into a nation of grumps. I chanced upon the 2019 survey of customer satisfaction done by the Shire of East Gippsland. The Shire is more than the city of Bairnsdale, of course, though Bairnsdale has one-third of its population. Only 51% of residents said they were satisfied with the overall performance of the Shire. Perhaps that low figure reflects the general loss of trust in authority figures and organisations. However, it's well below the average across the State for rural shires, and has been dropping in recent years.

Satisfaction with the Shire is a good deal lower in Paynesville and Lakes Entrance than it is in Bairnsdale. That's something I've found in many parts of Gippsland – places beyond a shire's central town feel neglected. It's an after-effect of the amalgamation of shires that was pushed through by the Kennett government in 1994. Resentment still lingers. Heyfield thinks they are hard done by in comparison with Sale; Drouin thinks Warragul is favoured at their expense; Paynesville believes Bairnsdale takes the cream. So it goes on. There are clear advantages especially in cost-saving in having larger shires, but we've lost some of the feeling of allegiance and sense of local responsibility we used to have. I don't think we've ever recovered from the enforced 20% rate cut that went with amalgamation, and now rates are capped as well. Local councils are continually squeezed for cash and many worthwhile projects go by the board, especially in the environmental area, where ratepayers often think expenditure is less warranted.

Bairnsdale was proclaimed a city in 1990. A city is "a legally defined entity with a structured system of governance, and which has delegated powers to oversee local legislation as well as the management of resources. Citizens of a city are responsible for electing representatives who form the local government that provides local services". When the then-four-year-old city of Bairnsdale became part of the amalgamated Shire of East Gippsland in 1994, were not these powers handed over to the Shire?

If so, the question arises as to whether Bairnsdale should still be called a city. Just asking!

Bairnsdale's best feature is Main Street, which is actually the Princes Highway. A street so wide needs a broad median strip, and this has one, with fine gardens and the Cenotaph and Band Rotunda. St Mary's Catholic Church on Main Street is the biggest tourist attraction. People come in busloads to see this red-brick Romanesque building and the beautifully adorned walls and ceiling of the interior. It's Bairnsdale's Sistine Chapel. The Michelangelo was an unemployed Italian man, Francesco Floreani. Floreani had had formal art training in Italy, but was reduced to painting houses and working on local farms before the Parish Priest, Father Cornelius Cremin, put him to work on this commission, paying him three pounds a week for his work. It took three years. The whole of Catholic iconography and theology is spread out in complex imagery.

To the south of the business centre is the Macleod Morass. You don't notice it as you drive through town, and many don't realise it's there. It was once a rich food source for the Gunaikurnai People. The Tatungalung Clan lived in this locality. The morass covers a huge area, and is naturally a freshwater swamp. The opening of the sea to the Lakes system years ago meant that salt water at times invaded these lands so they've built dams, levees and floodgates to preserve the freshness of the water. There are boardwalks and bird hides to help visitors get close to the wild life.

Bairnsdale is a retirement town. About a quarter of the residents are over sixty-five, and that means some 4,000 people. There is a long list of community groups in the town catering for these people. The Senior Citizens' Centre has a busy programme of euchre, 500, hoy and bingo. Newcomers are invited to "come along and have a chat and a laugh". Probus clubs covering the older cohort proliferate throughout Gippsland. There are two in Bairnsdale and three in some other towns, four in Traralgon.

The University of the Third Age is a more recent starter. Bairnsdale U3A began in 1987 and was the first one in Gippsland. It now has more than 400 members. They run dozens of different courses, six days a week. U3A has no stipulated age limits, but, like Probus, is for retired or semi-retired people. Courses can be on a multitude of topics, the key element being that rather bringing in outside instructors all courses are run by the members themselves. I know a lot of people are put off by the word, 'University', in the title, but in fact there are no entrance qualifications and no tests or exams. My experience with U3A is that it's a lot of fun as well as being a place to learn new things. There are eleven U3A branches in Gippsland – at Bairnsdale, Bass Valley, Drouin/Warragul, Latrobe Valley, Lakes Entrance, Mallacoota, Mirboo North, Phillip Island, Sale, Wonthaggi, and Yarram.

Bairnsdale has had more famous residents than any other Gippsland town. Matilda Emilie Bertha Kalkstein and Herman Bredt, both from Prussia, were married at St John's Church in Bairnsdale in 1872. Later in her life, Bertha became a socialist agitator and feminist, known throughout the land. Her husband, Herman, was Bairnsdale's shire secretary. They had two daughters. One married Jack Lang, afterwards the extraordinary Premier of New South Wales at the time of the opening of the Sydney Harbour Bridge (de Groot and all that!). As a boy, Lang lived just outside Bairnsdale for four years and went to school here. The other daughter married Henry Lawson. 'Nuff said!

You might add to the list of notable people from Bairnsdale Sir Albert Lind, Alfred William Howitt, Sir Keith Hancock, Bill Wannan, David Williamson, Sir Lance Townsend, Leigh Hobbs, and Hal Porter, not to mention the sportsmen and women. Hal Porter's book, *The Watcher on the Cast-iron Balcony*, tells much about Bairnsdale in the years between the Wars, but is really an autobiography, so it is more useful to go to his *Bairnsdale: portrait of a Victorian country town*, in which he casts the town against the backdrop of national and world events. The Bairnsdale Library, once Porter's place of employment, has a space set aside in honour of him. It's called the Hal Porter Study.

For some folk from Paynesville, Bairnsdale is the place you drive through to get home. It's not easy being a considerable town in the shadow of a larger one. Ask the people of Inverloch! Well, coming from the west, you *can* get to Paynesville without going through Bairnsdale. The wiseheads turn off the highway just after Stratford, and go across country through Perry Bridge, Meerlieu, and Bengworden, and join the Paynesville Road at Eagle Point.

At Eagle Point you see the famous silt jetties, going for miles out into the waters of Lake King. These are true delta formations, but instead of spreading out like at the mouth of the Nile the particles of sand and mud are deposited by the Mitchell River in a long thin line. That happens because Lake King is very still, whereas the Nile flows into the rough waters of the Mediterranean. If you're looking for all the good Gippsland topsoil washed away over the last few hundred thousand years, then here's where you'll find it. These are the finest silt jetties in the world. You may have been taught about them when you were in school.

Paynesville was once a sleepy fishing and boating hamlet, but it has grown in size and character over the last fifty years. People have more money and more fast cars, and an inbuilt desire to be beside the sea. Artificial waterfronts have been constructed through a canal system like on the Gold Coast. Property prices are so high the agents don't put them in their advertisements; they just put 'Contact Agent'. However, there are many ordinary homes and ordinary people in Paynesville. One special building is the Anglican Church, dedicated to St Peter, the patron saint of fisherfolk. The spire is a lighthouse, the pulpit is a ship's prow, the font is a ship's bell upturned, and the sanctuary lamp a ship's navigation light. As you sit in church, you see the water through the big windows behind the altar. Must be hard to concentrate on the sermon!

If some people pass through Bairnsdale to get to Paynesville, others pass through Paynesville to get to Raymond Island. You take a ferry across the narrow strait. The locals reject the idea of a bridge. They'd rather have the island the quiet backwater it is now rather than open it up to mass invasion by speed merchants and loud music freaks. There is a wondrous charm to living on a small island. In the case of Raymond Island, the charm is increased by the koalas. You're likely to find one in your back yard. They're everywhere. There's nothing quite so patronising as a koala serenely gazing down from its comfortable seat in the fork of a tree. However, there are too many of them here. A regular count is made, with the help of volunteers. The numbers are declining, and so is the koalas' food supply. Some have died from starvation.

The railway line from Sale to Bairnsdale runs through Montgomery (station closed), Stratford Junction (closed), Stratford, Munro (closed), Fernbank (closed), Lindenow (closed), Hillside (closed), to Bairnsdale. How the service is depleted! And the steam trains were as fast as the diesels, someone told me. Lindenow is the centre of an intensive vegetable-growing industry. All the produce is trucked out. Why such a concentration of vegetable-growing here?

Excellent soil, plenty of available water, yes, but there's another factor: like attracts like. Industries will agglomerate around each other. Take potatoes at Thorpdale as an example. Or asparagus at Koo Wee Rup. Or, in the past, chicory on Phillip Island. Or sugar beet near Maffra. A particular industry develops; services build up catering to it; marketing falls into line. So, by a delicate process of agri-commercial chemistry these nodes of production come to exist. Then a marketing reputation completes the process. These days, the industry is hi-tech and hi-speed. Vegetables may be hydro-cooled, packed scientifically, loaded into refrigerated vans and sent off to far-distant places within the day.

Bairnsdale City is moving out into its surrounding land as are many of our Gippsland towns. Some organisations in or near the centre of town figure out they can sell where they are and build bigger and better premises further out, where the population is moving, anyhow. The churches often find this an attractive idea. Thus, in Bairnsdale, the Uniting Church has moved out to a fine new building across the river in Lucknow. Similarly, the Church is now out in the 'suburbs' in Traralgon and Warragul, too.

By the time you get to the Uniting Church you're on the Great Alpine Highway, heading for Sarsfield and Bruthen. Here the 2020 fires raged as never before. They were so extensive I can't do justice to their severity in these few pages. I marvelled at the stoicism and wit of one Sarsfield fire victim. He lost his home in a

Queensland cyclone some years earlier. Here he lost his home again, totally destroyed. His response: "We've nothing left. It's just charcoal. Unless I go into the charcoal business, I don't know what I'm going to do."

If we turn off the Great Alpine Road at Lucknow and keep on the Princes Highway, we pass the Patties Foods headquarters on our left. Patties began in Lakes Entrance, but the business moved here early in the piece. It's a great Gippsland story of a family business being built up to become one of the world's biggest of its type. Not that it's owned locally any more. In 2016 they sold out to a Private Equity firm.

Further on we come to Nicholson, Johnsonville, and Swan Reach. One of the best features of Nicholson is the railway bridge. Engineers drool over it. Engineers are like that. One of my engineer friends used to park his car under the cooling towers at the old Yallourn Power Station and gaze at them for hours. This bridge at Nicholson was built during the First World War and represents the cleverest of engineering at that time. The river bed is 25 metres below the surrounding land so the approaches are very long - 180 metres long. The bridge is made of timber, steel and concrete in almost equal parts. Each span is an art work in itself, and the diagonal timber bracing gives an overall lacework effect. It is indeed a thing of beauty. As soon as it was finished, the first train to Orbost rolled over it. The trains run no more; the bridge stands in silent reproach.

Johnsonville may be a one-shop town, but that shop – the general store - is famous. The celebrated black stump stands outside. It's not quite original. There are other Black Stumps at Coolah and Merriwagga in New South Wales, Blackall and Mundubbera in Queensland, and Cowell in South Australia. No-one knows for sure where the term, 'beyond the black stump' originated, but the meaning is clear. If you're beyond the black stump you're in very remote and uncivilised country. Johnsonville? Never!

Swan Reach, nestling on the Tambo River, is the third link in the road chain beyond Bairnsdale – Nicholson, Johnsonville, then Swan Reach. Swan Reach played an important part in the fire storm of 2019 - 20. When the authorities made the decision to evacuate the whole of East Gippsland, Swan Reach was set up as the evacuation centre. Hundreds of tents were rigged up, stretching in rows as far as the eye could see. This was also the CFA base camp and control centre for the whole operation. Order amidst chaos!

Bruthen, Buchan and Nowa Nowa

Let's begin in Nowa Nowa. It's easy to speed through without a sideways glance, but a stop-off here is very worthwhile. We like to drive down to the Lake a couple of hundred yards off the highway for our driver-reviver. We're nearly always alone there. Most people don't realise that Nowa Nowa is actually on the Gippsland Lakes. The Nowa Nowa arm of Lake Tyers reaches right here to the town, where it forms the estuary of Boggy Creek The fresh water of Boggy Creek meets the salt water of Lake Tyers right here. No surprise then that the café and caravan park in town is called Mingling Waters.

Mingling Waters is the unofficial centre of town. The Jack Ramsdell Gallery is here. Jack Ramsdell ran a saw mill in town in the golden age of milling. On the side he polished gems and sculpted wood. His work is now housed here, along with his masterpiece, the Big Tree Root – the massive root system of a messmate that once stood here. It grew on a thin layer of topsoil above a hard rock layer, so the roots grew outwards instead of down. Now, it's been dug up holus-bolus, put on its side, and polished like burnished gold. It looks like a depiction of RA, the ancient Egyptian sun-god, and that's what it's named. It's claimed to be number 149 on the list of Australia's Big Things. I don't doubt it, but I couldn't find it in any of the lists I consulted. However, for the record, I could catalogue the ones from Gippsland that were on the list I found:

> *The Big Cigar, Churchill*
>
> *The Big Cows, Newhaven*
>
> *The Big Dead Fish, Fish Creek (on top of the pub)*
>
> *The Big Koala, Cowes*
>
> *The Big Pheasant, Tynong*
>
> *The Big Tap, Cowes*
>
> *The Big Wave, Newhaven*
>
> *The Giant Worm, Bass*

That's my final Gippsland 'BIG' list. No correspondence will be entered into! Nowa Nowa proclaims itself as an art town. There's been an annual 'Nude Nude Nowa Nowa' art show and even a whole house given over to art in every room. The town has a number of excellent walking trails. They take in the Boggy Creek gorge, the Stony Creek trestle bridge … and the petanque piste! The sculpture walk along the water has some wonderful silhouette figures looking for all the world as if they had leapt straight from an ancient Greek vase.

The Nowa Nowa State School has 50% aboriginal students. It's been steady at about that figure for a long time. Aborigines in East Gippsland make up a higher percentage of the total population than anywhere else. There are 1,290 people of aboriginal or Torres Strait origin in East Gippsland Shire. That's 2.7% of the total population, and compares with Latrobe City 1.6%, Wellington 1.5%, Baw Baw and South Gippsland both 1.0%, and Bass Coast 0.9%. Of East Gippsland's 1290 indigenous people, 538 are under eighteen – a good augury for the future. The Nowa Nowa Community Health Centre provides services specifically aimed at overcoming health disadvantages commonly suffered amongst koorie folk. All ATSI people are eligible for an annual health check. The aim is to detect early signs of disease and introduce treatment programmes.

The 2020 bushfire hit Nowa Nowa "like a tornado" and most people evacuated. Although the damage was widespread, the town was spared. Those who remained were in a parlous situation. All power and communications were lost so they were unaware of the official warnings being given by the ABC. They were literally and metaphorically in the dark. The store owner provided a free barbecue for everyone. They feasted on the food from the defrosting freezers.

The train line to Orbost came through Nowa Nowa in 1916. From Bairnsdale, it looped through Bruthen before arriving here. Buchan missed out on a rail service despite its pleadings. When black marble was discovered at Buchan, it had to be carted by road to Nowa Nowa and then railed to the city. Buchan was once a household name throughout Victoria because of its marble. In 1937, the Herald reported:

We have all seen its beauty in the Public Library and in those immense black pillars that look so imposing in the inner shrine of the Victorian War Memorial. All over Melbourne Buchan marble is adorning public buildings and business premises.

Tynong granite covers the exterior of the Shrine; Buchan marble lines the interior – sixteen vast pillars that encircle the most hallowed area within. They were quarried as blocks 5.7 metres long and almost one metre square. Each one weighed ten tons. Fourteen draught horses were assembled to cart each block separately to Nowa Nowa. Getting the load out of the quarry was the greatest problem. The Herald reporter breathlessly described the operation:

A crane was installed at the quarry capable of lifting 10 tons, and the first pillar was loaded. To back the waggon down into the quarry and lift the slab was easy enough. The problem was would the team pull the loaded waggon out. Every man stood by to watch that operation. The teamster climbed onto the footboard and gathered up the reins. The horses themselves seemed to know that an extra effort was required of them. They pricked their ears and looked round nervously. Every man was tense when the teamster called 'Giddup'. Every horse went slowly into the collar as good horses do. The teamster shouted encouragement. The horses bent to their great task. They dug their hooves in the earth and, with their noses almost on the ground, strained to their limit. Slowly the waggon moved to a low cheer from the onlookers. The teamster shouted again; the horses strained to it with their chains tight and the spreaders quivering, Out of the quarry lurched the waggon, and the rest was comparatively easy.

Marble is a rock formed from limestone. The limestone here is formed from sediments laid down beneath the sea that covered this part of Gippsland 350 million years ago. Limestone is porous and can be eaten away by water. In marble the limestone has been heated and compressed so that the crystals are realigned and the substance becomes 'rock-hard'. So it isn't surprising that close to the Buchan marble deposits there should be limestone caves where the soft rock has been dissolved to form immense caverns.

The Buchan caves were opened up soon after the turn of the twentieth century. The name most associated with the process is Frank Moon. He discovered the Fairy Cave, then named his daughter 'Fairy'. When Fairy grew up she named her son 'Cave'! The story goes that Fairy and her fiancé wanted to marry inside Fairy Cave. Permission was denied, but they had the keys and went ahead without it. The caves are very spectacular. Only their distance from Melbourne has prevented them from being more widely-known. The Buchan Caves Reserve is now jointly managed by Parks Victoria and the Gunaikurnai Land Management Board.

In normal times (sans bushfires and viruses) there are walks and picnic places … and kangaroos!

The 2020 fires swept through here. Buchan was at the centre of the inferno. Twenty-six houses were destroyed. One man lost his life. People from further out – from W Tree and beyond – evacuated to Buchan, and had to withstand a terrifying ordeal at the height of the fire storm. Many took refuge on the football oval "listening to the bangs of gas bottles and pops of stockpiled bullets in burning houses". There are many stories of disaster, bravery, and stoicism yet to be recorded. That stoicism and will to recover was highlighted when the Buchan Cup race meeting was held at Canni Creek just a month after the devastation of the fires. The judge's box was burned and most of the running rail. The winning post was half burnt away. It was a superb gesture of defiance and the will to go on. Thousands came in a show of support.

From Buchan the road goes on to isolated settlements at Murrindal, W Tree, Butcher's Ridge, Gelantipy, Wulgulmerang, and Suggan Buggan before sliding over the border into New South Wales. Just before Wulgulmerang, you can turn off through the Snowy River National Park and head over McKillop's Bridge, then through Deddick, Amboyne Crossing and Tubbutt to link up with the Bonang Highway at Bonang.

W Tree has become a place specialising in human and ecological harmony. One of the locals describes it thus:

> *W Tree has a small vibrant community of about 85 people. The valley is the home of two eco villages and one Tibetan Buddhist centre. ... Mt Murrindal is one of those eco villages. ... It consists of 5 houses built around a veggie garden and an orchard, surrounded by the Australian bush We live in a sacred land, a land protected by the ancestors of those who walked it since the beginning.*

Bruthen was on one of the early routes from the Monaro down into Gippsland. McMillan passed through here in 1840, and there's a monument to him in the main street. The first run was stocked in 1845, a time when some of our large towns westward and southward were still a smile on the face of their father. Again it was gold, however, that gave the impetus to Bruthen's development, as a supply town to the Omeo and other diggings. Before the Tambo silted up, small vessels including steamers were able to push up to Mossieface, just below Bruthen. One traveller of those times has described how the river was so narrow in places that the passengers would punt the vessel from the banks, at the same time pushing aside vegetation that overhung the narrowing stream.

Diggings arose and disappeared in quick succession. On the Haunted Stream, out from Tambo Crossing, a find was made in the 1860s. It followed the usual pattern of a rush to find alluvial deposits, a falling away, then the coming of reef mining. Many strange stories have come out of the Haunted Stream. One character in the early times was Ballarat Harry. He and his partner headed off to Omeo. The partner returned alone. Ballarat Harry was never seen again. All fingers pointed to the surviving man, but at the inquest an open finding was recorded. The spice in the story, however, is that Ballarat Harry was said by many to be, in reality, Roger Tichborne, heir to the Tichborne fortune in England. That *did* hit the headlines

Another dramatic story came out of the Haunted Stream in 1892. A "DIABOLICAL MURDER" there caught the attention of the nation. By that time the settlement was known as Stirling and had dwindled away until there was only a handful of buildings left. In the middle of the night a huge explosion rocked the whole settlement. Five pounds of dynamite had been detonated under the floorboards of a hut directly beneath where a man was sleeping. He was blown to smithereens. In that small circle, who could have done it and why? The whole country was riveted, but no one was ever convicted. Like the case of Ballarat Harry, it remains a Gippsland mystery.

All eyes were on Bruthen on another occasion. In 1958 an Air Force Avon-Sabre jet fighter was over Bruthen at 40,000 feet when the engine flamed out. The pilot, Flt Lt Ralph Oborn, jockeyed the craft down to 600 feet and managed to steer wide of the town before ejecting safely. It's claimed that this was the first successful aeroplane ejection in Australia. Oborn came to earth about three kilometres north of Bruthen. The local farmer gave him a cup of tea and rang the RAAF base at Sale! The nose cone is mounted in the main street of Bruthen as a memorial, and an account of the crash recorded on a plaque. The plaque was sponsored by the local undertaker!

Whenever we drive east, say going to Canberra through Cann River and Bombala, we have a moral choice to make when we reach Bairnsdale. Should we take the high road or the low road, through Bruthen or Lakes Entrance, through the quiet village of Bruthen or the fleshpots of the Lakes? It's the same distance either way through to Nowa Nowa. Today, we leave Lakes Entrance for another day and take the Bruthen road. This means going through Sarsfield. We had friends here once. Like many others, they built their own home amongst the trees. When the fire struck in December, 2019, Sarsfield was at the eye of the storm. Houses, crops, machinery, sheds, fences, and livelihoods were lost. A flower farm was destroyed – fifteen years of work and 15,000 plants. "There's no use moping around," the owner said. "You've got to move on and be positive."

From Sarsfield to Bruthen there are rolling hills and sweeping vistas. The road keeps in touch with the old railway line, now a rail trail. Then comes Wiseleigh, a gatepost to Bruthen itself. There are few places in Gippsland that have such a welcoming feeling as Bruthen – a wide green street as you drive in, shady trees, a pleasant shelter and garden seats, timber houses, shops with wide lattice-worked verandas supported by green pillars, modest business premises that don't shout out at you, and the war memorial. They like to keep their old buildings here. The general store was built in 1860, the Post Office in 1890, St Matthew's Church in 1892. Fairy Dell outside the town is a renowned beauty spot, though the fires have played havoc with this country. It will take years before the former glory is restored and the birds and animals which suffered so grievously re-colonise their territory.

They do allow some new things in Bruthen from time to time. There's the Bullant Brewery turning out boutique beers. Must have some sting in them. And be warned. There is a coven of geocachers in the district. I had to look that up. It seems these people hide things, then put the GPS location online. Other geocachers use their app and their GPS devices to find the cache, open it up, sign their name, and leave it there for others to find. They love it, these geocachers. I must try it!

Bunyip and Longwarry

Bunyip is a charming town, indeed 'a city set on a hill'. Like many of our towns, its earliest days were less agreeable. In 1878, at the time of the opening of the railway, a reporter from the old 'Argus' put his feelings this way:

> *On the whole the situation is very desolate, and the traveller tempted by railway timetables to run down into Gipps Land, will be strongly persuaded when he steps from the train into the open space which has been hewn out of the Bunyip forest to postpone his visit, and hasten back to Melbourne ...*

Nowadays the situation is reversed. The traveller scurries back to Bunyip after his or her visit to the metropolis!

Things changed for the better over the next decades. Compare this report in the Bunyip and Garfield Express of January, 1923:

> *The great stretch of swampland provides a continuous feast for the eye. In spring, the dominant note is the yellow of the wattles and this is soon followed by the alternative vivid green of the potatoes and the gold stretches of hay or stubble. Autumn gives us the dark tones of the ploughed fields and the pale gold of the ripened maize. It is a delight on a cloudy day to watch the purple cloud shadows speeding across the flats and the south westerly storms sweep across*

> *it with long trailing lines of rain, and depart lit with rainbows over the Drouin hills.*

Dull would he be of soul who could pass by a sight so touching in its majesty! Of course, the Swamp had been drained during the interim and small farmers tilled fertile soil where previously the bunyip lurked.

The bunyip is a mythical creature which dwelt in swamplands and waterholes, ready to devour unwary passers-by. The myth is found in many parts of aboriginal Australia. Today, it would be referred to as an evil spirit. I have heard the idea that the bunyip is an ancestral memory of the diprotodon that in truth did roam these parts. The word, 'bunyip', has seeped into local idiom. In early New South Wales the settlers with pretensions to class superiority were contemptuously called 'the Bunyip aristocracy'.

There's another secret of the Swamp that I alone have been privy to – up to now. The wonderful old stager, Bumper Gee, once told me when he was an old man and I was a young boy that in the days when the Swamp was in process of being drained the Bunyip fire engine, horse-drawn, was called to a fire on the still-dangerous ground out of Bunyip. It got off the hard track and sank in to the swamp, and remains there, totally covered, to this day. There'll come a time when a curious farmer will uncover some rusting machinery beneath his topsoil that will set his mind a-wondering.

Modern Bunyip, population about 2,500, has the trappings of a much larger town. There are two hotels for a start, the 'Top Pub' and the 'Bottom Pub', good educational and health facilities, and a highly-regarded Aged Care nursing home and hostel, 'Hillview'. Alongside Hillview is what I regard as Gippsland's most picturesque church. St Thomas's Anglican Church dates from 1902. It is built of timber in the Scandinavian style and is beautifully and appropriately appointed outside and inside, truly 'casting a dim religious light' as John Milton would put it.

In 1926, bushfire came close to burning down the township of Bunyip. Flames licked at the walls of St Thomas's. These fires were amongst the most damaging Gippsland has ever experienced. Hundreds of homes and timber mills were destroyed; Noojee was burnt out; thirty-three people died, including two tin miners, separately, in their isolated camps in the hills to the north of Bunyip.

Tragedy is never far away. In 1967, the township of Bunyip was rocked to its core when five of its young men, team-mates in the football club, died, together with the pilot, in an air crash near Daly Waters in the Northern Territory. I know men who still find it hard to talk about it today. One of the victims was Mike Breheny, captain and coach of the team. "Nothing was ever the same again," said his sister. A memorial stands at the entrance to the Bunyip football ground. I'm glad to report that the Club has won several premierships since that 1967 disaster. One earlier premiership, in 1939, was quite out of the ordinary. It was won when the opposing grand-finalist, Garfield, failed to turn up. They'd been told the match was off because of the drenching rain. You can't believe everything you hear!

Many of our smaller communities have their local Hall as the centre of their world. I can think of no other place in Gippsland where the Hall is so important in the lives of people than at Tonimbuk. Over the years it's served as church, school, dance hall, meeting place, and recently as the Recovery Centre from bushfire. Tonimbuk began to register as a locality when a Village Settlement scheme began in the 1890s. Even though the settlement failed after just a few years many people stayed on. They worked in the timber industry, distilling eucalyptus oil and orcharding until each of these industries diminished or petered out over time. Tonimbuk is now known for small scale cattle and horse activities. People are attracted these days not so much by job opportunities – after all, they can easily travel elsewhere to work – but by the lifestyle.

That Jindivick lifestyle has been menaced in recent times by two grave threats. The first is bushfire. West Gippsland has been described as one of most fire-prone regions in the world. Experience has proved the truth of that. For Tonimbuk the most recent fire attack was in the first days of March, 2019, when the Bunyip State Park fire wiped out the Tonimbuk community. By great fortune the Hall itself survived. The houses that were saved survived by the heroic work of CFA crews. One family came back to their home to find everything gone but the house itself. On the door a note, obviously written in haste, had been stuck: 'Your house was saved from the crew of Berwick'. We know what they meant! Since then the Hall has become the centre of the recovery effort for everyone in the district. Government, Shire, and local outreach services, formal and informal, have been conducted at the Hall. Blaze Aid immediately swung into action, headquartered at the Bunyip Football Ground. At the time of writing, very few of the fire victims have been able to rebuild. Government support packages have lagged badly. Many believe this has become a forgotten fire because of the overwhelming nature of the fires a year later. I note with a sense of grim irony that the name, 'Tonimbuk', comes from the aboriginal word for 'burn' or 'scorch'!

The other threat is to the Mount Cannibal Flora and Fauna Reserve. Properly speaking, Mount Cannibal is at Garfield North, but the threat comes from Tonimbuk which adjoins it. For some years a large overseas company has been working to establish a granite quarry close to the base of Mount Cannibal which would impinge seriously on the amenity of the reserve and on the ecological health of both flora and fauna. On average, 1,500 people visit Mount Cannibal each week. Two groups have been representing local residents in their strenuous efforts to oppose the granting of a licence to the company. They are the Friends of Mount Cannibal and the Save Mount Cannibal group. A third group has recently started up. Their arguments are built around noise (blasting), dust pollution, light pollution, introduction of foreign weeds, loss of green wedge land, deleterious effects on native wildlife, loss of lifestyle amenity, and truck movements. Hundreds of B-Double trucks would be operating into and out of the quarry each day. The matter is still unresolved.

It's hard to realise that Longwarry, now standing in the midst of smiling pasture-land, was to begin with a major centre of the logging industry, the largest in all Gippsland. Magnificent stands of mountain ash and stringybark grew close by, while narrow-gauge tram lines brought logs, by horse power or sometimes steam power, over longer distances to the mills and to the railway. The tramway to Harry Nash's mill in the Black Snake Range snaked twenty-nine kilometres in length. It was so far out that it took a day to take the timber in and another day for the return. The timetable always allowed for the drivers to be in town for their Saturday night spree! Sending sawn timber to Melbourne in the great building bonanza of the 1880s was the reason for the establishment of the town. Mike McCarthy has calculated that in total 486,000 tons of timber were sent out of the Longwarry railyards. The tramway system bringing in the timber operated, he tells us, for over fifty years, until 1933. McCarthy believes this may be a longer span than anywhere else in Australia. A copy of McCarthy's book, *Settlers and Sawmillers,* should be in every Gippsland home. The story it tells is of the essence of Gippsland.

With the forests cleared, the dairy cow came into her own. A co-operative butter factory began operations in Longwarry in 1921. It sold out to a private company in 1972, as is the way of most co-operatives. Bonlac, who eventually took ownership, closed the plant in 1999. Phoenix-like it arose some years later as the Longwarry Food Park, a division of the foreign-owned Parmalat. Again, like the Phoenix, it arose from the ashes of a major fire in 2012 when over-heated milk powder smouldered, burnt and exploded. Since then the factory has been a local success story, concentrating on milk powder, long-life milk and cream cheese.

The Longwarry shops, unlike Bunyip and Garfield, straddle the railway line. The Post Office and shops are on the northern side of the line, while the hotel and Hall, school and football ground are to the south. Something of a population boom is going on here, as with every town along this part of the line, although most development is on the south. Closer to the hotel than the store! The population of Longwarry and its environs in 2006 was 1187; in 2016 it was 2004. That's an increase of over 800 or 66% in ten years. Baw Baw Shire is faced with providing infrastructure for similar population increases all along the spine of the Shire. It faces a mammoth task, and will need huge support from government.

As you drive from Longwarry along the Drouin road, you pass the saw mill run for long years by the Proposch family and the air strip alongside. Both Longwarry landmarks. Going on, the road climbs quite steeply. The trains, taking a slightly different route, have cuttings built for their greater ease. Three million years ago a fault developed in the earth's crust along this line. To the east, on the Drouin side, the land rose up; to the west it sank to form the Koo Wee Rup Swamp. Today we call this line the Heath Hill fault scarp. The geologists get quite excited about it. As I drive up the hill I think about the rocks below and wonder if they're still grinding against each other. Wait till I get to the top, please!

Heading north out of the town along Sand Road (now bitumen) we reach the highway. A lot has been going on here. After much community action, an overpass was built to avoid the previously-dangerous intersection. Two Caltex fuel and food stops lie on either side of the flyover. A huge cattle sale complex has been planned for nearby, arousing a good deal of local opposition. People in Warragul grumble, too, as this development would mean the closing of the Warragul saleyards that have been a feature of local life for a century. Development always comes at a cost. Unfortunately the cost is often borne by a few individuals, not the whole community.

Past the flyover and still heading north, we reach the Old Princes Highway, now, without much traffic, a delight to drive along, turning right past the Longwarry North Hall, and then left and northwards again towards Labertouche. If we choose we could swing right and pick up the historic road to Jindivick, Jackson's Track. Labertouche, however, is straight ahead. Labertouche is named for Peter Paul Labertouche, who was Secretary for Railways in the boom period of the 1880s. Ironically, the place named after him never had a railway. Labertouche was a highly respected figure: he was "popular with all classes and possessed an extremely amiable disposition". He spent the last part of his life with one arm after a shooting accident.

Labertouche has historically had several large properties, some with city owners and run by local managers. It is very exposed to bushfire, and was severely affected in the 2009 Black Saturday fires and again in 2019. The local recovery and support effort was magnificent, from individuals in the community and from local government. Disaster often brings out the best in human nature.

The Labertouche Caves are notable in being granite caves rather than the much more common limestone caves. They're both popular and fiercesome. Cavers are faced with swiftly-flowing water, huge boulders, narrow crevices and darkness. Not for the faint-hearted. Two men were lost here in 2011 and spent forty uncomfortable hours before being rescued.

North of Labertouche we come to country that is very familiar to me: the Black Snake Ranges. My father worked for the Forestry

Commission in these hills for twenty years, and I often stayed with him at his bush camp on the slopes of Gentle Annie. On top of the mountain was the fire lookout tower. My dad would climb the mountain each morning in the fire season, then up the ladders to the cabin perched on top. If he spotted a fire he would ring down to the base camp and give the compass bearing. From there the information was radioed through to headquarters at Neerim South where the location would be cross-checked with other reports to determine the precise location of the fire. I remember the call signs. "VL3BJ calling VL3AL. Over," the operator would say, then wait for the reply. No two-way radio in those days. It was a hard life for these men - away all week in their very rough huts, living on basic rations, working on fire spotting, keeping the roads open, measuring the logs on timber trucks to assess the royalties, and being on call for any emergency that might arise, including fire-fighting. Apart from their workmates the only others for miles around were the tin miners, eccentric men living alone in even more basic circumstances, hoping one day to strike their El Dorado. Most died a lonely death in the forest. Some died in bushfires. The Gippsland bush can be very unforgiving.

Cann River

Unless you live there, Cann River is a long way away. It's 444 kilometres from Melbourne, 582 kilometres from Sydney, and 383 kilometres from Canberra. To go by public transport from Cann River to Melbourne, by bus, then train, takes seven hours, give or take a few minutes. But then, the folk from Cann River don't spend much time thinking about Melbourne ... or Sydney ... or Canberra. The further you are from a metropolis the more you're caught up in your own local affairs and the greater you find community spirit to be. Yet the outside world is forced on the people of Cann River because of the constant stream of travellers through their town. On the other side of the coin, most of these travellers hardly give a thought to the town itself; for them it's just a wayside place to fill up with petrol or buy a pie. No wonder the locals stick together so resolutely.

I've always loved Cann River. The Cann Valley is like all Gippsland farmland should be – deliciously fertile and green, and bordered by true-blue eucalypt forest. Then you come to the town, and if you can shrug off all the advertising signs, you have an attractive group of street buildings. The prettiest place in town is the little church at the far end of the street. Most people who head up the Cann Valley Highway would miss it. It's perfect – white picket fence, lych gate, a stained timber building, set back from the street front a little, with shady trees, not shouting at you, but inviting you in. The other place I'm very fond of is the Bush Nursing Centre. In a place without a doctor, the Centre has awesome responsibilities, but they handle everything that comes to them with professional aplomb. I know. I went there once with a tick bite. The wretched critter was beginning to eat its way into my insides until the nurse there kindly gave it its comeuppance.

Cann River is the jumping off point for one of Australia's most famous spots. Captain Cook was not the first European to hit upon Australian shores, but he was the first to discover and chart the east coast, and it was his voyage that led to British settlement. On 20 April, 1770, the second-in-command of Cook's ship, the *Endeavour,* Lt Zachary Hicks, sighted the coast at the point now named after him. Point Hicks is almost due south of Cann River. Sadly, Hicks died of consumption on the voyage back to England and was buried at sea. If you go to Point Hicks, you must go through Cann River. It's a dirt road, and you have to walk the last couple of kilometres. A lighthouse was built here in 1888. It's different from others you might have been to. It's concrete for a start, and the staircase is iron, adhering to the outside walls, not a central pillar as with most lighthouses. The area was badly burnt in the destructive bushfires of January, 2020. At the time of writing, it's not clear if access to Point Hicks is still open.

Those fires were particularly fierce around Tamboon, nearby. The Cann River drains into Tamboon Inlet. On the day of the fire, the situation was so horrendous that the fire was creating its own weather system – huge internal updraughts of heated air, with shards of vicious lightning. Tamboon has no permanent residents, but about a dozen people were there at the time of the fire attack. They survived by clinging to the waterfront. Ordinarily, Tamboon Inlet is a fishers' paradise, black bream being the chief prize. Like many water areas around the coast, the Inlet is cut off from the open water in dry seasons, when it can be rather clogged with weed. But the setting is glorious – deep water surrounded by dense forest ... and very still!

Back on the highway, if we trace our way westward along the highway from Cann River, we get to Tonghi Creek, then through the Lind National Park. Off the road to the north is Club Terrace. This little place was once a goldfield and a throughway to the goldfields at Combienbar and further north. I was amazed to discover there is a 'Friends of Club Terrace and Combienbar' group online, with nearly 600 members! How these small towns continue to tug at the heart of folk whose families once lived there. Club Terrace and Combienbar were badly burnt in the recent fire storms, though fortunately there was no loss of life. I came across an account of Combienbar, written in 1931, but describing the scene in 1911. It gives an insight into the difficulties of life in those times:

> *The valley, set between high, rugged hills was then a most isolated place. The only means of communication with the*

outside world was by a bridle track 14 miles long over the range to Club Terrace. ... I left Orbost with buggy and pair one sunny morning in July, 1911, our equipment consisted of two saddles and bridles, an axe, and a rope, and two bags of chaff in case of need for the horses. For food ourselves we had to rely upon three hotels in the huge, remote district we were to traverse and upon the hospitality of settlers. ... The Princes Highway was then only a vision. If I remember rightly there was then but one motorcar in Orbost.

Today there's a good road into Combienbar from Club Terrace, following the Bemm River upstream. When you come to the junction of the Bemm and the Combienbar River, you go either up the Combienbar to Combienbar itself or continue up the Bemm to the Errinundra National Park. The last time we were at the National Park it must have been spring because the waratahs were in full bloom. Their bright red florets lit up the understory beneath the eucalypt canopy. It was stunning. I've read later that the name, 'waratah', means 'seen from afar'. They certainly are. On the same trip we saw a protester camped high up on a platform built into the branches of a huge mountain gum. It was the time when environmentalists were engaged in a strenuous campaign to save the old-growth forests of the region. The movement is well-organised now and has achieved most of its early aims. One effect of the 2020 bushfires has been to once again open up the future of the logging industry to furious debate.

Pushing further westward along the highway, we come unexpectedly to the Bellbird Hotel. "We had been driving for a few hours, saw this pub in the middle of nowhere and popped in for a well earnt beer," someone wrote on Facebook, and that's been the experience of many travellers. We stayed the night here once. After the meal the cards came out and we joined fifteen or sixteen others sitting round in the bar playing euchre. The prize went to a couple who'd come up for the evening from Bemm River, twenty miles away. Next morning we had a look at the tunnel – three round culverts, actually – they've dug under the highway to allow long-footed potaroos to cross safely. The results have been disappointing. The potaroos prefer to dodge the cars on the open road, it seems.

Some really big timber has come out of here. Take, for instance, this newspaper story from 1941:

> *Three yellow stringybark trees, which grew within 20 feet of each other, passed through Orbost. They were fallen by a Bairnsdale contractor for the defence authorities for use as aerodrome wireless poles. They were taken from a gully near the Bemm River at Bell Bird. Each weighs approximately six tons, and will be sunk 14 feet in the ground. The contractor, who said that he had marked them out 15 years ago as giants, said that in his experience they are the best three "sticks" to have come out of the forest in*

Gippsland. The poles were 85 feet in length [26 metres – six metres longer than a cricket pitch!]

Sydenham Inlet is similar to other estuaries along this coast in that the entrance tends to be blocked by shifting sands. It is now kept open to prevent flooding in nearby low-lying land. The artificial opening is often made several times a year. Fishing has long been important in the Inlet for both professionals and amateurs. Conditions have not always been easy, but the results worth the while. From 1916, we read that:

> *The late rains have opened the entrance to the lake and two fishing craft have come in, the Ruby and the Maria. Both crafts are running regularly to Cunninghame* (Lakes Entrance) *with full freights of fish. Messrs Croft and Gilbert are making great hauls and Messrs Morgan are kept busy with a four horse wagon carting to Marlo. The quantity of fish in the lake is extraordinary and the fishermen are having no trouble in getting as many as they want.*

Sydenham Inlet was a long-time food source and gathering place for the indigenous inhabitants. When fish stocks in the Inlet were high neighbouring tribes were summoned and great gatherings took place. These were very important in indigenous culture. Abalone was harvested here. Bruce Pascoe, in *Dark Emu*, explains that the first Europeans couldn't stand the taste of abalone. They boiled it, so no wonder! They called it 'mutton fish'. It was only when they learnt from the aborigines to cook it gently in its shell over hot coals they discovered its superb taste. These days there is a strict limit on how many abalone can be taken – three a day for each person, with a maximum of twenty-four in a year. The inspectors keep a close watch. In one recent case a Sydney man was gaoled for six months and banned from abalone fishing for ten years. He had 120 abalone with him when arrested.

Cann River folk sometimes speak of their home town as a 'café town'. It's not a title many places would want. Socially isolated, yet a transit town. These are issues that are inevitably faced by the school. There's only one school. It runs across all ages, so is called a P-12 college. With a very small enrolment – fifty or sixty in all – it is both culturally limited, yet wonderfully caring. Everyone knows and understands everyone else. The staff stay for years. But there is quite a high drop-out rate before Year 12. Parents are often unemployed, largely because of the closure of timber mills in recent times. Despite such difficulties, schools like this can develop a powerful esprit de corps, and from everything I've seen this is the case at Cann River.

The children from Noorinbee School, seven kilometres up the Monaro Highway, come in to the College in Cann River for some specialist classes. There's only a handful of them. Many people have taken a fond glance at the Noorinbee school as they've sped by on their way to Canberra. It's beautifully placed in its forest clearing. Alongside it is the original school, now on the National Trust heritage register. The citation reads as follows:

> *The former Noorinbee School, constructed in 1899, is historically significant at a regional level as a near original example of a parent-built school leased by the Education Department while still being used for community purposes. Although once a common practice in remote areas, particularly in north and east Gippsland, intact examples of parent built school-halls are rare, especially located on their original sites and used for school purposes. The building also has great local significance as an early centre for community life in the district.*

Both Noorinbee and Cann River were severely impacted by bushfires in January, 2020. Heroic tales have been told of the battle to save both places. They were at the epicentre of the Gippsland fire tragedy. Fighting the fires was only the first of the troubles. Roads in and out of both places were closed for safety reasons after the main danger had subsided. The residents of Noorinbee were most affected. Many had evacuated first to Cann River and then further afield. With the road closures they were unable to return to their homes for many days, causing them extreme stress. Some were very vocal in their complaints. The authorities, in such cases, are bound to put safety first, of course, safety of their own personnel as well as the public's. The particular danger after the fire had passed was from falling trees along roadsides. Of those who died fighting the Gippsland fires, one – Bill Slade from Wonthaggi - was killed by a falling tree near Omeo.

The road north along the Cann Valley Highway is one of my favourite drives in Gippsland. You get intermittent glimpses of the Cann River, sweeping vistas in some places and close forest in others, together with outposts of settlement. It's our practice to pull into a little roadside stop about twenty miles north of Cann. (See how I use the local lingo!) It's marked on the road as 'Beehive Falls', but it's easy to miss. Immediately off the road you have a sandy beach on the river, a perfect spot for a break. If the weather's good and the road firm and you have time, you can drive on another mile or so to the Beehive Falls themselves. We did it once, in a two-wheel drive car. It's worth the trip. The water cascades down, pure as crystal. Driving further north, you're getting into what's been described as the most remote and inhospitable region in Victoria, though you don't get that feeling from the highway. The Coopracambra massif is the source of many of the creeks and rivers that plunge towards the coast. There are no roads, only timber and fire-fighting tracks through the bush, then, further off the road, nothing. Just the wilderness. And its denizens.

As we zoom across the state border into New South Wales, we little think of the herculean efforts that led to the establishment of this boundary. When Victoria separated from its mother colony in 1851, the eastern boundary was fixed as a direct line between the headwaters of the Murray River and Cape Howe facing the Tasman Sea. Easy! Except that that line went through some of the most rugged country in the continent. Two men had the task of surveying the line – Alexander Black, who later became the Surveyor-General of Victoria, and Alexander Allan. They took the best part of two years, from 1870 to 1872. A series of cairns was built along the route, which you can still find today. Officially it's known as the Black-Allan Line. Curiously, due to legal wrangling, the line was not confirmed and gazetted until 2006, when a ceremony took place near Delegate, where the line crosses the Bonang Highway. The two State Governors shook hands across the dividing line.

Corner Inlet

I have to admit that I'm a land creature, primarily. There's no salt in my blood, so when I think of that part of Gippsland around Corner Inlet I think first of Foster and Toora rather than the Inlet itself and the little ports that front it, Port Welshpool and Port Franklin. In that, I'm doing an injustice to the facts of history, as it was the sea that dominated the opening up of this region to white settlement. The whalers and sealers knew this wild southern coastline before any settlers appeared, and when a permanent foothold *was* made, the sea was its lifeblood. The shipping lines from Corner Inlet were quickly established, first with Sydney and Hobart, then increasingly with Melbourne. In a perceptive comment, Cheryl Glowrey has written:

> *In order to understand the strategic importance of Port Albert and Corner Inlet to the merchants we need to view it from the sea and realise that at this time Gippsland was more connected to the north and south than to the west, where natural barriers of mountains, forests, rivers and swamps limited overland routes.**

In reading the history of Gippsland, I'm constantly amazed at how quickly the natural resources of newly discovered places were exploited, and how shrewd merchants were in getting goods to market and supplies into the new settlements. The story of the settlement of the region has been well documented by many writers, from George Cox, an early churchman, through John Adams and Patrick Morgan, to Cheryl Glowrey. The most tragic part of the story is the high cost to shipping and human life brought about by the dangers of this coastline before the days of lighthouses or other navigational aids. Jane Lennon, in her essay in *Earth and Industry*, has pointed out that three schooners were wrecked on the Corner Inlet coast within twelve months in 1847, while between 1860 and 1900 twenty-three more came to grief on these same shores.

The first wreck occurred before any settlement was made – and remains the best known of all. The *Clonmel*, a paddle steamer bound from Sydney for Melbourne hit the sands of the island named after her in January, 1841. There were eighty souls aboard (as they say) – 42 crew and thirty-eight passengers. Picture the scene! The vessel was travelling at 10 knots (18 kilometres an hour) and weighed 500 tons (old tons!). It was the middle of the night. Without warning, with everyone asleep, they ploughed into the sand. However, everyone got to shore, fortunately with some supplies and shelter, like Robinson Crusoe. The ship's whaleboat set out the next day, with seven crewmen, to seek help. After several hair-raising adventures they got to Melbourne and a rescue vessel eventually picked up the stranded party. I can't help but think of the seventy-three people waiting on that barren and inhospitable shore, week after week, not knowing if the whaleboat had itself survived the waves and if they would ever see their homes and families again. All ended well. The episode actually opened up interest in the region. Permanent settlement quickly followed.

It's stories like this that make me wary of the sea. Shark attacks are worse. Years ago I came across a chap in National Service. His name was Bob Kay. There were scars all over his body from when he was mauled by a shark in these same waters. He was rushed to Port Welshpool and somehow survived to tell the tale. You see why I try to stay well inland!

One more thing about Corner Inlet before we step ashore. I was intrigued to learn about a novel programme that's restoring a healthy fishing industry to the Inlet. There aren't many places left that provide fresh – fresh! – fish to city markets, and Corner Inlet is one of them. However, the industry has suffered recently through the decay of the seagrass beds on the sea floor. They're vital to the whole life cycle of fish, but were being gobbled up by sea urchins. Tens of thousands of urchins were removed by divers a few years ago, but the sea grass beds still need to be brought back to their former extent and health. It's a simple process. Sea grass seeds are gathered by fishermen, fixed into sand bags onshore, taken out to sea again and dropped overboard to rest on the denuded bottom areas. Hundreds of hectares are being regenerated, and the fish are coming back. There's a big environmental spin-off. One hectare of sea grass captures up to 830 kilograms of carbon each year. That's thirty-five times more than rainforest. Landcare groups and other volunteers are pitching in to help. A really good news story!

Foster began as a camping spot for drovers taking cattle to Westernport, and was known as Stockyard Creek. It was given an adrenalin shot when gold was discovered in the late 1860s and 70s. This is unlikely gold country – rolling green hills and gullies rather than the blocky, stony country we usually associate with gold. It wasn't as big a find as further north, but enough to bring a flood of fortune-seekers. Foster was well-placed. It had a direct connection with Corner Inlet. Boats could navigate upstream to a landing near the town, though that was available only while the tide was at the flood. The landing is still there, out from town, and you still see some boats moored there.

Foster is one of the prettiest towns in Gippsland. Many people living there enjoy its proximity to the coast, but most like the town for what it is. The community organisations refer to it as "Victoria's secret", and there's some justification for that. This is probably the least known part of all Gippsland. I like the neat comment of the locals: 'People come here for the beauty - and stay for the lifestyle'. We can make some allowance for the puff-piece elements of the following blurb, but it's truer, in my opinion, than just about any other place in our region:

> *Living in Foster and the Corner Inlet District is all about discovering a simpler pace of life. No traffic lights, no*

> *traffic jams and definitely no stress. People love the uncrowded streets and their peaceful, relaxing ambience – and the parks and gardens that are maintained to perfection year round. This is a friendly, welcoming and open-minded community, where people have a sense of peace and belonging – and feel privileged to live here.*

There's a good feel as you walk the streets. Pearl Park is indeed a gem. You read about their history in the park, then you step straight into it, behind you - Stockyard Creek itself, where it all began. There's a painting on a shop wall showing the original landing, with a very poetic caption, simply, 'On the morning tide …' The Post Office calls itself 'Mailbox Corner'; there's a comfortable bus stop in the main street, two good op shops, and a free book exchange in the main street!

Near town, they've put up some standing stones to acknowledge the indigenous heritage, together with this explanation of the local dreaming:

> *Boorun the Pelican flies in from the east across the mountains. Tuk the Musk Duck joins him as they travel in their canoe around the islands and the waters of Corner Inlet. Mother and Father of the Gunnai Kurnai, they carry the stories of the land and sea. Bunjil the eagle flies in from the west. He circles above us on powerful wings. Creator*

> *Spirit of the Kulin, he remembers the creation of the rivers, the mountains, the creatures and the people.*

More towns should make people aware of the living legends of their land.

It rains a lot in Foster. I was amused to come across these lines from Nathaniel Spielvogel's *The Gumsucker at Home* (1913):

> *A fortnight have I been in Foster, and every day it has rained ... Once upon a time, long years ago, there was a week in which no rain fell – of course, anything under half an inch is disregarded here – and, lo, there was a drought in the land.*

The forgotten ones of those old days are the womenfolk. They bore the brunt of the loneliness and anxieties on bush farms, often miles from neighbours and isolated by muddy and ill-formed roads. Many of them had come from more salubrious circumstances, some directly from England. Ruth Ford records one woman writing from this Gippsland bush. She wrote to a newspaper in 1938 under the pen-name, 'Orchids':

> *On arriving at our dairy farm in the bush (after living in Melbourne) I felt very lonely. I was listening one day to a concert over the air given by members of a friendly circle. They all sounded so carefree and happy that I found myself in tears. I felt so lonely. My husband came in in the middle*

of it, to make things worse, and after trying to comfort me and murmuring something about being a brute to bring me to this, I felt really ashamed and resolved to keep a stiff upper lip from then on, which I have done.**

The pathos is only too clear. More needs to be written about the ordeals of our Gippsland women. Henry Lawson's 'The Drover's Wife' has always appealed to me as the quintessential account of the character of women of the bush.

Toora is the only town in Gippsland that owes its development to tin mining. There has been low-key interest in tin mining in other places. I remember my dad telling me about the tin prospectors in the Black Snake Range north of Labertouche in West Gippsland. They lived like hermits in the bush, appearing occasionally in town to get supplies. They were regarded as eccentric loners. The mining at Toora was a different kettle of fish. This was large-scale mining, operating from 1884 until 1942, and involving intensive dredging and sluicing. Water was brought in a race from the Franklin River. In one year alone, 1909, twenty-three tons of tin were produced, worth £1,555. A school was established - the Tin Mine School, which ran from 1907 to 1967.

One of the sore points around Toora is the Wind Farm – twelve gigantic towers generating enough power for over 6,000 homes and greatly reducing greenhouse gases. Much ink has been spilt over the rights and wrongs of these wind farms. I acknowledge the sincerity of the nay-sayers, but my feeling lies strongly on the side of those who believe we must develop alternative sources of power on a large scale and urgently. Local opposition to the Toora development has largely faded. Tourist buses take their clients to view it. Now, other wind projects on the drawing board put this one at Toora quite in the shade.

Toora can tell of two interesting residents in its past. The first was Harold Lasseter, a drifter, who spent his life thinking up outlandish schemes. His greatest hoodwink was to convince some people that he had discovered an Aladdin's Cave of gold in Central Australia. The other was Randolph Bedford who owned the local paper for a short time. Bedford was a drifter, but a productive one - a member of the Queensland parliament, an ardent nationalist, a prolific author, and friend of people as widely different as Lionel Lindsay and John Wren. Bedford was an inveterate proposer of wild schemes, not altogether unlike Harold Lasseter. Must be something in the Toora air!

The Agnes River curls its way from the Strzeleckis down to Corner Inlet. On the way it tumbles over a steep escarpment north-east of Toora. A dam supplies small local towns with drinking water before the water crashes straight down some sixty metres. It was in full flood the last time I was there - a truly awe-inspiring sight. There's a well-kept reserve set out in the hook of the river just above the falls, with a rotunda and beautifully-placed picnic tables.

The reserve is looked after by the Friends of Agnes Falls. How good are these Friends groups – Friends of Mount Cannibal, Friends of Mount Worth, Friends of Drouin Trees, Friends of Agnes Falls! When last there, I drove from the Falls along Agnes River Road, then down into Welshpool. It must be one of the prettiest roads we have … and I had a feast of wild blackberries on the way!

A glimpse at the small coastal towns before we leave the area. Port Franklin has somewhat more than a hundred residents, largely dependent on the fishing industry. They send their catches, including King George whiting and rock flathead, packed in ice directly to Melbourne. Mangroves line the water's edge. Welshpool, a short distance away on the South Gippsland highway, is larger, with a number of community activities and facilities. The school brings in pupils by bus from outlying areas.

Back on the coast, we come to Port Welshpool, once vital to the coastal shipping trade. Like Port Franklin, this is a town with a purpose – fishing! It reminds me of one of those English towns facing the North Sea, with its long row of sea-front houses along Lewis Street. The Long Jetty is remarkable, crooking its way far out into the shallow water. A fast car and passenger ferry service ran between Port Welshpool and Georgetown in Tasmania for a short period in the early 1990s, using 'Seacat' catamarans. It failed due to the lack of patronage … though it was a very rough ride according to the survivors!

You drive out of Port Welshpool across a low-lying coastal plain. It must be very close to sea level. How will this land appear in a hundred years? It must be one of the most vulnerable parts of our Gippsland coast, given the inevitable rise of sea level. One day, Welshpool itself, now five kilometres inland, may be re-named 'Port Welshpool'!

Close to Port Welshpool lies one of Gippsland's most important infrastructure nodes – Esso-BHP Billiton's Barry Beach Marine Facility. It services the vast network of oil and gas platforms offshore. 70,000 tonnes of cargo each year is shipped from here to supply and service the twenty-three production platforms in Bass Strait. At times there are 300 workers on these floating bases. The largest ones are able to sleep eighty men. They have gymnasiums and recreation rooms, as well as kitchen and dining facilities. Helicopters operating from Longford ferry the men on and off work, while heavy material is handled by two supply ships from Barry Beach.

* Cheryl Glowrey, "Port Albert and its strategic role, 1841-1860", in *Earth and Industry: Stories from Gippsland*, Erik Eklund and Julie Fenley, eds; Monash Publishing, Melbourne, 2015, p. 82.

** Ruth Ford, "Nature is around us in her loveliness: Settler women in the Gippsland bush in 1930s Australia", in *Ibid*, p. 50.

Drouin

In the sweet long ago, Drouin was a place of pure loveliness. E J Brady, writing in 1926, was in rhapsodies:

> *This is one of the sweetest villages in all Australia. It is placed in the heart of beautiful agricultural country, and is seemingly prosperous and content. Vividly green hillsides, with scattered trees on their slopes, chocolate fields in fallow, fat stock and fertility are its features.*

Drouin is now, however, all hustle and bustle. The main street is choked with traffic. You often find it hard to park your car. The railway car park is filled with commuters' vehicles. The schools are overflowing. The red farming soil around the town edges is being eaten up by 'suburban sprawl'. Drouin is within the South-Eastern Growth Corridor and is subject to a Precinct Structure Plan set out by the Victorian Government. See how these phrases slip so easily from the tongue. It boils down in layman's terms to Drouin becoming a huge place, probably bigger than Warragul, which itself is growing at much the same rate. The Shire is planning for 7,400 new homes in Drouin.

I've always been of the view that each country town develops its own spirit, and that once it's well and truly established nothing can ever shake it. That goes for organisations, too, big ones like Rotary and little ones like a local cricket club. Well, I used to think that, but I'm beginning to have some doubts in the case of these Gippsland towns that are growing so fast and furiously in the Great Population Upsurge we're experiencing. Drouin is a test case, in the middle of this huge population explosion, which comes not from the native-born, but from immigrants.

Can the character of the old town be preserved? I have hopes that it can. There are several groups in town that are quietly doing their bit to keep up both the appearance and spirit of the town. The first is the Friends of Drouin's Trees. These people have latched on to the notion that there's an intimate bond between the soul of a tree, the soul of a person, and the soul of a community. After all, each tree is a small wonder, and many trees are objects of great beauty. Hans Heysen, who spent his life painting trees, spoke of the combination of mightiness and delicacy in the gum tree – "mighty in its strength of limb and delicate in the colouring". He went on, "I know of no other tree which is more decorative, both as regards the flow of its limbs and the patterns the bark makes". The Friends of Drouin's Trees have made a register of the town's significant trees and produced a booklet showing a series of walks that take you by Drouin's treasury of trees. They've even give names to some of these trees. For instance, there's the Settlement Giant and the Bill Kraft Giant. My favourite amongst the walks is the Trees of Many Nations Walk that takes you through the Alex Goudie Reserve. Drouin has a number of quiet backwaters, and this Reserve is one of them.

The same people have put out a companion volume on the Birds of Drouin – seventy or so species, with beautiful photographs and hints on where to find them. Look out for the spotted pardalote when you're next in Drouin.

There's another livewire group in Drouin that has recorded stories about the people of the town. People can be as beautiful as trees … or birds! The Committee for Drouin teamed up with the local History group and the community radio station, 3BBR, to record on CDs detailed interviews with people of the town and district whose families have been part of the history of the district. They got some funding from Melbourne and from the Bendigo Bank. I went to the shindig when some of these stories were presented. The place was crowded. A woman sang a song she'd written for the event. There was back-slapping all round, and thoroughly deserved. I can't think of a better project than this for pulling a community together.

That radio station is, again, something special. They operate out of a building in Oak Street, and have turned some rough customers (including me) into silky-smooth presenters (ahem!). I suppose there must be hundreds of people – all volunteers – who've been involved with the station over the past twenty-five years that they've been running. It's a great local success story. They play "easy-listening" music during the day, but the night-time and weekend shows are much livelier. There's one presenter, for instance, who advertises his weekly show as "about 60% smooth modern jazz, and most of the rest is a mixture of cool funk, R&B, maybe a bit of blues or pop, and about 10% of the show is the rare and spicy part". Well, variety is the spicy part of life, they say!

Drouin, like a number of towns along the line, started off some distance away on fresh streams of water, then migrated to where they are now when the railway came through. That means that they are now located far away from their water supply, so reservoirs have to be built and water piped a good distance. That's a cloud on the horizon for Drouin as the population soars and water for domestic supply becomes more of a problem, to say nothing about the supply for public and private gardens. You could say that Drouin's problem is Australia's problem in miniature, as climate change brings hotter and drier weather.

People talk about Drouin and Warragul one day merging into one metropolis, not that anyone I've spoken to wants it. Each town likes to preserve its own distinctive personality. There's a huge amount of traffic between the towns. How different from the old days on that road, when we'd wave to each driver we met! I hope we can preserve the green belt that now separates the two towns. There are hopes that a new hospital will be built on that land. Is that a legitimate use of green-belt country? At least, it will be equidistant from both towns. One thing that does effectively link Drouin and Warragul is the aptly-named Two Towns Trail. It runs near the main road for a good part of its length, which is bad for the walkers and cyclists because of the noise, but good for the drivers because the sight of all this energy hits their consciences and makes them more inclined to get out and do some exercise themselves!

The biggest thing that happens in Drouin each year is the Ficifolia Festival. Ficifolia are native to Western Australia, but someone brought them to Drouin and they do exceptionally well here (although I've seen some brilliant ficifolias in South Gippsland, too). The State School children once planted a fine avenue of them and there are others in quite a few streets. You see their red flowers – or cream or pink or orange – all round town. The Festival is in February when the trees are at their best. There are talks and demonstrations, art shows, garden displays, open days, a dinner, and, sometimes, a grand parade down the main street, culminating in a festival in Civic Park. The good thing about that is that the people watching know most of the people in the parade. It's the town showing itself off to itself, which is the best kind of parade.

A little bit of serendipity occurred for Drouin in 1981. Two packets of old forgotten photos unexpectedly turned up. They were taken towards the end of the Second World War by the Department of Information. The purpose was to show the world, particularly Australia's allies, that all was well and normal Down Under. The Department chose Drouin as a typical country town and dispatched a photographer, Jim Fitzpatrick, to take a series of eighty-eight photos of typical, up-beat local people going about their day-to-day activities. They're extremely good photos and give a marvellous snapshot of life here – and indeed, everywhere – at that time. They're often put on display in Drouin, and you can see them online. One of them shows a petrol station, with petrol at 2/11 a gallon. That's about nine cents a litre by my calculations!

There's a sad chapter in Drouin's otherwise happy history. In the 1940s, Daryl Tonkin and his brother established a timber mill on Jackson's Track, north of Drouin, at Jindivick. Over the years, many aboriginal people came to live and work there. A congenial and well-ordered community developed. Daryl married one of the aboriginal women, Euphemia, and Euphie produced a large family. Some of those children are now local elders and play an important part in the community of West Gippsland. Outsiders, including some church and civic leaders, tended to see the settlement through prejudiced Western eyes. They campaigned for its destruction. The Aboriginal Protection Board did little to help the Jackson's Track people. Eventually, the camp was bulldozed and burnt with very little warning. The residents were shifted into tents around Drouin before being scattered, largely in Drouin and Warragul.

I've talked to some of those responsible for breaking up the settlement. Most of them now regret their actions; they say they did what they thought best at the time. I visited Daryl in his shack in the bush long after these events. He was a quiet and gentle man, without rancour. Carolyn Landon coaxed his life story out of him and wrote it up, with Daryl's co-authorship, in a book called *Jackson's Track*. It's on the way to becoming an Australian classic alongside books like AB Facey's *A Fortunate Life*. You must read it!

One of the young fellas who grew up on Jackson's Track was Lionel Rose. He was there until he was ten. He suffered the uncertainties and indignities of life that are common for aboriginal people until his stellar boxing career took off. In 1967 he had a notable win over Rocky Gattellari, then in 1968 beat Fighting Harara in Tokyo for the World Bantam-weight Championship, the first indigenous Australian to hold a World title. He came home to a public reception in Melbourne before 100,000 people. The same year he was Australian of the Year, and given an MBE. Lionel came to live in Warragul rather than Drouin, and it's there that a fine statue of him has been erected, in Queen Street Park. It's the first thing people see of Warragul as they get off the train, which is very appropriate.

Drouin West lies to the north of the town of Drouin. I think it got that name because the name 'Drouin North' was already taken. What we now call Buln Buln East was once known as Drouin North, amazing as that seems. There was little logic and less sense of direction amongst our early settlers, it seems. Drouin West is a proud settlement, revolving around the school, the fire brigade, and the cemetery. Like most of these little village areas, it once was more populous. In the first decades of the twentieth century, the Drouin West football team used to defeat all comers, including Drouin. In one match, in 1914, the team included two players from Neerim, three from Bunyip, and two from Jindivick. A kind of Drouin West All-Nations! The umpire for that game was A Brown, and "some of his decisions received rather adverse criticism", the paper reported. The more things change, the more they stay the same! Hard by Drouin West is the Glen Cromie Caravan Park. It's a lovely spot – shady trees, open grassy areas, the Tarago River running through. In 2009, it was a blackened ruin after the Black Saturday bushfire; now it's risen from those ashes. Resurrection!

There can be no doubt about Drouin South – square south of Drouin. As with Drouin West, there's a scattering of houses, a fire shed, and a school. No cemetery, however. It's a good school. Many parents from larger towns like their children to go to the smaller schools some few miles away. They think the children will benefit from the community atmosphere and the greater individual care that might be given, and perhaps there will be smaller classes. Some of these things are debateable, but it's safe to say that some children will benefit from smaller schools and other children will do better in larger schools. And it's the quality of the teaching rather than the size of the class that's important. There, now I can put my old teaching perspective back in the saddle-bag!

At Drouin South, the road forks. You can go left to Lardner and on eventually to Korumburra. That way you can get to Lardner Park, which has become one of the premier show places in rural Victoria. It's known mostly for Farm World, held in autumn each year, and for the music festival, Beyond the Valley, over New Year. Both bring in thousands of people, some more sedate than others. They both offer something to outsiders rather than to the local citizenry.

If, however, you go right at that fork, you can get to Athlone, which is a place with a long history and a pronounced local spirit. Like so many small towns, they've gradually lost their facilities. At Athlone, first, the Post Office went, then the church, and then the school. But the Hall remains, and it's still a focal point for the district. Badminton has always been a big thing at the Hall, and I notice that last year they received a $50,000 grant to do up the kitchen (how wise!) and put in a super-duper playground alongside. These small towns need a helping hand from time to time.

Finally, we come to Jindivick. Yes, I know Jindivick is closer to Neerim South than it is to Drouin, but I'm including it here because it has the same postcode as Drouin, and also because, in one of those illogical quirks of local doings, the people of Jindivick look to Drouin much more than they do to their closer neighbour, Neerim South. You can fall in love with Jindivick in an instant. I have done. It happened one balmy December evening. The hills were in dappled sunshine. There was a perfect combination of aspect, relief, the natural order, and human habitation. I drove out from Warragul, already in a state of gladness, but when I stepped out of the car my gladness turned to joy. I walked alone through the beautiful gardens of 'Makendye', where a couple from Africa have shown their delight in this land by making a lovely garden. Then, in the middle of town, as the sun moved further down the sky, I parked my car at the little church and wandered around the town. Not a car, not a soul, was about. I was in a timeless capsule - the old store, proudly bearing its date of birth, 1889; the AG Pretty Memorial Reserve, carefully tended, bearing the names of four Jindivick men who gave up their lives in war for a greater good; the Hall, bearing witness to the past both in its own self and by the photographs of pioneer days it contains. And is there anywhere a prettier cricket ground than this one, looking out over the slopes and plains below? Fortunate are those who live their lives out here in Jindivick. If E J Brady were to reappear in Jindivick, he might be inclined to describe this place, instead, as "one of the sweetest villages in all Australia".

Heyfield

Heyfield was originally 'Hayfield'. The MacFarlanes, first settlers in these parts, found the land rippling with knee-high grass, just like the hayfields they were used to at home in Scotland. Hence the name they gave to their station. Their experience was common. Nearly all the explorers and first settlers in the colony wrote about the open grasslands they found. Thomas Mitchell, for instance, in the 1830s:

> *We crossed a beautiful plain; covered with shining verdure, and ornamented with trees, which, although 'dropt in Nature's careless haste' gave the country the appearance of an extensive park.*

I'm indebted to Bruce Pascoe's brilliant book, *Dark Emu*, for much of this information. The open nature of the country was the direct result of aboriginal land practices. Charles Sturt saw

> *... grassy plains spreading out like a boundless stubble field, the grass being of the kind from which the natives collect seed for subsistence at this season of the year ... large heaps that had been thrashed out by the natives were piled up like haycocks ... the plains were verdant indeed, the luxuriant pasturage surpassed in quality anything I had ever seen.*

Pascoe tells of the experience of settlers in Gippsland. He writes:

Old settler families of north-east Gippsland have told me that when their forefathers were shown the country by Aboriginal people in the 1840s, all the plains were clean and well grassed, including the narrow river valleys. Looking at those valleys today, it is almost inconceivable, and modern, long-term farmers of the district are incredulous when they are told what their farms used to look like.

The aboriginal people used fire as the principal means of keeping the land in this condition. They maintained a rotating mosaic pattern of low-level burns, which kept the land free from scrubby infestation, while allowing plants and animals to survive in refuges.

The white settlers abandoned these practices. They put up fences, which inhibited burning. They brought in sheep and cattle which ate out the native grasses. Further, their weight and heavy hooves compacted the ground so that water ran off rather than sinking into the soil. The overall result was a rapid deterioration in these former grasslands. Farmers have battled ever since at huge cost and by the use of chemical additives to maintain the productivity of their land. Maybe it's time to listen to the earliest Australians and learn from them.

James MacFarlane sold to Robert Firebrace, who in turn sold to that legend of Australian squatting, James Tyson. At his height, Tyson held twenty-eight leasehold and freehold properties extending over nearly five and a half million acres in several colonies. Heyfield was, however, his only Victorian holding. He once referred to it (14,000 acres) as a 'cabbage patch'. Tyson had a reputation as a hard man, although he gave generously to charity. He never smoked or drank or used bad language. After he died, Banjo Paterson wrote a poem called T.Y.S.O.N., which ends:

> *But in that last great drafting yard,*
> *Where Peter keeps the gate,*
> *And souls of sinners find it barred,*
> *And go to meet their fate;*
> *There's one who ought to enter in,*
> *For good deeds done on earth ...*
> *But through the big gate, opened wide,*
> *The grizzled figure, eagle-eyed*
> *Will saunter up – and then*
> *Old Peter'll say: "Let's pass him through,*
> *There's many a thing he used to do,*
> *Good-hearted things that no one knew;*
> *That's T.Y.S.O.N."*

After Tyson died in 1898, the station was bought by a syndicate for £7/16/0 an acre. They promptly split it into 114 blocks which sold at a single mammoth auction sale – and brought a handsome profit to the syndicate members. Heyfield has been a place of small farmers ever since.

It's in the nature of cities to grow and keep on growing. It's in the nature of smaller country towns to grow and then subside, perhaps several times over, according to the strength of the local industries they depend on. And if the basis of their economy disappears, then the towns disappear as well, like the gold-mining ghost towns of North Gippsland, Jericho and Red Jacket and others. Over the course of its history, Heyfield has had a solid base in the agricultural industry. Dairying and beef, in particular, and sheep to a less extent, have provided that base. On top of this – like the cream on the cake – has been the timber industry. Underpinned by these resources, the town has grown to its present size. Just now, the timber industry is under threat, bringing the prospect of the town of Heyfield shrinking to a size more appropriate to its agricultural base.

Heyfield has long been a timber town, but it received enormous impetus after the 1939 fires. After the turmoil of war, the mills were moved out of the bush into fire-safe towns. Seven mills began operations in Heyfield in the one year, 1950. Now, one mill dominates the town – Australian Softwood Holdings. It is under some threat, however. The Victorian government has been moving over time to reduce logging, and actually bought out the ASH mill in 2018. Then, in 2019, the decision was made to ban logging of old-growth forests and to end the logging of native timber ten years later. The town is still coming to terms with what this might mean for its future. Community feeling, however, remains strong. In

2018, a Municipal Conference named Heyfield as Australia's 'Strongest and Most Resilient Community'.

People look back fondly on the golden years of timber-milling. Golden years for the town, but at huge personal cost. Men were killed by falling trees, in milling operations, and in transport accidents. Lives depended on quick wittedness and quick movement. Take one example. At Licola in 1954 a log carter died from his injuries after he'd winched the trailer clear of his truck. He released the safety bolt to let the trailer down, but failed to jump clear quickly enough. The swinging handle of the winch struck him with great force.

The timber workers, though, had their heady moments. For three years in the early 'fifties, they formed their own football club in the Cowwarr and District League. That meant playing against the older Heyfield team. Rivalry was intense. In 1952, the two teams played off in the Grand Final. Heyfield won. The next year the Timber Workers were premiers, but then, strangely, promptly disbanded.

These evocative but savage timber days have been memorialised by the construction of the Victorian Timber Workers' Memorial. It's in just the right place in Heyfield; native trees have been planted around; a stylised bush hut has been placed there, while the names of those killed in the industry are listed. I've seen the National Timber Workers' Memorial at Eden in New South Wales, and that's a beautiful place. But it's good to have our own Victorian memorial – equally beautiful - right here in Gippsland.

Heyfield is watered by the Thomson River. It begins above Mount Baw Baw, the birthing ground for much of our State's river system. The Yarra starts here and flows westwards, the Latrobe flows southwards, and the Thomson makes a magnificent arc as it swings northwards, then east, and southwards, through the Thomson Dam, on to the Cowwarr Weir, past Heywood, then on to join the Latrobe near Sale, and down to the sea. The Thomson Dam sends water to Melbourne, first through a twelve-mile tunnel to the Upper Yarra Dam, then on to the Silvan Reservoir. Its water is one of Gippsland's many gifts to Melbourne. As well, the dam feeds power into the State's grid through a small hydro-electricity plant at the base of the dam wall.

For the people of Heyfield, the Glenmaggie Weir on the Macalister River has their more immediate attention. The irrigation water that flows from here is the lifeblood of the intensive farming region that stretches from here down to Sale, and from Boisdale to Denison. If you look at a road map of Gippsland, you'll be struck by two areas where the road markings form a dense grid pattern – here and on the Koo Wee Rup Swamp - both areas of small farms and intensive production. I used to know some of the men who built the Glenmaggie Dam and the women who shared their life. They told an amazing tale of building the dam wall and then the irrigation channels with horses and scoops, picks and shovels. What they remembered best was the camaraderie that developed and the sense of pride they felt in what they achieved. They must all be gone now, those people, but they've left us an example of mutual endeavour that is not so easy to find nowadays.

Licola, on the Macalister north of Heyfield, is unique. If you leave out the mining towns, it's the only privately-owned town in Australia. The Lions Club bought the settlement here - formed around Saxton's timber mill – in 1965 and made it into a camp for children. It caters for the "underprivileged, deserving, special needs and disengaged young people" in particular, but has an eye out for tourists as well. You can get married here in the old church – if you're free!

By the time you get to Licola, you're entering serious high country territory. Lake Tarli Karng is not far away. It's a jewel. I'd been mad about Tarli Karng from the time I saw a film on it when I was a boy, though it took me fifty years to get there. I was in a two-family group, a male bonding group, which included surveyors, military men, and bushwalkers, but we still managed to get lost on the way in and had to traverse some very rugged country as a result. Don't be put off by this. For Gippslanders, Tarli Karng must be number one on the bucket list.

North of Licola and covering 646,000 hectares is the Alpine National Park, the largest of Victoria's parks. The road from Licola into the high country was built in the early 'sixties to tap the timber resources there. The Heyfield sawmillers paid part of the cost, the Forestry Commission the rest. The road takes you over the Tamboritha Saddle. There you're in the Market Square of the High Country, with Mount Tamboritha to the west, Mount Wellington away to the east, Tarli Karng below you, while McMillan's famous Track passes close by. Mount Wellington is better known to Gippslanders because it can be seen from large parts of the east, while, from a distance, other peaks tend to be lost in the line of the high plateau. This alpine region is important to the Gippsland psyche. Someone in the Alpine National Park service understands this. They have written, with some feeling:

> *From the time people first set foot on the Australian continent, they have sought the alps for social, spiritual and survival reasons. Their presence in these wild and wonderful mountains has left us a rich cultural heritage – from the rock scatters of the Gunaikurnai people on lofty vantage points to graziers huts nestling in protected folds of the high country.*

Cowwarr is a leafy oasis on the Traralgon to Maffra road. We always look out for the Cricket Club hotel and the Catholic Church, both living remnants from the past, but we also watch the speedo. Cowwarr has been renowned for the police intercepting speeding drivers. Cowwarr started as a staging post on the way from the coast to the Walhalla diggings. Here, goods had to be unloaded from wagons to pack-horses in order to negotiate the mountainous country from this point on. Today, there are no pack-horses, but there are racing lawnmowers. It's a growing sport. Take the cutters off your ride-on mower, change the steering wheel for bike handles, and you're away. It's popular in Cowwarr. For a different kind of culture you can take in the Art Gallery in the old butter factory, while for haute cuisine there's High Tea at the Cricket Club Hotel. Not a bad smorgasbord for a little village!

Tinamba is a little close to Maffra to have developed a great deal of individuality, but it has one particularly building of note, and that's the pub! In my days in this area the Tinamba Hotel was run by the Schoenmakers. Being Dutch, they established a very Dutch flavour about the bar and dining area. It was the place to go. Now the Schoenmakers and the Dutch element are gone, but the reputation for good food is greater still. Apparently, there is a craze these days for 'destination dining'. You drive a long way, eat and drink a lot, then drive home (not through Cowarr – see above). The place has attracted the attention of the food critics. One of them wrote up the pub in colourful terms, surprised that Gippsland could offer such fare. She finished her review, a little superciliously, in these words: *So what's a pub like this doing in a place like Tinamba? Getting the balancing act right, essentially: being a place where sheep farmers and poncy food snobs can be equally happy.* (Not many sheep around Tinamba, we could have told her!)

Ben Cruachan is north of Heyfield. You can see it from all over the district. There are two other mountains like that in Gippsland – Mount Worth in the Strzeleckis and Mount Cannibal at Garfield North. The name, Ben Cruachan, reminds us of the powerful Scottish element in early Gippsland. There's a Ben Cruachan in Scotland, too. *"CRUACHAN!"* is the battle cry of the Campbell clan. No such warlike aspects for our mountain. The Ben Cruachan Walking Club is a particularly peaceful bunch. In melodramatic fashion, the Club was formed at the top of the mountain in 1965. They're still very active, which is a good trait in a walking club. The Club took on a mighty work in 1983. The pioneer Angus McMillan had cut an eight-foot track along the lower flank of the Dividing Range, running for over 200 kilometres. The Walking Club rediscovered, then cleared and marked the old track, an enormous job. It runs from Woods Point to Omeo. Club members – or some of them - do the complete walk every ten years. Every decade. Decadent!

Koo Wee Rup

First, let's get the spelling right. It's the '*Kooweerup* Regional Health Service', the 'Royal Hotel, *Koo-Wee-Rup*' and '*Koo Wee Rup* Dental'. Three spellings but only one correct: the third. Three distinct words, it should be, all with capitals, and no hyphens. The name is from the Bunurong word for blackfish, which abounded in the swamp waters before nature was pushed back into second place. The name of this district was Yallock in the early days. The original run was Tobin Yallock, and there's Yallock Creek nearby. Yallock is another aboriginal word and has to do with water.

At Koo Wee Rup, there's been more concern with the future than the past, particularly the future of Melbourne's third airport. In 2013, the Guy government announced grand plans for a new Melbourne airport 'between Koo Wee Rup and Lang Lang'. It would cater for one-third of Melbourne's air commuters and team-tag with a developed port at Hastings. Later a private investment company offered to build the airport without cost to the taxpayer. It would be "at least as big as Tullamarine". However the Andrews government has shown no inclination to take up the idea. In 2019 the announcement was made of a third runway for Tullamarine, which took the wind out of the sails of the third airport proponents, for the time being, at any rate.

During the last war, there *was* an airfield here, at Monomeath Park. The Japanese threat was at its height and air protection was needed for the Yallourn power station as well as Melbourne, and the sea approaches, too. Four runways were planned, but the number was reduced to two as the Japanese menace receded. After the War, in 1947, a DC9 aircraft made a forced landing on the now-disused airstrip. The passengers stepped out into "a field of curious cows". Robert Bourke witnessed it; his grandparents owned the land originally.

The other wartime facility here is one I have direct knowledge of. A prisoner-of-war camp was established in August, 1944, between Ballarto Road and Backhouse's Road. It followed on the North African campaign, where Australian troops were pitted against Italian troops. Some of the Italian prisoners-of-war were brought back to internment in Australia. This was one of their camps, built to house 100 men – eighty-eight prisoners and twelve staff. The men worked on farms round about, in particular on the potato and asparagus farms - the Kinsellas' and the Roxbughs' - and were paid 1/3 a day. They were given a good deal of latitude. Some Saturday nights they'd come across to the pictures in Garfield, wearing their maroon (or was it orange?) sloppy Joe uniforms. Some people were nervous about the freedom they were given. It was a time when gossip readily was blown into a conspiracy theory. The bootmaker in Garfield at the time was Mr Interlighi, an Italian, and suspicions circulated about his loyalty, groundless, needless to say. When the camp was dismantled in 1946, one of the huts was bought by the Athlone Presbyterian Church. I've been to services in that church without realising what its background was. Other prisoner-of-war camps were built at Bete Bolong, near Orbost, Leongatha, Foster, Yarram, Warragul, and Maffra.

Koo Wee Rup has an excellent community newsletter, *Blackfish*. Imaginatively named, and full of interesting material – and easily available online. Heather Arnold, the Laura Tingle of local investigators, has a regular column in it. She touches on some of these matters. I heard her speak about Carlo Catani not long ago. I'll come back to Signor Catani.

While I'm on the subject, community newsletters have sprung up in most of our towns in recent years. To give you an idea of their spread, if we take Baw Baw Shire alone, here's the list of community newsletters: Hill End Herald, Jindivick News, Longwarry & Labertouche News, Narracan News, Neerim Star, Noojee News, Ridgey Didge Rag, Thomson Times, Traf News, Yarragon News, and Walhalla Chronicle. Some of them have particular features, like the Garfield Spectator (Cardinia Shire) which has a police round-up with every misdemeanour and crime, large or small, set out for everyone to tut-tut about. Generally speaking, though, I'd like to see our community newsletters grow more teeth – to express more forthright views and challenge more reflection amongst readers. But then, perhaps they'd no longer be community newsletters.

Carlo Catani was the man in charge of draining the Great Swamp, now called the Koo Wee Rup Swamp. After arriving from Italy via New Zealand, he became an engineer in the Victorian Public Works department. He was "visionary, well respected, amiable, generous and kind". And good at his work. Catani was responsible for a vast sheaf of engineering developments throughout Melbourne and Victoria. He opened up Mount Buffalo, for instance, and Lake Catani there is named after him. With the Great Swamp, he masterminded the channelling of the Bunyip River, which became the Main Drain and hundreds of miles of subsidiary drains, so that 40,000 hectares of valuable land was gained for farming purposes. It wasn't just the opening up of the land. A Village Settlement Scheme went along with it, and this was very close to Carlo's heart. The six designated villages that he brought into existence were Koo Wee Rup, Five Mile, Cora Lynn, Vervale, Iona, and Yallock. Heather Arnold quoted from H J Boxshall's early reminiscences:

> *Mr Catani was well known to most of the men employed on the drain work, no matter how far away or how small the drain, he would insist on having a look at it to see how the work was progressing. He got to know many of the men by name and would sit on the drain bank and have his lunch with them. These trips meant long rides on horseback and often longer distances on foot, but it was all in a day's work for Mr Catani.*

All hail to Carlo Catani. These days, there's not just the town of Catani to remember him by. There's also a potato. In 1986 a new potato was developed out there and named the Catani potato. It's just the right size for fish and chips!

It may because of the general flatness around Koo Wee Rup, but they like to get up in the air when they can. First, there's the Observation Tower a couple of kilometres out of town on the South Gippsland Highway, built to mark Victoria's 150th anniversary. The structure itself, architecturally, is adventurous, and from the top you can look out and imagine the Swamp as it used to be. The history of the Swamp is explained down below, and it's a good spot for a picnic. They say there's a man selling donuts, but he's never been there when I go. In the town itself are the Clocktowers, built from Federation Commemoration funds. These are a very attractive set of interesting – even perky – towers that give a lift to this otherwise low-level town. The Clocktowers double as the bus station – and the comfort station!

The 'Swamp villages' maintain a strict individuality. Catani's pride rests soundly on its Football/Netball Club. They've punched well above their weight in both codes, despite the cruel burning-down of their clubrooms, *twice*, in 1970 because of a lightning strike, and in 2001 through an arson attack.

Cora Lynn used to have a great cricket team and maybe still does. Once, as a boy, I rode my bike – without a light – for miles across the dark Swamp roads to the Cora Lynn Hall to hear Lindsay Hassett and Ian Johnson talk to the cricket faithful. The football ground here is one of the best for miles around, and many of the finals are played on it. Like all places on the Swamp, Cora Lynn has suffered terrible floods. In 1911, the brand new hall, Keast Hall, had three feet of flood water in it the day it was due to be opened. The 1934 flood was particularly bad in Cora Lynn. The Main Drain broke through its levee banks and poured on to the surrounding low-lying countryside. One of the old landmarks of Cora Lynn, the cheese factory, has been transposed into a modern home, and has been used for public functions and overnight accommodation.

Bayles, the original Yallock, was re-named after a soldier killed in the First World War. A railway line once ran through here (and Catani), enabling the transport of farm produce and leading to the building of the Butter Factory here. The best thing about the present town is the Fauna Park, built on and around the old railway land. It's old-fashioned enough to have an honesty-box for admission. The Park boasts deer, emus, geese, ducks, bandicoots, and kangaroos. My advice is not to go actively searching for these creatures. Just wander along the quiet pathways and let them appear if they will. It's one of West Gippsland's little-known delights, and a tribute to the voluntary work that's gone into it.

Westward from Koo Wee Rup the South Gippsland Highway takes you along the coast to Tooradin. It's low-lying country and the coastal fringe has mangroves and mud flats. At Tooradin itself, Sawtell's Inlet empties into Westernport. There are boating facilities here – a jetty, boat ramp, a boardwalk –and a place for a picnic, though you should go at high tide or your view will be limited to a square mile or so of mud flat. Despite this, Tooradin has always been a favoured getaway place for the fun-starved people of West Gippsland. Growing up not far away, I always felt it incongruous that hardened old dairy farmers should take their delight in going to Tooradin, hiring a boat, and spending the day on the water chasing fish.

The Tooradin Airfield is a private business, though subject, of course, to strict governmental controls. It has one bitumen runway with lights, one grass strip, and one gravel strip. You can hire a plane there or have a meal. The restaurant is aptly named, 'Wings and Fins'. They specialise in Flinders Island crayfish. Wonder how they get there! The landing strips run towards the water, and there, at the end of the runway, in the mangroves, lies the vessel, *Edwina May*. She was in the process of being restored in 1974 when a family tragedy led to work being halted and never resumed. She lies there as the planes take off over her hulk, slowly rusting away, officially recorded as a shipwreck.

The strip of country along the coast from Tooradin, through Koo Wee Rup, to Lang Lang, and on towards Phillip Island and Wilsons Promontory is changing rapidly as more and more people seek to live a rural lifestyle yet be within easy reach of Melbourne. Tooradin had 1,568 residents at the last census, and Koo Wee Rup an astounding 3,579. Tooradin actually is in Casey Shire, Koo Wee Rup in Bass Coast. The huge population growth poses material problems to these shires, but also cultural problems as newcomers arrive with little knowledge of local tradition. I have a good deal of confidence the newcomers will be absorbed into their new communities and that the old spirit will live on … but all the more if the past is remembered with affection and with imagination. To this end, I'm going to put in here a few paragraphs from one of the best accounts of growing-up I've come across. Mick De Vries lived most of his life in Drouin, where I came to know him. However, he grew up in Koo Wee Rup, and his book, *My Story: the Life and Times of Mick De Vries*, brings to life his early days there in his natural and unaffected style:

> *I was born in Koo-Wee-Rup on April 22nd 1927. There was no electricity, we had candles, kerosene lights and in the lounge (with its big open fire) we had a kero or shellite light on a long chain and to light it we pulled the chain and it came down from the ceiling, when lit we pulled the chain again and it went back up to the ceiling … The only hot*

water was in the big cast iron kettle that was always boiling on the stove. To make toast we cooked it on the toasting forks in front of the fire and instead of a fridge we had a meat safe hung up on a hook under the veranda ... The baker used to come around in his horse and cart and you would go out and choose what bread you wanted – the butcher and milkman did the same. The Indian Hawkers came around in the old horse and covered wagons selling everything you could imagine – pots, pans, materials, cane baskets, kettles, everything under the sun ...

I don't know how Bill and I survived our boyhood days, between the swamp and the main drain was where we spent most of our time and nobody seemed to worry about us. We used to take a frying pan and some bread and butter and catch minnows in the main drain, fry them up and that would be our dinner. We would spend all day playing Tarzan in the Blackwood trees which lined the drain, and watch the dredge which used to pump the sand out of the drain and load it into little railway trucks ... Rules and regulations have taken all the fun out of kids' lives these days. When we were kids we made Shanghais, Bows and Arrows and we had little Daisy Air Guns. We made our own billy carts. One would sit in the seat and steer with his feet on the front axle while the other would pull him along with a rope.

Then there was the 1934 flood. It was about 7 o'clock in the morning Bill was outside yelling "Mick, come out here." I ran out [to find] a wall of water about two feet high. We rushed inside and woke the family up. We had time to get the Pianola up on a couple of bricks then we got on the roof. We were on the roof only for a little while when chairs started to float out the door, so Dick got down and shut it. We were on the roof for eight hours and finally a boat came and took us to the railway station as it was the only place that wasn't under water. Mum, Bill and I were sent to Dandenong by train, I remember looking out the window and seeing cows and horses floating past. We slept in Dandenong Scout Hall on the floor ...

I'm actually writing this on Australia Day, when we reflect on our past and our traditions. We can learn a lot from Mick De Vries about what Gippsland – and our nation - is built on.

Korumburra

Korumburra lies in the heart of what was once the Great Forest of South Gippsland. The rolling hills that we see now bear little resemblance to what once was here. To discover that we need to go back to the old photographs and the old records. The best of the early records is *Land of the Lyrebird*, published in 1920, written about the time of the first settlement in the 1870s and later. This was indeed primal land, too thickly forested for the indigenous first people to occupy. The selectors were fascinated by the forest, yet they had to destroy it in order to make their living. One of the first men in the Moyarra area, out from Korumburra, James Rainbow, wrote in *Land of the Lyrebird*:

> *It was very interesting to walk through this great bush and observe the habits of the various animals and birds and note the various kinds of trees, shrubs, ferns, and mosses, etc. which grew in such profusive luxuriance everywhere; from small ferns and moss at your feet to the tops of the trees, the tallest of which were the bluegums and the blackbutts, one hundred and fifty feet high, and as close together as they could grow.* *

The early settlers broke their backs clearing their land. The general picture of them is that they were sturdy sons of the soil, well-used to their tasks. Such was generally not the case. Many of them were more used to town life, and came from business and professional families. They had an idealistic rather than a practical outlook on life, and were inexperienced in the bush. They learned the hard way! The forest was not their only problem. Most had no capital behind them and had to borrow in their most difficult early years of struggle. And for many there was the loneliness of their isolated surroundings. Think, too, of the pioneer women in their very trying circumstances.

The new selector's work was never-ending. First a hut had to be built and the bush cleared away. Clearing the land meant, in approximate order, burning, felling, heaping the fallen timber, burning again, clearing undergrowth, harrowing, ploughing, and fencing. Fencing might be by post and rail, pickets or palings, or simply logs piled on top of each other or loaded into trestles. Then came the first crop, usually potatoes, and/or pasture grasses. Perhaps the first cow could then be purchased. The Selection Acts required improvements to be made if the block was to be retained (or purchased) after six years of residence. I've seen photos of the homes of the early selectors around Korumburra, surrounded by tall timber, still green or ringbarked. The largest trees were left where they stood. To our modern eyes the scene is totally dismal, the task impossible.

To many modern eyes, however, those cleared hills appear equally dismal, ecologically disastrous. Attempts are being made to recover something of their pristine condition and bring back the birds and animals that once proliferated here, at the same time restoring ecological balance. One of the organisations engaged in this task is Greening Australia which has restored hundreds of thousands of hectares of degraded country throughout Australia, including land around Korumburra. I've seen a video showing how Greening Australia took a barren hillside in this district and over years converted it to its original primitive state. Bird calls now echo through the bush, native animals have returned, and carbon dioxide is sequestered in the best possible way. In the wider district the greater glider has been saved from extinction through planting trees and building nest boxes for them. The greater glider is a magnificent creature, sometimes soaring a hundred metres between trees. Maybe in another hundred years we'll see these Korumburra hills being farmed in harmony with a restored natural landscape.

The opening up of coal mines in the Korumburra district provided a boost to the struggling dairy farmers. Timber was needed for the mines and farm produce for the workers. Mines were opened in many places - at Korumburra, Wonthaggi, Jumbunna, Outtrim, Kilcunda, Woolamai, and Coalville. Smaller mines were at Berrys Creek, Boolarra and Cape Paterson. Over time, production from Wonthaggi, Jumbunna and Outtrim increased at the expense of Korumburra.

Korumburra, however, retains the Coal Creek Community Park and Museum. I know many people who've never been there; they think it's the same as the State Coal Mine in Wonthaggi. The two places are totally different. Coal Creek is more like wandering through an old village with various exhibitions on the side. It's actually a public park, run by volunteers, and it's FREE! Something for nothing! In this day and age!

The Primary School is housed in a grand building. Its most famous student was (Sir) Stanley Savige, who is commemorated in the entrance gates to Coleman Park. Then there's the railway station. Korumburra has one of Gippsland's finest railway stations, built with multiple tracks and a turntable, to cater for shipping out coal. The station building has a grand entrance portico, patterned brick work, and stately chimney pots. It's said to be built in Queen Anne style, and I must say it bears some similarity to English manor houses of that style. Today there are no trains, except for occasional tourist ones. The building, however, remains. It's heritage-listed, and contains an interesting collection of railway memorabilia.

In March each year the Karmai Festival features the Giant Earthworm. The Giant Earthworm is an extraordinary creature – up to two metres in length, living in dark loneliness entirely underground. David Attenborough came here to check them out. He was amazed. He could hear them gurgling their way through their subterranean passages as he walked down the gully. He found an egg, and then a full-size specimen, which he gently pulled from its inch-wide hole. The worms flourish in the damp soils of these Korumburra valleys where the average rainfall is 1135 mm a year.

Following the success of the Light-Up-Melbourne Festival, Korumburra instituted its own Festival of Lights in 2019. It was held in June as a gesture of defiance to mid-winter. Virus permitting, it was due to be repeated in 2020 with "warm fires, live music, food vans, market stalls, fire twirlers, lantern parade, carved fire drum competition, glow in the dark merchandise, kids activities and more …". What more could there be?!

Burra Foods employs 150 workers in Korumburra, turning out cheeses, milk concentrate and milk powder, 50,000 metric tonnes of product annually. In 1987 the old Korumburra butter factory lay empty. It was taken over by a family company from Shepparton, which joined up with Japanese backers in 2009. To ensure a power supply, the Company put down an underground power cable from Leongatha. One thing bothers me, though, about this otherwise transparent company: their logo is a kookaburra. Which 'Burra' does 'Burra Foods' represent? Korumburra or Kookaburra?

How different our society is from former times! I've been looking through the old newspapers about Poowong and reading how people used to entertain themselves. There was a Mutual Improvement Society which held its meetings at the Athenaeum. In 1932 they held a mock Federal election, while Miss Gregg spoke about her trip to England. At the Talkies, Laurel and Hardy were starring in 'Their First Mistake'. The Rifle Club competed with Outtrim and other clubs around the district. In 1930, electric light came to the town. In 1927, the Swimming Basin was officially opened; swimmers and divers came from all around, including Melbourne. And where was the swimming basin? In a pool at the Bass River. Athletic sports were held every year. Going further back, in 1900, they played a fancy-dress football match here. It's hard to imagine that!

But there was a sombre side. In 1900 the Shire of Poowong and Jeetho was officially declared "infected" because of the prevalence of typhoid fever, diphtheria, and scarlet fever. Not such good old days, in that respect. And snakes abounded. One correspondent declared Poowong to be "the headquarters of the snake family", and called for a bounty on their heads. Snake-bite was indeed common. One farm worker in 1900 after being bitten had the wound scarified and burnt with gunpowder. He was kept from going to sleep and "well-dosed with brandy". He survived. The local papers of the time tell of many recoveries from snakebite, but also of several deaths.

Despite its small population, Poowong today has very good facilities, especially for sport – tennis courts, basketball and squash stadium, netball courts – as well as an outdoor swimming pool (not in the Bass River) and the football ground. Poowong has always been home to many Wesleyans and Uniting Church folk. The old

Wesleyan Church is now the Pioneer Chapel, home of the Historical Society and used for community events, including concerts, church gatherings and funerals. Out of town is the Sculpture Park, on the Nyora Road.

The Burchett family has made a big imprint on Poowong. Caleb Burchett was one of the early settlers and very influential in the community. His son, Franklin, wrote the history of early Poowong, and his grandson, Wilfred Burchett, became world-famous as a journalist. He was in Japan at the end of the Second World War. When the atomic bomb was dropped on Hiroshima, he walked into the ruined city. His report on the front page of the Daily Express has been called 'the scoop of the century'. His later career was dogged by controversy because of his sympathy with Communist countries. Burchett wrote about his years in Poowong in his autobiography, *Passport*. Another son of Poowong is Don Watson, renowned as Paul Keating's speech-writer. The book of his that will resonate best with Gippslanders is *The Bush: Travels in the heart of Australia*, a beautifully reflective work about the nation's past and present.

Nyora, further west, lies on McDonald's Track, now a track no longer – a sealed road and much used transport route. While Poowong remained relatively unchanged over the years, Nyora benefited from its location, closer to Lang Lang and the city. Poowong missed out on a railway connection, but Nyora was on the Koo Wee Rup line and was also the change station for the branch line to Wonthaggi. As motor transport became common, Nyora was favoured by many who wanted a small rural holding. A speedway was opened in 1960, bringing crowds into the town. Maybe you would like to go? One of their recent advertisements announces that "Crash and Bash will tear down the house as they smash their way around the Speedway'. Not today, thanks! Nyora gained some fame through the ABC series, 'Something in the Air', that was set here, but given a new name, 'Emu Springs'. It featured a bunch of weirdos (most unlike the actual residents!) around a radio station. Annie Phelan was one of the stars. I met up with her through the Rural Australians for Refugees. She used to come down to Gippsland to support the work of RAR.

Loch is at the base of the Nyora-Poowong-Loch triangle. It gets its name from Sir Henry Brougham Loch, Governor of Victoria from 1884 to 1889. Loch was Scottish and a renowned empire-builder. Once, held in a dungeon in China, he was released to a safe haven ten minutes before an order arrived for his immediate execution! Here in Victoria, he was ineffectual but amiable, and was well thought of. He liked shooting and used to come down into West Gippsland shooting ducks.

Loch is a small town, but significant in the local area. It has a lot going for it as an 'art, craft and eat' town, like Yarragon. It also does some smart publicity. The Loch Express cleverly mixes advertisements with community news. They have a Food and Wine Festival in June, offering "the flavour and sensation of our region". Sensational! There's a suspension bridge across the leafy gully. Very peaceful, and part of the war memorial. The highway by-pass allows the place to be itself.

Kongwak sounds Chinese but is actually aboriginal by name. It's a tidy town with a considerable past. The old butter factory building dominates the town, but has long since closed its doors. Nowadays Kongwak is a dormitory town for Korumburra. The town "bursts into life" each Sunday when the Market brings in customers from the larger towns like Korumburra, Wonthaggi and Inverloch. Kongwak is known as 'the Valley of Peace'.

Outtrim was named for the Minister of Mines, Alfred Richard Outtrim. The town should be proud of its eponymic. Outtrim was an honourable man and effective politician, who stood up for the welfare of rural towns. Like Jumbunna, Outtrim rose and fell with the development of black coal. Old photos show the magnitude of the earthworks and bridgeworks that came with the mine and the railway. Almost nothing now remains of that bustling past.

My RACV map shows Jumbunna and Moyarra as 'localities'. At the time of Federation Jumbunna was a busy coal-mining town with a railway line and hundreds of residents. Now it's a locality! Sic Transit Gloria! It remains, however, a place of much beauty. Jill Durance wrote an affectionate piece about one of the old homesteads here, 'The Pines'. Moyarra lies, she says, 'in the heart of rural south Gippsland where today, from each side of the winding road, stretch green rolling hills dotted with dairy and beef cows and the occasional house fringed with trees'.* That's South Gippsland! She writes of the beauty of the original forest, the clearing of the land, the impact of the coal mines, and the Great Fire of 1898. She details poignant stories, such as the family in the Great Fire who carried their valuable possessions from the house to a ploughed paddock before fleeing. They returned later to find their possessions all destroyed but the house saved! Her account ends with a tragedy - a triple drowning in a farm dam. How often in the old days did such tragedies occur! However, Jillian Durance hints at a brighter future. 'Reforestation,' she writes, 'is bringing back pockets of natural vegetation and a slow increase in bird life and the odd koala'. **

*Quoted in Jillian Durance, "Nothing we liked better", in *Earth and Industry: Stories from Gippsland*, Erik Eklund and Julie Fenley, eds; Monash Publishing, Melbourne, 2015, p 242.

***Ibid*, p 255.

Lakes Entrance

Lakes Entrance bids fair to be our most celebrated town. People in other states might not know where Gippsland is, but they'll know where Lakes Entrance is. To the outsider, it's a fabled place, like Coleridge's pleasure-dome in Xanadu.

One of the first to write about it used words that would still grace the tourist literature:

> *One of the finest views in Gipps Land and Australia is to be obtained from the heights of Kalimna, or Jimmy's Point. The whole expanse of Lakes King and Victoria, the Back Lakes, the wooded islands, the undulating shores, the low lands around the rivers northwards, nearer at hand a dense redgum forest, valuable, they tell me, as that of Bullarook, Mount Taylor showing up beyond Bairnsdale, the Alps fringing the horizon in one direction, and in the other over a narrow strip of sandy bank covered with stunted scrub one sees the white-crested breakers of the Southern Ocean rolling in on the Ninety-mile Beach with a chorus of never-ceasing thunder.*

That was written in 1886. What a description! And what a sentence! Ninety-two words! Others have been attracted not so much by the beauty of the area as the town itself. Chester Eagle, in 1971, wrote:

> *This is Gippsland's best known town, the only one to make any promise to the visitor ... Lakes is said to offer play, love, life larger than the working week world knows it.*

Chester Eagle is a good case study in understanding how people react to Gippsland. He came from Melbourne to Bairnsdale as a teacher, but hated the place. Yet he stayed, and over the twelve years of his residence came to understand and appreciate not only Bairnsdale but Gippsland as a whole. He fell in love with it. I'm not like Chester Eagle. I've always been in love with Gippsland. But then I grew up here. I absorbed the landscape and the mindset of Gippsland as a child. My feelings for Gippsland were set hard before I knew of other places. Yet those other places are as deeply loved by others as is Gippsland by me and countless others.

I know of people who have never felt at home in Gippsland. They've longed for the other side of the Dividing Range, for the open plains of the interior, for the subtleties of colour there, for the dryness and distance of the landscape. I know one woman who lived in the prettiest spot imaginable near Neerim. Yet she pined for the drier country of the north and moved away to live somewhere out of Bendigo. Others I've known who've chosen to make their homes in the blocky, sandstone 'lizard country' in the inland foothills of New South Wales. And although Dorothea McKellar does dip her lid to "the sapphire-misted mountains" and the "green tangle of the brushes where lithe lianas coil", it's clear from her famous poem that her heart really lay with the "sweeping plains" and the "far horizons" of her wide brown land. As Gippslanders we can truly love our home, yet avoid the parochialism that one comes across at times.

Back to that view from Jimmy's Point (now mostly known as 'Jemmy's Point'). I'm astounded to discover that if I click on the right buttons on my mobile phone I can see a video of this view looking down over the actual entrance as it is at the very same moment. In real time, I think they say! There's another view from Flagstaff, more dramatic, with the white horses tossing their manes as they crash into the shore. Live streaming indeed!

The entrance is an artificial opening between the Lakes and the sea. Up to 1870, the entire Lake system drained into the open sea through a sandy barrier which was constantly shifting. Sometimes boats could get through, at other times they were blocked. They were sometimes held up for months, unable to work their way inwards or outwards. Lives were lost in the uncertain waters. The contract to open the Lakes in a permanent fashion was won by John Carpenter. Carpenter was one of the finest of Gippsland nineteenth-century men, a hard-headed, practical businessman, an all-rounder. He had previously operated a steam-driven flour mill in Maffra and then a timber mill in Heyfield, among other concerns. At Maffra, he had been a stalwart member of the Church of England, and actually designed the first church building there in 1870, and then the parsonage.

Lakes Entrance looks outwards in three directions – to the sea, to the Lakes, and back to its hinterland. Fishing is a huge amateur as well as professional activity. It's fascinating to read the weekly fishing reports provided for tourists:

> *The footbridge for trevally. Kalimna jetty for whiting and for the boaties Fraser Island and Nungurner for whiting all on pipi and fresh prawn. Offshore they are getting plenty of snapper at 6 Mile Reef. The Pipeline for snapper. Gummy shark closer to shore on pilchard and squid.*

Who worries about punctuation when the whiting are biting?! But who could not smell the smack of the sea in those lines?! There's been constant friction between commercial and amateur fisherfolk. You can read about it as far back as the 1870s. The railway had extended to Sale and it was then possible to get fresh fish to Melbourne. But at the same time Lakes Entrance was being promoted as a wonderland for amateur fishers. It was:

> *... the paradise of pleasure-seekers, for you have mountain, sea, lake and river so closely associated that hunting, shooting, fishing, boating and bathing can all be combined without great effort in one day's amusement.*

That's from 1876. The current position is that the State government has sided with the recreational fishers against the professionals. Or with the conservationists against the exploiters, as some would see it. A ban has been declared on commercial fishing in the Gippsland Lakes, to take effect from April Fools Day in 2021. The commercial fishers have been offered compensation, but that's poor recompense for those who have been part of the local fisheries scene for generations. Like most things in life, there's no easy answer to this problem. We're private individuals but we live in a commercial world. Where do we draw the line?

The waters of the Lakes themselves cover over 400 square kilometres. The water is not deep, but deep enough for keel boats to be used with careful management. However, this is the Mecca of the trailer-sailor. The best-known competitive event on the Lakes is the Marlay Point yacht race, from Marlay Point on Lake Wellington to Paynesville, the meeting-place of Lake King and Lake Victoria. It's been sailed on the Labour Day weekend in March for over fifty years. I've known men who've sailed in it; their eyes glaze over just thinking about it. It's the only sailing event in Australia that starts at sunset. That's the first point of excitement. Then it includes the narrow five-mile stretch of the McLennan Straits, where there's every possibility of grounding your craft, hitting the bank, or crashing into another boat. In the dark! People call it the 'Sydney-Hobart' for small boats.

Next, there's the region round about. Nungurner is some little distance from the sea, but many people like that. There's a good feeling about Nungurner. It comes from the comfortable balance between the permanents and the holiday-makers. Neither crowds the other out. Metung, on the other hand is all glitz and glamour. Well, nearly all. The locals have given the waterfront over to the tourists and retreated to the back streets. Still, Metung is a beautiful place ... and the sun always shines! The Bataluk Cultural Trail runs through Metung. It connects Cape Conran, Orbost, Buchan, Lake Tyers, Metung, Bairnsdale, and Sale, following ancient indigenous trading routes and highlighting Gunaikurnai archaeological sites and special places of the Dreaming.

One of these special places is Legend Rock in the heart of Metung. The aboriginal legend is that one day some fishermen had a great catch and feasted sumptuously. But, in their greed, they failed to feed the dogs. The women, keepers of the moral law, were angered and the men were turned to stone as a punishment and a warning to others to be compassionate. The three rocks here were the three turned-to-stone men. Sadly, two of the rocks were blasted away in the 1960s when the road was being widened. Only one remains. The lesson about respecting Koorie culture may be more powerful than the original legend itself! I don't think that destruction would happen today.

North of Lakes Entrance is the rugged country of the Colquhoun State Forest. Granite was once quarried here. It was brought down to Lakes Entrance by a tramway and used to replace the original wooden pylons at the actual Entrance to the Lakes. In 2000, the State Government set about developing rail trails in rural Victoria. Now the old tramway has become the route of the Gippsland Lakes Discovery Trail. It's not for the faint-hearted. You'd best take a mountain bike on this track, but it's more rewarding than the silkier ride you get on most of the rail trails.

The Discovery Trail links up with the East Gippsland Rail Trail which follows the route of the former line from Bairnsdale to Orbost. That's a ride I'd thoroughly recommend, even though there are some quite steep gradients. I've seen a cross-section of the track. If you're riding west to east, you go from 10 metres to 130 metres above sea level in less than 15 kilometres. Those steam trains had plenty of ... steam power! Soon after you get over the highest hump, at the old Colquhoun railway station, you come down to cross Stony Creek. Here the trains went over a trestle bridge. It's still there. This isn't your common or garden trestle bridge. This is the grandfather of trestle bridges, the biggest in the State and maybe beyond. It is 276 metres long and 19 metres high. Noojee's bridge is slightly higher, but much shorter. Think of those bush engineers first designing their bridge, then having to find the matching logs up to twenty metres and more in length, and the intermediate planking, then securing the bolts, some of which were almost a metre in length. The last train passed over the bridge in 1988. Since then maintenance has proved too costly and the bridge is now locked against human or wheeled traffic. So you won't have the thrill of riding high above the forest floor and the gurgling waters of the creek. There is a handy detour provided.

Heading west from Lakes Entrance you come to a more open landscape, the sort of country you might expect to see comfortable old homes and buildings. Nyerimilang is one of these – one of Gippsland's graceful homes, beautifully situated above the water, and with lovely grounds. I always feel it is very Gippslandish in its softness and understatement. Very feminine, really. It was built as a family home, not for ostentation, though Melbourne money was behind it. Frank Stuart, who built the original building, later added to by his son, was a colourful businessman and parliamentarian, who used Nyerimilang as a retreat. Access was by steamer through the Lakes. Today it's a government property – Nyerimilang Heritage Park - run by a band of volunteers. They don't charge to go in, though they do ask for a donation. The Gippsland Opera Company performs here every year. You do have to pay for that!

Let's return to Lakes Entrance itself. The settlement used to be called 'Cunninghame'. I've got a book published as late as 1947 that still refers to the town as Cunninghame. Millions of people over time have driven through this main street, tourists and locals, old and young, saints and sinners. It must be one of the best-known main streets in the land ... winding down from Kalimna, across North Arm, past the Park, Bullock Island on the right, turning into the Esplanade, past the eating places and the shell museum ... there's the Uniting Church, the Post Office, the newsagent (I know someone who thinks Lakes Entrance is a lucky town, so he buys a Tattslotto ticket here every time he passes through) ... now Mechanics Street and the library on the left; the Anglican Church is up there, too, called St Nicholas', the patron saint of fishermen and women – nice touch! ... past Bulmer Street, named after John Bulmer from Lake Tyers ... now the famous footbridge appears, taking you over to the ocean – the Ninety-mile Beach and to the Entrance itself ... there are the World War 1 statues, carved by John Brady from the cypresses that once stood here as an Avenue of Honour, and there's a plaque commemorating those who died in the wreck of the *Glenelg* ... and all the while the waterfront to Cunninghame Arm calls our attention away from the buildings across the street.

Now we're winding up the hill and out of town to St Brendan's Catholic Church. Father John Shanley was a charismatic priest here for over thirty years and introduced some very imaginative features, like a baptismal stream flowing through the church. Annie Rijs used to play the organ. She and her husband, Peter, bought a cake shop in Lakes Entrance in 1966 and developed it into the Patties Food empire, now a multinational concern employing 500 people.

Soon we come to the Lake Tyers turn-off. Lake Tyers is one of those hideaway places that regular holiday visitors keep secret. It's far enough off the beaten track to have kept much of its charm. You can sail and swim and walk, but most of those who take holidays here seem to just hang around. But maybe that's what holidays are for! The lake is blocked off by shifting sands from the ocean most of the time, but every now and then it breaks through to the sea. That's when the mingling of waters brings a revitalising of marine food stocks. The indigenous people who have been here for aeons knew all about that. It was a time of feasting and tribal gathering.

Lake Tyers is associated in most Gippslanders' minds with the Mission Station here in the nineteenth and twentieth centuries. Its founder was John Bulmer, a churchman, one of the gentlest and greatest of men. The government let him down, first by forcing native people to come here, and later by making many of them leave. Families were broken up, hearts were broken. John Bulmer's too. There are still a large number of aboriginal folk here. In 1970 they were given title to their land, and the name was changed to Bung Yarnda – 'Big Waters'. Go and see it. You'll be welcome, but only if you go in a spirit of humility.

Lang Lang

We're sitting outside the Palace Hotel wondering how such a splendid building came to be in this small town. Perhaps weary travellers on the highway needed a break and came here to be fed and watered. What visions of the future – or what delusions of grandeur - those early settlers had to call the pub the 'Palace Hotel'! We try to imagine the first Palace Hotel, the one that burnt down in 1933, forcing the one and only guest to shin down a veranda post, leaving his clothes behind him, as well as his watch and chain. It was in May, and very likely chilly. How long did he stand there shivering before the locals took him in? Did Mr Lang the Post Master look after him? What a sense of humour in the Post Office, to send Mr Lang to Lang Lang! People liked Mr Lang; they gave a party for him when he left.

And this name, 'Lang Lang'? What does it mean? Some say 'stones'; it means 'stones' or 'stony place' in the local aboriginal language. But others say it means 'clump of trees'". How can we tell? Is the old language lost, as it is in many places? It seems to us the latter meaning is more likely. You don't see many stones around Lang Lang. Sand, yes, but not stones. And there are clumps of trees, and rows of them. Some were planted by Mr Hunter, the school teacher, in the 'thirties, and his pupils went along and helped him. Could those trees we passed along the road be part of those plantings? They seem to be the right age.

How important the teacher was in those times, in these little towns. And their wives. They brought skills and interests often little known in the country districts to enrich the local cultural scene. But their teaching was always under scrutiny from townsfolk. When people from Lang Lang, in 1914, sent a critical report on the teacher to the Education Department, he sued them for libel. The case was spread over the pages of the local press.

We leave the hotel and continue along the main street, imagining the scene here in November, 1918, when news of the Armistice came through. Flags were strung up all along the street, a procession was got together, and people marched along singing patriotic songs. Did they manage to arrange a band with such short notice? And what were the 'patriotic songs'? 'It's a Long Long Way to Tipperary', perhaps, or 'Pack up your Troubles', with 'God Save the King' to finish with?

Some years later, in 1935, a huge crowd – a thousand, some said – was here in this same street for the long-awaited coming of electricity to the town. The ceremony was held in the evening. Proceedings began with a bonfire and fireworks display on the edge of town. Mr Ridgway and Councillor Stafford made speeches, then Mr Madgie from the Electricity Commission took a pair of silver scissors and cut a ribbon, turning on the lights in the street and in the shop windows, "presenting an animated scene". In high mood, people turned to the sports. Keith Harris won the wheel-barrow race, pushing Mr Stephenson. Was Mr Stephenson a little man and Mr Harris the town's strong man? And where are those silver scissors now? Did Mr Madgie keep them? Does some descendant of his now cut up the beans on the kitchen bench with a splendid pair of scissors and wonder where they came from?

The country round about was once much more forested. A hundred years ago, deer camped amongst the timber, and descended on the crops and gardens of the householders to wreak destruction. Protests were made to the authorities, and permits were given for shooters to destroy them. The deer were brought here under the madly wrong idea that this land should be stocked with English creatures. The Acclimatisation Society was behind it all, and one of the leading members was William Lyall, who built the fine house, 'Harewood', and who brought deer and rabbits to Lang Lang, as well as hares and sparrows, thrushes and goats.

The timber was cut out and shipped off to build the burgeoning metropolis of Melbourne. The logs were hauled down to Jam Jerrup from miles around, including the far-off hill country, by narrow-gauge trams hauled by bullocks. Jam Jerrup was the outlet for this part of Gippsland, just as Port Albert was for the country further east. One of the early settlers used to swim his cattle from here across to French Island.

Jam Jerrup was first called Lang Lang. It played a key role as the gateway to McDonald's Track and so on into the wilder country of

West and South Gippsland. The name and position of Lang Lang was tossed around with gay abandon in those early days. There was an East Lang Lang and a West Lang Lang at one time. East Lang Lang became Nyora. And the present Lang Lang was once called Carrington. Lord Carrington was Governor of New South Wales and was a capable and much-admired man – he did much to pave the way for Federation, for instance – but it's hard to see how a struggling bush township in faraway Gippsland should have been honoured with his name. Well, it wasn't. Not for long, at any rate.

Surrounding the town are the hobby farms and small-holdings, then the real farms. Lang Lang is constantly changing. In the first place the land was held by large landholders – squatters, really – who had the land by leasehold until they or their successors managed to buy it or some of it. So it was like East Gippsland – squatters with huge acreages, building fine homes, employing large numbers of workers - men like William Lyall we've already mentioned, and Mickle and Bakewell who were in partnership with Lyall, and who intermarried with his family. So Harewood and Warrock Homestead were built. Warrock ended its days in ashes, but another lovely home was built in its place. Many city-dwellers come there now to re-connect with their rural roots. The car park is full every weekend.

But the old land-holdings are gone. They couldn't withstand the demand to give land to the returning men of the First World War so they could farm the soil they'd fought for. The distributions around here went on right up to 1939. Men who were employed as farm-workers before the war now took up the plough for themselves, growing potatoes and milking their cows in the small barbed-wire-fenced paddocks all around the town. In the potato season an army of diggers came into town. There used to be a Potato Diggers and Fancy Dress Ball every year. The barn dance was the highlight of the evening.

Now the potatoes have given way to asparagus, which can be whisked to Melbourne in no time, and overseas in little more. "It's the biggest asparagus region in the Southern Hemisphere," one man told me. "Here and Koo Wee Rup. There's one of their trucks now," he added with a turn of his head. A cattle truck followed it, and we inhaled the not-unpleasant aroma of cattle manure and straw and warm animal bodies. Not that you can find too many dairy farms at Lang Lang either. There's more money in small crops like vegetables, and when a dairy farmer retires, he goes over to beef. Less money, but you can stay in bed later in the morning.

The Greaves family have had a continuing connection with Lang Lang for more than a century. They took over land from another pioneer, Alexander McMillan – no relation to that other Gippslander, Angus McMillan – and have been movers and shakers as we say nowadays, though the term would have horrified, say,

William Clement Greaves, who was a leader in agricultural circles – he was a superb judge of cattle - and in the community. He died at Warrock Homestead in 1936. "A loyal member and generous friend," the Presbyterians recorded. His funeral there was the biggest ever seen. His son, also William Clement, picked up his father's mantle, and was equally honoured when he died in 1973.

Eric Kent worked a farm not far outside town. Eric's contribution was more political. He worked on behalf of farmers all his life, especially during his years as Minister of Agriculture in the State Government. Eric lived to be almost 100, always as sharp as a tack and just as ready to prick any notions of pomposity or stupidity as he ever was.

They have a pistol club, a golf club, and a coursing club in Lang Lang. They've raced just about everything here – dogs, horses, pigeons. I've read about the races here in 1915, when Mr Glasscock was Secretary. The final event was the big event of the day. Well Aware, at two to one, triumphed over Gay Boy at evens. The winner was ridden by Mr Glasscock himself. There were two other runners, Excell and Darkie. Half way through the race Darkie's jockey took a short cut through the centre of the course. We don't see such enterprise amongst today's jockeys!

The Lang Lang Show is now one of the big events in town. Some of the small agricultural show societies are struggling to hold on, and some are folding up. But Lang Lang flourishes. Another Mr

Greaves demonstrates his pottery, the stock events are as good as ever, and the produce stands are full. The Lang Lang rodeo is famous throughout the land. Buses used to run here from all the towns round about every Easter Monday, but people travel in their cars nowadays. I went to my first Lang Lang rodeo as a young lad more than half a century ago, and still recall the tingling excitement I felt.

Now we move a couple of miles out of town. Had we been here a century ago, we would have been in water. This was the Great Swamp, a vast morass of mud, reeds, paper-barks and bulrushes, some 40,000 acres in all. No one could cross it. You had to go round it to get into Gippsland, or go by sea. But human will and ingenuity have dried it out. Cardinia Creek and Toomuc Creek and the Bunyip River were channelled and tamed, and the deep black soil made available for the cows and the potatoes and the asparagus. Not without a struggle. Building the railway through here was a nightmare. The horses were sometimes stuck in the mud, up to their bellies. The navvies worked in water all day. The railway, however arrived … and later departed! The Swamp, though vanquished, has sometimes struck back. In 1904 there were disastrous floods, and again in 1934, even worse. The Lang Lang River burst its banks and spilled over the low country for miles around. The river can be treacherous in flood, and the Bass River, too. A Lang Lang lad drowned here when he went swimming with two pals, and a farm worker, "under the influence of drink" tried to swim his horse across. The horse struggled over, but the rider was lost.

Now to the Lang Lang cemetery ... and thinking of the other peaceful places of rest we've come across in Gippsland. But none more peaceful than here. In season the ficifolia florets fall to form a colourful quilt over the graves. The names repeated over and over again catch the eye, and also those we've heard over time and instantly say, 'Ah! That's a Lang Lang name!' Names like (and I'll put them in alphabetical order) Bell, Boxshall, Emmett, Gardiner, Glasscock, Glover, Greaves, Harker, Head, Kitchin, Leeson, Lineham, Male, McCraw, Motton, Patullo, Ridgway, Thwaites, and Wildes. There's a plaque recently placed here. It records the burial of the first person to be interred in this cemetery, a two-year-old girl, Louise Mary Pickersgill, who died of diphtheria in 1886. It's a sad story. The little girl's father was away, so when the little girl and her brother, Samuel, contracted diphtheria, their mother wrapped them in blankets and drove them in the jinker to the doctor's in San Remo. San Remo! Mary died on the way, and Samuel later. The children are buried together here, along with their mother, Jane. The plaque reads, '*A cemetery exists because every life is worth loving and remembering*'.

The line of coast at Lang Lang, right through to Coronet Bay and inland to Bass is becoming victim to the spreading tentacles of the City of Greater Melbourne. Bass Coast Shire has one of the highest growth rates in Victoria. Thousands of tourists head this way as well. On the weekends this strip of land changes its nature altogether. At Grantville, well-placed to take advantage of the passing tourist cars and buses, the Maru Koala and Animal Park beckons Japanese tourists in particular. Who could resist the combination of the names, 'Maru' and 'koala'? Further on, at Bass, is the Giant Earthworm Museum, where "you can climb inside the giant worm, into its simulated stomach, and get ready to learn more than you ever wanted to know about the monstrous Gippsland Giant worm". Did they ask the Giant Earthworm about that? [These places may very well have been temporarily closed because of the coronavirus pandemic.]

The publicity folk speak of Corinella as a hidden gem and Victoria's best-kept secret. Well, we've all heard that before, but the little town is indeed very pretty. You can take sandy, ti-tree-lined walks, and the salt air fills the nostrils. I like best the gently-sloping drive down to the jetty with the blue water glimpsed further ahead. O for a boat! If you haven't got one, you may like to take a ferry across to French Island. Some claim Corinella as Victoria's first settlement. There *was* a garrison stationed here in 1826, eight years ahead of Melbourne or Portland, but they were taken off two years later, and the buildings fell in to ruin.

Coronet Bay, a few miles further on, is Corinella writ small. It's a place where the folk who live here know each other very well, but keep out of each other's way. Live and let live! BUT, a huge $42 million tourist development has been proposed for the town. The Shire seems to be strongly supportive, but local groups have strongly opposed it. "If you've experienced Coronet Bay and love it for what it is now, please lodge an objection …" writes one correspondent. Here is one of Gippsland's great dilemmas. We have a place of great beauty. How can we share it? How can we preserve it? Do we live for the past or for the future? Is there a modus vivendi between these two poles?

Leongatha

Wow! Leongatha is "the civic, commercial, industrial, religious, educational and sporting centre of the region". Must be some place. Rather odd to see, then, that the population is a mere 5,119 people at the 2016 census. The explanation, I think, is that whereas Leongatha was once much the same size as many other regional centres in Gippsland, the others have grown – think Drouin, Warragul, Moe, Morwell, Traralgon, Sale, Bairnsdale. Leongatha has remained solid old Leongatha, the same now as it always was, faithfully serving the district round about, without any one single factor pushing it towards growth. Everybody knows Leongatha, however. Main roads go through it. You pass through Leongatha if you're going to Korumburra or Inverloch or Warragul or along the highway to Foster or down to Wilson's Promontory or over to Mirboo North or even to Phillip Island. People are always going through it. More should stop over!

Leongatha folk are proud of their town, but it's not only those who live there now. I've known quite a few who live elsewhere but spent a period of their lives in Leongatha and they all speak about it in the warmest terms. One man who went to school there and much later worked there for some years says it's the friendliest place he's ever been in. He couldn't quite say why that is; it's just the way the place has developed. Each country town seems to develop its own particular set of characteristics and, once established, they last for ever. Leongatha generates a good feeling. Perhaps it comes from that solidity I've mentioned above. The best elements of the past have come down unfiltered to the present.

The cleared hills surrounding the town were once covered by majestic eucalypts. It was a mighty struggle to clear the land. Some regret that it was ever done. One monarch of the Strzeleckis was so tall it was cut down so it could be measured! And once the land was cleared other problems appeared, like rabbits, blackberries, and bracken. The bracken was a particular curse for the early settlers on those steep southern hills. It kept on coming back. Bernard Cronin, who worked on farms round Leongatha a hundred years ago actually wrote a book called, 'Bracken', in which he dramatized the plight of the struggling hill farmers:

> *The weary guillotine of the fern-hook was powerless against the snake-like rhizomes that writhed a tenebrous passage beneath the soil ... From every bud and joint and spur hidden from his sight, the evil thrust itself anew in tendrils of exquisite green frondule ... Close at hand was a riot of old fern, rearing itself with the poisonous arrogance of conquest. For a whole season this patch had evaded the fern-hook ... A year since, the land where he lay had been good grassland. Now there was no grass at all. The bracken had strangled it.*

Those years of intense struggle with the land have now passed. The nation has been blessed with good years, and places like Leongatha have taken part in the greater ease with which life is lived.

I've made out Leongatha to be a place of some respectability. It has had its charlatans, however. I was amused by this report in the Morwell Advertiser in 1903:

> *Joseph Wilson was before the [Leongatha] Court on Tuesday, charged with being a rogue and vagabond. Accused had posed as deaf and dumb, and successfully solicited alms from townspeople. He was sentenced to six months hard labour.*

Perhaps they took him to Port Arthur and put him in the deaf-and-dumb cell!

Much worse was to come. In 1935 a serial child-killer, Arnold Sodeman, murdered his fourth and last victim in Leongatha – a twelve-year-old girl, June Rushmer. His previous murders had been in Melbourne and Inverloch. Sodeman, who was married and had a small daughter, was working in Leongatha on the roads. He pleaded guilty and was executed in Pentridge Prison in June, 1936. In 1965, an episode of the TV show, 'Homicide', was based on the case.

It's time to pick up that claim that Leongatha is the civic, commercial, industrial, religious, educational, and sporting centre of the region. The claim to 'civic' primacy is valid enough. The huge South Gippsland Shire has its seat here in the town, and covers Foster, Korumburra, Meeniyan, Mirboo North, Poowong, and the whole of Wilson's Promontory. Sad to say, the Council was dismissed by the State government in 2019 after a 'toxic intractable culture' developed among councillors. The Shire is to be run by an administrator and three appointed commissioners until October 2021.

As to the commercial supremacy of Leongatha, certainly the town has the largest commercial area of any town in the Shire. However, Council surveys have drawn criticism of the town centre as being "boring', bleak", "grey", and having "no heart". Leongatha, like several Gippsland towns, has inherited a structural problem in that the streets were originally planned to allow cattle to be driven along them. Now we are left with wide streets that are not friendly as close and companionable pedestrian and shopping places. We can't blame Leongatha for that, although it is time a highway by-pass was built. It's been on the drawing-boards long enough.

The claim that Leongatha is an industrial centre is principally based on the huge Murray-Goulburn Dairy Processing plant on the northern side of the town. It's said to be the largest of its kind in the Southern Hemisphere. Murray-Goulburn was a co-operative of dairy-farmers from its beginning, but many became disenchanted with the company and were willing sellers when the Canadian firm, Saputo, bought the company in 2018. There is still a lot of grief surrounding the demise of Murray-Goulburn. Catherine Watson, who wrote a history of the firm, commented, "How can it go down the drain over two years and just disappear from the scene? ... It's like a death in the family. I feel so sad about it."

I'm not too sure about the 'religious' claim. How do you measure that? I see there are seventeen "churches, temples and mosques" listed in the Yellow Pages directory for Leongatha, which seems a lot. One church for every 300 people. In the old days there were just 'Catholics, Protestants, and Others'. Perhaps I'm remembering that from my army days! Somebody told me that "all the doctors go to church in Leongatha". Could that be true?

The church folk of Leongatha were shocked one Sunday in 1936 when some fanatics drove into town with a van and loudspeakers, and began blasting their propaganda outside two of the town's churches. Not only the church attenders but players on the tennis courts (tut-tut; Sunday morning!) were shocked by the "subversive and insulting blasts from the microphone". The police soon advised these "anti-religious gangsters" to vacate the town with all speed.

Certainly, Leongatha is an educational centre, with a strong spread of primary and secondary, government and independent schools. In recent years there has been an upsurge of small alternative schools in rural areas. One such is the Village School in Koonwarra, a little south of Leongatha. A sister school is at Ventnor on Phillip Island,

and in 2020 a secondary school began at Ryanston, near Wonthaggi.

Leongatha has a fine sporting record, particularly in Australian Rules football. The club was formed in 1894, so it has been putting teams on the field over three centuries! Known as the Parrots (grass parrots, I'd say, from their green and gold gear), they played off in the Grand Final every year from 2015 to 2019, winning on two of those five occasions. Maffra have been their great rivals in recent years, and it's worthy of note that these two towns are much smaller than most of the other teams in the Gippsland League. Who said a champion team will always beat a team of champions? Dyson Heppell and Jarred Roughhead, two AFL stars, are products of Leongatha. There's a host of other sports played in and around the town, from basketball to badminton, gymnastics to golf. Leongatha may well claim to be the sporting centre of the region.

Leongatha occupies one little niche in history. During the 1890s Depression, thousands of able-bodied men were thrown out of work in Melbourne. The government set up settlements throughout the State where men could do farm and timber work with a view to them becoming land owners. I've counted well over twenty of these settlements in Gippsland alone. A settlement of a different type was established on 800 acres at Leongatha where the Secondary College now stands. Its aim was not to bring city men on to the land as settlers, but to give them training and experience that would allow them to find employment in the country. It was known as the Leongatha Labour Colony and gave employment to more than 9,000 men over the years of its existence, 1891 to 1919. The colony was virtually self-sufficient. The men cleared the land, grew oats, wheat, potatoes and onions, and had twenty-one acres of garden and fruit trees. There were pigs and poultry, a dairy herd and creamery, a slaughterhouse and bakery. Each man had to leave after six months or when he had accumulated thirty shillings from his wages. There were always plenty more on the waiting list.

South Gippsland led the fight against unconventional coal seam gas production – 'fracking' – in Victoria in the middle-2010s, and Leongatha was in the thick of it. The protest movement got underway locally when the legendary Drew Hutton, President of the 'Lock the Gate' movement, came to Leongatha to speak to Gippslanders in 2011. 200 people attended. The magic of the movement was that it brought together an unlikely pair of protagonists – environmentalists and conservatively-minded landholders. "You must fight this fight for yourselves, because once you allow them into your property, they will never leave," Hutton told the Leongatha crowd. "The crowd of landholders, environmentalists and National Party voters cheered in response," the ABC reported. The movement spread across Gippsland. Poowong was at the forefront. The Bishop of Gippsland declared his opposition. 'Lock the Gate' signs appeared all over the region. Protesters at Seaspray formed a human sign: 'NO GASFIELDS', it read, photographed from the air as people lined up on the beach. The government crumbled. A permanent moratorium was declared on fracking and a hold put on conventional gas exploration, although it was announced in 2020 that the ban on conventional gas exploration would be lifted. Most people will accept that, I believe. However many still don't understand the difference between conventional and unconventional (fracking) exploration.

One of the attractive aspects of Gippsland is the way some small towns have become low-key tourist attractions. Not necessarily for the big-ticket travellers, but for people who are in the know about these 'boutique' villages. I'm thinking of places like Yarragon, Stratford, and, here in South Gippsland, Loch, Fish Creek, Meeniyan, and Koonwarra. I could almost add Noojee and Yinnar to the list. Koonwarra is a very pretty township that's developed a name for its progressive environmentalism. It's claimed the shops won't serve anything in a plastic bag, although when I was there the shop girl knew nothing about it! It has a farmers' market each month. Someone said it was the first one in Australia. It was the first waste-wise village in the land. There was a training day here not long ago on civil disobedience, to prepare protesters for street demonstrations!

How many towns are there where the big banks and the big supermarket chains fear to tread, but the Bendigo Bank and the IGA chain of grocers provide their vital services? This is the case in

Meeniyan, a small town with a big name in a variety of ways. It's become known as a 'foodies' delight' and an 'artists' happy valley'. The Lyrebird Arts Council puts on good music; the Dramatic Society presents local drama; there's an annual art and craft exhibition; and the Tavern Nights give a platform for local performers. Straw figures propped up on street corners ogle you as you walk past. There's a garlic festival every February. Thousands come. Meeniyan is a stop-over point on the Great Southern Rail Trail that runs from Leongatha to Foster. Tanderra Park is alongside, which adjoins a fantastic pleasure ground with a bicycle theme. There's a bike rider up a pole, a sunflower bed within a framework of old bike wheels cunningly fixed together, straw ladies stand idly around, while a straw hobo slumps on a bench. The place doubles as the community garden. It's the sort of place you'd only find in Meeniyan.

There are several other small towns near Leongatha that deserve mention. One of them is Nerrena, where you'll find a fine public hall, a large quarry, and a heritage-listed farm complex, designed in the 1920s by James Knox. It was far ahead of its time. It was also the home of the Gippsland Light Horse. That was in 1941 and was the last gasp for the use of horses in war or training for war. The Nerrena-Tarwin Landcare Group is working to preserve the Black Spur Creek Wetlands, which contain original vegetation. They give a glimpse of what the pre-settlement landscape was like.

Dumbalk has all the trappings of a self-contained town. It's lost its butter factory, but retains a lively neighbourhood identity. It feels good to be there, or even to drive through it. Though they played against each other for years, Dumbalk and Meeniyan have joined forces to become the Meeniyan Dumbalk Union football team. Koorooman, further out, is notable for its First World War Avenue of Honour, consisting of chestnut oaks. Ruby, on the Korumburra side is more of a locality. There is a Ruby, Canada as well as a Ruby, Australia. Make sure you know which one you're going to!

I grew up when country racetracks were found "all over the place". However there was a rationalisation which saw many of the old tracks disappear. One of the old stalwarts – the Stony Creek track - was above rationalisation. It's part of the fabric of Gippsland. There are five race days each year, the highlight being the Stony Creek Cup in March. The biggest news story ever to come from here was the triple dead-heat of 1987. Chester Field, Mr Spectre, and Fast Seal couldn't be separated. The event made headlines around the world. I've been to the track only once. If I'd backed the favourite in every race I'd have won handsomely, but I didn't ... and I didn't!

Maffra

Boisdale Street cuts through the heart of Maffra from south-east to north-west. You can't miss it. It's three chains, sixty metres, wide. That's the width they allowed for a cattle track in the pioneer days, the official government regulation. And that takes us to the heart of the original Maffra story.

We're not in the hilly, forested West Gippsland country. We're not in the hills and small farms of the south. We're not in the industrialised Latrobe Valley. We're on the edge of the squatting country of East Gippsland where herds of cattle and flocks of sheep were moved into this land that was opening up for settlement.

This is the country of Angus McMillan and Lachlan Macalister and their men, who wrested these plains from their aboriginal occupants for good or ill, and gave us the first shaping of modern Gippsland. The course of Boisdale Street through the town is a monument to those far-off days. In 1886, a visitor described Maffra:

> *The main street is a three-chain road, bordered with English trees ... Not so many brick buildings here as at Stratford, but there is a live, smart look about the place which makes up for the lack of prominent edifices.*

One smart edifice that is there in Maffra is 'Duart', a reception centre now, but originally home to Allan McLean, the most prominent person ever to come from Maffra. McLean began as a squatter in the classic sense, but he became a highly successful stock and station agent. Scottish like many other Gippsland squatters, Catholic like few others, and a poet, he charmed people with his Scottish burr. One account describes him when a young man: "… a dashing young station hand who could tame a wild dog, put a mob of cattle over a river, dance a reel, play the bagpipes until the skirl came screaming back from the hills, or sing a Scottish ballad in broad Gaelic with the fire and pathos of an ancient minstrel". Ah, they don't make them now like they used to! McLean entered local politics, became President of Maffra Shire, then was elected to State parliament as the Member for Gippsland North. He served there for twenty years, becoming Premier for twelve months, before entering the first Federal parliament in 1901. He became Deputy Prime Minister to Sir George Reid, but was defeated in 1906 and returned to private life. He died in his Melbourne home in Beaconsfield Parade, Albert Park, which he also called 'Duart'.

Maffra might have ridden on the sheep's back, to steal someone else's phrase, in the pioneering days, but other economic impulses have driven the town forward. The first of these was sugar beet, championed by Allan McLean and others. Maffra is the only place in Australia ever to have had a viable sugar beet industry. In State school, we all learnt about it, and our Gippsland hearts swelled with pride that our own Gippsland should have a place so important. Even today, sixty years after the industry collapsed, folk all over the country will instantly say 'sugar beet' when you mention Maffra. Or vice-versa. Sugar beet contains as much sugar as cane sugar, even a little bit more. It was seen as a useful crop in this district – the soil was suitable, irrigation was on hand, and the climate was perfect. When the closer settlement schemes were set up by the government, it was stipulated that each settler had to grow ten acres of sugar beet. Without that, I don't think any of them would have grown it. Growing beet was back-breaking work, and the financial return was meagre, especially in the first years. Some of the old-timers have told me they could barely stand after a day's work on the beet. In the end, dairying proved more profitable than beet, and sugar became a memory, kept in the public mind by the Sugar Beet Museum near the town centre. It's just a tiny part of the huge establishment that once stood here.

Providing water for sugar beet was the main reason for the development of the irrigation scheme that now dominates the district. The authorities first thought of building a dam on the Avon River, but the higher annual flow in the Macalister swung the decision that way. In constructing Lake Glenmaggie they flooded some good country. A man passing through left a record of his impressions of old Glenmaggie before it was submerged beneath the water:

> *No lovelier glen than it, at that day, could, I think, exist anywhere, immense quantities of fern trees, innumerable*

> *red gums, straight as gun barrels, their big trunks shining white as silver, towering to heights of 100 feet, rose from the flats, all shades of lightwoods and wattles, with their golden bloom, and tapering sassafras trees, filled the eye with satisfied pleasure.*

At the same time a settler named Robert Fullerton was battling the odds on his selection block a few miles away. His daughter was Mary Fullerton who wrote about her early life there in her *Bark House Days*, one of the most remarkable Gippsland books ever to be written. Her book tells of a Gippsland we will never see again. From its first page to its last, it brings on the nostalgic shivers in me. She begins:

> *The old house is no longer there. The structures of pioneer days are not for permanency. We were born to it, the whole wild, shy, little seven of us, and when it began to tumble and lurch itself out of plumb, hands, I know not if desecrating or reverent, were laid upon it, and it was demolished.*

On the last page, she writes of a beautiful Glenmaggie evening:

> *Around us the world lay melting into evening's magic, darkling yet clear. Across the opaline sky towards the distant lakes was flying one waterfowl, a dark speck in the wide, clear expanse.*

The retaining dam for the weir took seven years to build. A tent city of workers was set up; 400 horses were put to work, and the old town of Glenmaggie and the surrounding farms were flooded. It was tough going, though now part of the folk-lore of the district. The workers –'navvies'- were a mixed bunch. John Shaw Neilson, as famous for his poems as Mary Fullerton is for her prose, was one of them. He wrote about the men he worked with:

> *When I think of the way some navvies behave I am reminded of a saying .... 'I can't love the human race, I've seen it.' But I must not be unjust to my fellow-workers. Most of them especially the young fellows & the bushmen were decent chaps. I like the bushborn ones much the best. They were more modest & more efficient at anything.*

After seven years of construction work, in 1926, the first water from Lake Glenmaggie was sent out through the Northern Channel to Boisdale. Over the years, the dam wall has been raised to increase capacity and even a small hydro-electric plant installed. Many farms have been laser-graded to make more efficient use of the water. The Macalister Irrigation District now has 33,500 hectares under irrigation. Just about as big as McFarlane's original squattage here.

As you travel round the district you find yourself driving alongside or crossing the irrigation channels. There are 592 kilometres of them! At the outlet to each farm you will notice a device that they use to measure the water being taken out. They're called Dethridge wheels, and they were the invention of John Dethridge, an engineer who worked for the Water Commission around the state and eventually became the Senior Engineer for the whole show and one of the three Water Commissioners for the State. In 1910, when working in the Goulburn Valley, he invented his water wheel. Some have called it one of the great icons of rural Australia, alongside the stump-jump plough and the Furphy water tank. Dethridge's wheel was a drum with eight external fins that was placed on an axle into the flow of water. The water filled the vanes and so turned the wheel. The number of revolutions was recorded automatically and so the quantity of water could be measured and costed accordingly. Good old Dethridge refused to take out a patent on his work, and so his water wheel spread around Australia and across the world in hundreds of thousands.

After the beet sugar declined and disappeared, dairying became the backbone of Maffra and the irrigation district. It still is. The Murray-Goulburn factory, with its slogan, 'Healthy Cows, Healthy Milk', is on the southern edge of town. It dominates the place visually and commercially. Around it is one of the most concentrated dairying regions in Australia. No pretty little Jerseys to be seen here, only big black and white Holstein-Friesians. Bulk milk is in demand, not the creamy offerings of the Jersey. You'd think the football team should wear black and white in honour of the dairy cattle instead of their red and black. That said, the Maffra football team is renowned Gippsland-wide. Is there any other team that has a higher success ratio to town size than Maffra?

Where does public spirit come from? It's something a town gets without trying for it, but once achieved, it sticks. Maffra has got as much town spirit as any place I know. Some put it down to the distance from Melbourne – 220 kilometres to be precise. Others put it down to being off the main highway and railway line – 20 kilometres away. Others still talk about strong local leadership over the years. There was a lot of angst here when the town was handed over to be part of Wellington Shire when the Great Amalgamation occurred, and there is still an undercurrent of complaint that Maffra doesn't get a fair deal. The annual Mardi Gras is as good a reference point for local spirit as anything else. It's run through the Rotary Club, but it's a whole-town event. For six weeks the girls representing their particular charities compete – in good spirit – to see who can raise the most money. The culmination is the festival and street parade, always in March. The show's been going for sixty years and many hundreds of thousands of dollars have been raised for good works over this time.

Maffra has 200 Japanese visitors each year, but they bring no money with them. Nor do they worry about passports or custom duties or the Border Force. They're the Japanese Snipe (properly called Latham's Snipe), a beautiful little speckled brown bird with a round head, short legs and wings, but a very long beak which they use to grub out feed from the marshy ground they frequent. Each year they migrate between the wetlands of southern and eastern Australia and Hokkaido in northern Japan. 9000 kilometres. They do it in three stages. They'll leave the Maffra Wetlands, say, in February, fly to Southern Queensland, rest for a few weeks, then fly to Torres Strait, take another rest, then over New Guinea and the Pacific to their breeding grounds in Japan. After some months they set out on their return journey, and eventually come back to the same place, in this case, Maffra, in September. I wonder what the young ones who've never done it before think of it!

Several satellite towns surround Maffra. Each has its own history and its own pride. The old names go on. I was reading a newspaper from 1927 recently, about Newry. The names of Clyne, Manson, Webster, Horstman, Bowman, and Weir were prominent in it. There's something about country towns that never changes. Newry is a place with long memories. I'll pick out two people to represent the town and apologise to the others I might have chosen. Jack Dwyer farmed this land all his life, like his father before him. Strong in his Catholic faith, but known as a friend to church folk of all persuasions, he is an embodiment of the spirit of Newry. Not that he was ever provincial; he is as well known in Maffra as in Newry. Jack was instrumental (amongst a host of other things) in having Bellbird Corner, where Newry Creek joins the Macalister, set aside as a public reserve. It now delights many people.

There's a poignant tale set here. A two-year-old girl, Eliza Amey was drowned at this place, near her home, in 1867. With no other materials at hand, her father stripped the bark from a redgum tree, wrapped her in this bark shroud, and buried her here by the Newry Creek. The site has now been beautifully marked by the Bellbird Corner volunteers, and the gum tree still stands, bearing the scars where it gave its bark to be a final shelter for this little one. Someone has written a little poem for her, ending with these lines:

> *Now, if people passing by should pause, to gaze and quietly ponder,*
>
> *The little girl who knew so few may hear them call – 'Eliza'.*

The other name is that of Ivan McNally who worked as a butcher for seventy-two years, first in Stratford, then in Newry for the last forty years. When he retired and closed the shop in 2017, aged eighty-six, he was the oldest active butcher in Australia. The supermarkets drove him out of business.

Boisdale was first a sheep run, Lachlan Macalister's originally, before it passed into the hands of the Foster family. Askin Foster broke the property up into small-holdings, thirty-five in all, which were leased to individual dairy farmers. It was a rare thing to do in Australia. The only similar action I can think of was when the Tooth family, the Sydney brewers, developed a number of small farms on their run near Bega, where they looked after their tenants in a genuinely caring way. It was much the same here. The Foster farms were the heart of Boisdale. On the ridge above the Boisdale flats Askin Foster built his 'Boisdale House', where the family have continued to this day. Boisdale is named after a place on the island of South Uist in the Outer Hebrides.

In 1991, I took the ferry from Oban, plunging for six hours across the fierce Atlantic to reach fabled South Uist. The people there were faintly interested to hear that someone was visiting from their twin-town far away. Near there, in 1830, a mermaid was found, deceased, and was buried in the sand. Much later, in 1941, a ship carrying whisky ran ashore, giving the locals a whale of a time. Compton McKenzie wrote a book based on it, 'Whisky Galore', which was made into a film. Remember it? As far as I know, my wife and I are the only ones from this Boisdale ever to visit the other Boisdale.

Mallacoota

There's an argument that Mallacoota was the first permanent settlement in Victoria. I came across it in George Cox's papers on early Gippsland. The argument goes that there were people living here permanently before the Hentys at Portland in 1834 or John Batman in Melbourne in 1835. That's doubtful. It might even be called 'fake news' in America. Certainly there were whaling depots here before Portland was settled. Ben Boyd and others put them here, but whether you could call that permanent settlement is doubtful. The first true settler, Captain John Stephenson arrived in 1841, and stayed. He had been one of those whalers, and liked what he saw. Captain Stephenson's Point commemorates him today.

I used to have a rather jaundiced view of Mallacoota. It came about because on my first visit here, as a young man, I was in a boat that put out into the Bay on a pleasant December morning. There were five or six others aboard, and we cruised gently about, the still waters lapping at the gunwales. I looked over the side to study something or other, when one of the other passengers accidentally bumped me, and my glasses fell into the blue waves. I watched in horror as they did a slow spiral descent to the floor of the Bay. There was an off-duty abalone diver on board, and I fully expected him to volunteer to strip off and dive down and retrieve them. To my dismay, he politely declined to do so. I was left rueful and spectacle-less. They will be there to this day, I have no doubt, barnacled and broken.

But my early sour view of Mallacoota has been changed over the years by many very happy visits since, during which I have clung tightly not only to my glasses, but also to my hat and my teeth. One thing that delights me about Mallacoota is that it has been a mecca for literary figures. The principal one was E.J. Brady. You might know these lines of his, inspired by Mallacoota. They have been used in tourism advertisements in Melbourne just recently:

> *I'll call you to the beaches,*
> *And you shall bide with me*
> *Along the river reaches*
> *And by the open sea.*

Brady spent the last forty years of his life in Mallacoota, living close to nature, and attracting a host of leading writers to join him. The most famous of these is Henry Lawson. There's a wonderful photo of Brady and Lawson together. Brady's doing the talking, and Lawson, with shoulders hunched and bushy moustache prominent, doing the listening. They say Lawson was recovering from alcoholism at the time. Katherine Susannah Prichard also came, as did Louis Esson. It was a literary fellowship, centred on E J Brady. In a later age, they might have called them Brady's Bunch! Towards the end of Brady's life, Edward Harrington visited him, and wrote this description of Mallacoota by night:

Mallacoota in the moonlight

Has a glory all its own

When the mighty sea is muttering

In a muffled undertone

And when rain is on the waters

And the heavens give no light

Then the light from mighty Gabo

Like a great sword cleaves the night.

Gabo Island is away to the eastward, not far, and decidedly part of the Mallacoota scene. You can fly to the island, but many prefer to go by boat from Mallacoota. The world's largest colony of little penguins is there. They were in danger from feral cats until a campaign in the late 'eighties got rid of them, the cats, that is. The beams from the lighthouse, built from the local red granite, still cleave the night, as Harrington's poem puts it. A lighthouse was built after the wreck of the *Monumental City* on nearby Tullaberga Island in 1853. It was replaced by the present structure in 1863. The same year, the artist, Samuel Calvert, did a brilliant engraving of the lighthouse, showing the skirl of the sky above and the swirl of the waves below, sea-birds skimming the water. The *Monumental City* was an American vessel, a modern screw steamer, and had arrived in Australian waters only a few weeks earlier, carrying diggers from California to the Australian goldfields. It was the very first steamship to cross the Pacific. En route from Melbourne to Sydney on a Sunday morning, it hit the rocks at full speed in the darkness of early morning. Some fifty people managed to get safe to land due to the bravery and skill of one man, Charles Plummer, who managed to get a line and bosun's chair ashore. However, more than thirty perished.

There are several other wrecks in nearby waters. The *Schah* was wrecked in 1837 near Ram's Head. This vessel had a wretched history, having been used as a slave-trader before being put to work on this side of the world on the Hobart-Sydney run. Several lives were lost, including women and children. The *Riverina* carrying brandy, whisky, and paint, hit the rocks at Island Point in 1890 in a 'Whisky Galore' parallel, though none of the Mallacoota residents got hold of the cargo in this instance. The *Iron Prince*, a BHP limestone carrier, was wrecked near Cape Howe in 1923. The wrecks these days provide sport for divers, though professional salvage teams have attempted to take off metals. Some have used explosives to assist their recovery efforts, though to little avail.

The tranquillity of present-day Mallacoota jars with its history as a military base during both World Wars. It's hard to think that our Gippsland seaways were threatened by the German navy in the First World War, but so it was. The German raider, *SMS Wolf*, wreaked havoc with Allied shipping in the latter part of the war. She disguised herself as a commercial vessel, which in fact she was, originally. With false sides to conceal her weapons and false funnels, she was indeed a wolf in sheep's clothing. Her tactic was to locate trading vessels, helped by a two-seater sea-plane she carried on board. She would capture the unarmed vessels, take the crews prisoner, transfer precious goods, especially coal and metals, and then sink the ships. The *Wolf* also laid mines in strategic zones off South Africa, India, Australia, and New Zealand. One of the mines off Gabo Island damaged the *Cumberland*, carrying precious metals, in July, 1917. The ship was beached near Gabo Island, and an attempt made to refloat her. However she sank in heavy seas while being towed to Sydney. After a fifteen-month voyage, the *Wolf* returned to her home port of Kiel unscathed, with 460 prisoners-of-war. She had destroyed some thirty Allied vessels, and taken much precious material, especially rubber and copper.

The impact of the Second World War on Mallacoota was more immediate. The RAAF built an Advanced Operations Base here. It was one of many such stations established along the coast. Others in Gippsland were at Bairnsdale and Yanakie. The bases listened in to coastal shipping and sent intelligence information to Headquarters in Melbourne. German warships were active off our coast during the first two years of the War, and then Japanese submarines. These submarines carried mini submarines like the ones that caused havoc in Sydney Harbour, and also little seaplanes which were launched by catapults. Twenty-two ships were lost to these submarines along our east coast, including two off Gabo Island. One of these was the *Iron Crown* where thirty-eight lives were lost. There's a memorial to these men in Mallacoota.

That's only part of the story. An aerodrome was built alongside the Advanced Operations Base, from where Avro Ansons and Wirraways and Beauforts patrolled the coastline. There was also a seaplane depot on Mallacoota Lake, from where Sea Gull flying boats operated. Exercises were constantly carried out, including mock training 'attacks' on inland places like Benambra. It must have been frightening for the local residents. Much of this wartime military apparatus remains. The airfield is now the Mallacoota aerodrome. The bunker housing the communications and intelligence equipment is still there, just as it was. It's a large underground concrete structure in very peaceful surroundings, and is operated by the Mallacoota Historical Society as a museum, a reminder of those dramatic years of war. Truly, the swords have been beaten into ploughshares.

The Wallagaraugh River joins the Genoa River just above Mallacoota. Both are interstate interlopers. They begin in New South Wales and, like many of their human counterparts, finish up in Victoria. But then, the interstate boundary here is simply a line on the map – the Black-Allan line, it's called. Black and Allan were the two men who surveyed the line between Cape Howe and the headwaters of the Murray River that marks the border between the

States. At the confluence of the two rivers you find what I think is the most luscious little spot in Gippsland – Gipsy Point. If I didn't enjoy the trappings of modern society as much as I do, this is where I'd live. I'd paddle my canoe over the still waters and watch the sun go down over the green hills!

Genoa itself straddles the Princes Highway. The first time I came through here, the highway was a dirt road. Genoa is worth looking around. The old bridge across the river is no longer in service, but still stands as a monument to past times. Another monument to past times here is the sculpture of a tetrapod, a very ancient creature, the first animal to have four legs, as its name indicates. To my untrained eye it looks rather like a blue-tongue lizard. A few miles out of Genoa, towards Orbost, quite close to the main road, are the Genoa Falls. They're amazing. For a start you'd never know they were there unless someone told you. One of East Gippsland's best kept secrets. The Falls themselves could almost be called the 'Horizontal Falls' because the river – the Genoa River – tumbles over a hundred yards of boulders set in its bed rather than actually fall over a rock outcrop. But it's here you find the water dragons, who must surely be direct descendants of those tetrapods of ancient times, they look so similar. When I first came here, there must have been more than a hundred of them, scrambling and scorching around the rocks, totally unconcerned by our presence. Will there be a sculpture of a water dragon in Genoa in several hundred million years' time?

I can't leave Genoa without mentioning an extraordinary event that took place here forty or so years ago. Now I can't vouch for this tale. It could be an urban myth, but the person who told me about it swore he was there at the time, and that this is absolutely true. A certain Mr North happened to meet a certain Mr South here in Genoa. They were unknown to each other. Just then a man came along, who, upon questioning, told the other two his name was East. Finally, another stranger – no doubt passing through to or from Eden – came on the scene. You've got it. His name was West. You can't verify this tale from Google. It's not there. It's just one of those curious old Gippsland stories that needs to be recorded before it sinks into the mists of time.

Many people from Mallacoota and Genoa drive to Eden in New South Wales to do their bulk shopping. It sounds crazy until you look at a map. Eden is far closer that Orbost, the nearest Victorian town to offer similar services. Crossing the border leads to the same conversation in every car: the road surface either improves or deteriorates according to your particular prejudice! You see a sign to Timbillica not far from the border. On one trip we decided it would be interesting to visit the place so we drove in … and out. We failed to find it. The census says that nine people live there. Sorry, folk. We missed you.

The eyes of the world were on Mallacoota over New Year, 2020. In a few lines, I can't do justice to the trauma, then the courage and resilience of the locals and holiday-makers who endured the New Year's Eve bushfire horror. The fire bore down relentlessly, its fearsome tentacles reaching out to consume the town like a hound from hell. Thousands huddled on the foreshore as the flames advanced and the sky turned blood-crimson/purple. In the end, no lives were lost, though some hundred homes were destroyed, and the livelihood of residents decimated. The most vulnerable were evacuated by naval craft and helicopter, while the rest were marooned in town until the roads were made safe many days later.

The event brought out the nobility not just in local people, but across the nation. Millions of dollars were donated towards the work of recovery, while there were countless acts of kindness. A good example is of the two young women in Melbourne who founded the Empty Esky movement. Over 50,000 signed up. The principle was that those unaffected by the fires should visit the places where the fires had raged, taking an empty esky with them to load up with goods to take home, thus helping local producers and traders to recover. But the people of Mallacoota themselves were quick to bring things back to normal. They promptly organised several gatherings to rekindle public spirit. The biggest one was the Wild Harvest Seafood Festival that was originally set down for early April, 2020, but had to be postponed for six months because of the coronavirus outbreak. The double-whammy of bushfire and coronavirus pandemic has hit Mallacoota harder than any other place in the region.

Fire and pestilence aside, Mallacoota remains a place of supreme beauty. Its charm comes from the landscape – the harmony between sea and land – but also from Mallacoota's location, far from the beaten track. That has always been the case. A newspaper correspondent of a hundred years ago – in 1919 – made this observation:

> *In one respect there is reason for regret that the iron road from north to south does not hug the coast with sufficient closeness to make ... Mallacoota Inlet available to the public. Practical considerations aside, however, this would be a rash experiment for in the very aloofness of these quiet places lies much of their charm, and, touched by the 'civilising' element, they are never the same again.*

To me, the miracle is that 'civilisation' *has* found Mallacoota, yet it has retained its pristine loveliness. The scars of the recent bushfires will heal; the residents will once more delight in their surroundings; and people, like me, who come and go, will find rest for their souls.

Mirboo North

I drove up from Meeniyan to Mirboo North recently and marvelled at the road builders. Many of our Gippsland roads began as tracks following ancient aboriginal trails, then developed into cart tracks, later to be improved, straightening bends, cutting through hills, and building up low places. It was done using horses and scoops where possible, but a lot of it was pick and shovel and wheelbarrow work. Those early back-breaking endeavours were very clear as we swept up from the lower land into the Strzelecki slopes.

At Mirboo North we reached the Grand Ridge Road at about its mid-point. In the same way that Blaxland, Wentworth and Lawson followed the ridges rather than the valleys to cross the Blue Mountains in 1813, so the Grand Ridge Road follows the ridges of the Strzeleckis to link east and west over the 130 kilometres of its length, from Seaview to Carrajung, connecting the towns and localities of Ferndale, Trida, Hallston, Mirboo North, Boolarra South, Gunyah, Balook, and Blackwarry. The road has served very practical purposes in the past, like transporting the disused Callignee South School to Jumbuk in 1947 or, infamously, transporting nine kidnapped Wooreen schoolchildren and their teacher by their captor, Edwin John Eastwood, in 1977. Most traffic, however, is much more benign!

By the 'thirties the road was being billed as a tourist road. "It provides a scene of panoramic grandeur equalled by few places in the State," one motorist wrote to the Argus in 1935. Baw Baw Shire still dangles the road as an attraction for tourists: It is "one of the great tourist drives of Victoria ... it offers visitors a journey and a destination that exceeds all expectations". I'm not quite sure what that means, but certainly the blurb writer got it right when he or she added that they'd find "a surprise around every corner". A log truck, maybe!

The place where Mirboo North now stands was 'discovered' by Count Paul Strzelecki, but it took a long time for settlement to occur. The dense forests and steep hills were not the first choice of the settlers. Strzelecki was here in 1840, but it was 1880 before permanent settlement took place. The bush featured prominently in early accounts of the district. By the end of the 'eighties the poet Nellie Clerk had written and published her *Songs from Gippsland Forests*. Nellie felt a spiritual connection with the towering gums that surrounded her at Mirboo North, and was saddened by the knowledge that the bushman's axe would before long them take them away:

> *But armies of these ghostly eucalypt trees*
> *For years their sad guard will be keeping.*

In 1918, with much of the forest cover removed, EJ Brady, in *Australia Unlimited*, still found beauty in the landscape. He was travelling the same road as I had, from the southern plain into the Strzelecki hills:

> *From Leongatha to Mirboo North a more-than-usually bad carriage road winds and climbs through new country, from which the original forest has not all been removed. The cuttings show the richest of rich chocolate land, with friable soils to any depth; the flats are green and moist - it is as good as anything in the world. Go through it, as I did, on a dew-wet morning with the magpies carolling and the lories flashing their splendid plumage from tree to tree, willows waving gently by many a creekside, smoke issuing from the chimneys of farm-houses ...*

The Grand Ridge Road is the setting for contemporary poet, Chris Wallace-Crabbe's poem, *Real Estate*. It's redolent with local imagery. Amongst his philosophical reflections, he speaks of 'sad, galvo-and-weatherboard sheds and halls'. Sounds like the Grand Ridge Road all right!

Mirboo North is an attractive town. Most outsiders come into it either from the north, from Morwell or Thorpdale, or from the south, from Leongatha or Meeniyan. Both entrances are very welcoming, especially the Morwell road approach. You climb gently to the hilltop, the curves preventing you from seeing what you know lies just ahead. The town suddenly presents itself. Strangely, although the street pattern is simple and regular, I've known more people lose their way in Mirboo North than any other town of its size. I think it's the slope that puts people off.

One of the reasons for the good feeling about Mirboo North, I believe, is its location, away from the two spines of Gippsland – the central and the southern – but also because it has no other towns 'in competition' with it. It seems a long way from other places through distance and difficulty of convenient access. It's also the best size for community spirit. I put Mirboo North into the third tier of Gippsland towns. That's based simply on size.

Tier 1 includes the places over 10,000 – Traralgon, Sale, Bairnsdale, Moe, Morwell, Warragul, and Drouin, in approximate order of size.

Tier 2 has the towns below 10,000 and above 2,000, again in approximate order of size – Newborough (7,000), Inverloch, Maffra, Lakes Entrance, Leongatha, Wonthaggi, Churchill, Cowes, Trafalgar, Korumburra, Koo Wee Rup, Paynesville, Stratford, Bunyip, Orbost, Yarram, and Longwarry (2,000).

Tier 3 contains the towns between 2,000 and 1,000 – Heyfield, Garfield, Mirboo North, Metung, Yarragon, Rosedale, Lang Lang, Tooradin, Yallourn North, Nyora, Neerim South, San Remo, Foster, Nar Nar Goon, and Mallacoota – again in rough order of size.

Tier 4 has all towns with fewer than 1,000 people. These are too numerous to mention, but they range from Bass with 937 residents to Walhalla with 20. This listing is based on the latest Census figures, but that was in 2016. The next Census, due in 2021, will show significant changes, particularly in the western, peri-urban region of Gippsland.

The spirit of Mirboo North is epitomised not by the Brewery (though that is something special), but by Baromi Park, which adjoins the main street and the shopping centre. It's a wonderful location and the pivot of Mirboo North's self-awareness. Community festivals are held here, but the Park serves more as a place for private and individual relaxation. This mix of public and private accessibility should be the main object of all town planners. I've spent quite a few rest stops here. I particularly like the predominance of indigenous trees which bring in native birds. Then there's the way in which features like the skate park, the playground and the Senior Citizen's Centre have been incorporated without affecting the open nature of the Park as a whole. Too many of our war memorials are in busy places, sometimes in the middle of the street, but here the Cenotaph is in a green place of quiet peace. This is how it should be.

The locals like to remind you – and themselves - of their past. They do it through some very detailed historical plaques in significant places and by means of murals depicting historic scenes. After all, as Manning Clark once said, 'Men make their own history more wisely when they know what their history has been about'. Women, too, of course! One event well-remembered here occurred in 1908. It was a time when Australia depended on the British fleet for its ultimate protection. However, in that year, President Teddy Roosevelt sent a fleet from the United States on a world cruise to demonstrate America's rising might. It was known as the Great White Fleet, and in due time it arrived in Melbourne. It caused a sensation. Delegations from the Fleet went to the major country centres of Victoria ... and to Mirboo North! The invitation was the subject of a good deal of mirth in the Melbourne papers, and even the Premier, Tommy Bent, at first thought it was a joke. Ten officers and over a hundred men arrived in Mirboo North by train, were met by a band and a children's choir, marched to the reception marquee, were feasted and lionised, then spent the afternoon engaging the locals in a tug-of-war, foot races, and demonstrations. On the way from Melbourne and on their return, hundreds crowded around them when they stopped for refreshments at Warragul and Morwell, while girls decorated them with flowers. "Three cheers for Mirbee!" called a sailor at the end of the journey.

One last glimpse of Mirboo North. During a back-burning operation in Samson Road a few kilometres north of the town at the time of the 2009 fires, a female koala suffering with scorched paws was discovered by a fire crew. She allowed herself to be petted by a fireman, David Tree, and drank copiously from a bottle of water he held to her lips. A mate filmed the episode on his mobile phone. It 'went viral'. The koala became a media darling all around the world, and was made the centrepiece of a fund-raising campaign that raised hundreds of thousands of dollars for the CFA and a bushfire recovery appeal. She was named Sam (for Samson Road), and was taken to the animal rescue centre at Rawson. Sadly, Sam died only months later after being diagnosed with chlamydia. Now, preserved, she rests in the Melbourne Museum, while in Baromi Park, there stands a magnificent depiction of the incident in bas-relief. It's worth a visit to Mirboo North just to see that.

A winding road south-east from Mirboo North takes you to Mirboo itself, some dozen kilometres away, on the headwaters of the Tarwin River. The Tarwin River is home to what is perhaps Gippsland's most acclaimed, though not particularly glamorous fish, the blackfish. Partly because it stays in its home stretch of river rather than migrate, the blackfish has been in decline. The West Gippsland Water Catchment Authority is making efforts to rehabilitate the stream and bring the fish back to its previous numbers.

The name, Mirboo, comes from an aboriginal word for 'kidney', though I've heard no explanation as to why this name was applied to the town. You can find the indigenous Mirboo Lily here – a light-purple and gold flower that closes up at night time like the chemist's shop. This process is called nyctinasty, a word I didn't know yesterday! Mirboo was the original settlement in these parts, but when the railway came to what is now Mirboo North, most of the people migrated to the railhead there. It's an old story in Gippsland! Today, Mirboo is a close-knit farming community, dependant on Mirboo North, but perhaps more inclined to look south, with the river, to the coastal plains and the sea.

Most people are more familiar with the northern approach to Mirboo North. That's where you'll find the golf course. There are excellent facilities for a town of Mirboo North's size. You can play there and eat there and even stay there. Further on you come to the Lyrebird Walk, not as dramatic as, say, Glen Nayook near Neerim, but more accessible. You can use a wheel chair for part of it. From here you can take a bike ride along the Darlimurla Road and pick up the Grand Ridge Rail Trail, but you should really begin where the trail begins, behind the Brewery in Mirboo North itself. The trail is thirteen kilometres long and takes you through a good variety of country to Boolarra. They recommend mountain bikes, though my road bike handled it easily. You may prefer to walk, of course. Half way along you come to the little settlement of Darlimurla.

The old railway station at Darlimurla is a good stopping point. It's hard to imagine that trains ran through here as late as 1974. Amongst the goods carried was cricket bat willow from a farm at Mirboo North. There are no cricket bats made in Australia any more. Cheap (and inferior) Indian imports have ruined the local craft. I have a friend who lived in Darlimurla some time ago, alongside the hall. She tells me the community is very active. The gazetteer says that there are thirty people living hereabouts. That's more than Walhalla! There was once a famed Big Tree at Darlimurla. It was a regular stopping-place for walkers and cyclists on the rail trail. Its height was sixty-one metres (three cricket pitches), and it was estimated to be more than three hundred years old. Sadly, it was lost in the bushfires of 2009.

The road from Mirboo North to Churchill takes you through Boolarra and Yinnar. Boolarra is now a pale reflection of its former importance as a regional centre, but it has built on its strengths to become a cultural centre. Many would know it because of the annual folk festival, but it is also home to artists and fabric workers. You can buy art works in the Community Hotel and at the General Store. For sixty years one niche industry was carried out on the Morwell River on the outskirts of Boolarra – the fish farm. Over three generations the farm supplied goldfish to the aquarium industry. They bred and supplied many kinds of fish – fantails, comets, shubunkin, nymphs, red caps, orandas, calico and black moors, as well as axolotls. It regularly supplied 40% of the Australian market. Russell Wucherpfennig, the grandson of the founder began phasing out production over the second half of 2019. A feature of the Boolarra landscape is now lost, although you really had to get up in the air to see the magnitude of the operation. The farm has been connected with the introduction of the 'Boolarra' strain of carp – a non-indigenous fish - into Victorian streams and rivers. It now dominates all other strains. Carp have been called the cane toads of freshwater streams, and huge efforts are now made to eliminate them. In environmental river circles, 'Boolarra' is a dirty word!

Yinnar, too, is home to a vibrant arts community. It's built around the arc Gallery in the middle of town. Back in the 'eighties, some enterprising folk in the arts world took over the old butter factory and turned it into a hive of artistic activity. They have exhibitions, theatre, music, work spaces, demonstrations ... and much much more! It's like a mixture of the Melbourne Meat Market and the Biennale of Sydney. I was there a year or two ago for a daring performance combining music and art. Brian Chapman, a pianist from Drouin, played a Franz Schubert song cycle, while his wife, Lucy, an artist, exhibited her interpretation of each of the twenty-four poems. Nathan Lay's fine baritone voice completed the magic. Wundebar!

Moe and Newborough

Some towns are at the end of the line, like Portland in Western Victoria. You go there because you mean to go there. It's the same with Mallacoota. The road doesn't go any further. No one goes there by mistake. But a lot of people who go to Moe are on the way to some other place. Maybe they're going to the snow. Maybe they're going to Walhalla. Maybe they're just travelling down the freeway and Moe is not much more than a signpost on the road. That's a shame, because Moe's got a lot going for it.

But being on the way to somewhere else is not all bad. In Moe's early days, the railway was the most important thing. The town got a kick-start through the railway. Moe was the middle point of railway lines going to somewhere else. One line went to Walhalla. One line went to Thorpdale. Later, another line went to the brown coal fields. The main line actually came from the east. Most of us presume that the Gippsland railway line crept out from Melbourne, forging its way steadily eastwards. But that wasn't the case. The line was built in separate sections, which were linked up later on. The section that got to Moe came from the east, from Sale.

Moe has, I believe, tended to look eastwards rather than towards the west. Moe is at the western end of the Latrobe Valley, the western end of the City of Latrobe, so the civic mind turns that way – eastwards – naturally. And Moe is far enough away from Melbourne not to be dominated by it. In my way of thinking, all the main line towns in Gippsland from Nar Nar Goon to Yarragon look westwards. Trafalgar looks both ways – towards Warragul one way and towards the Latrobe Valley the other way – but by the time Moe is reached, it's the east that is the prevailing element in the communal mindset.

In 1994, the Victorian government forced through a process of shire amalgamation throughout the State. Many people thought it was a good idea – it would bring about savings because the scale of operations in each new shire would be much bigger – but, likewise, many people thought it was a bad idea. Smaller places would lose their identity, they argued. They weren't listened to. It's part of the tragedy of history that the little people aren't listened to. The locals aren't listened to. So the City of Latrobe came into being, and the town of Moe has been the poorer for it ever since.

We've all heard that a camel is a horse designed by a committee, and in the same way, the City of Latrobe is a region designed by the theorists. It's never been a happy arrangement. There's constant talk of Traralgon breaking away, and Moe, too. The matter was seriously raised in 2014 when a Traralgon secessionist movement gained strength, and at the same time a former Mayor of Latrobe urged the people of Moe to break free from Latrobe City. He wanted Moe to align itself with the Baw Baw Shire to the west. And now, to back up that idea, Moe is in a different State electorate from the rest of the Valley, even different from Newborough. But the idea came to nothing. So Moe has ended up rather as the poor relation in the Latrobe Valley family. That's what outsiders think, but not the people of the town. They're a very proud lot.

We're very used to saying Moe and Newborough in the one breath. Maybe that's an injustice to both towns. Is this one town – Moe/Newborough - or is it two towns – Moe and Newborough – that have run together? Victoria always has had difficulties with two communities existing close together. Albury-Wodonga has never been a satisfactory creation; Warragul and Drouin, increasingly being driven into a single community, live in an uneasy relationship; and here in Moe and Newborough, almost everybody I've talked to is sharply conscious of a divide between the two.

It began, I think, with the establishment of Newborough as a dormitory town for SEC workers after the Second World War. Many of these were folk newly arrived from England. Even today there is a distinct English element in the town. Gippslanders in general have always looked askance at newcomers, and the people of Moe did so at that time. On top of that, the managers in the SEC project tended to live in Newborough, while the hands-on workers tended to live in Moe. The white-collars drove home from work in a different direction from the blue-collars. The edginess is still to be felt.

The whole of the Latrobe Valley is still mourning the loss of Yallourn. The spirit of Yallourn still haunts the region. Moe and Newborough felt the loss more keenly than other centres, however, because they were closest. More residents of the old town came to live in Newborough than anywhere else. More of the Yallourn houses came to Newborough than anywhere else, stark reminders of the old days. The space that was once Yallourn is still there, to be seen and felt when you drive by. There's been a double bereavement, actually. After the demise of Yallourn came the demise of the SEC itself. It's as if two dear old uncles have departed the family. Gone, but not forgotten! As I walk and drive around Moe and Newborough, I can feel a lingering sadness covering the place, or is it just my imagination?

If you look down on Moe from above, or just look at a map – it's simpler – the place is dominated by two things – Old Gippstown and the Moe Race Course. At Old Gippstown you'll find many of our old buildings – Angus McMillan's Bushy Park homestead, the old Sunny Creek School, the National Bank from Meeniyan, the Narracan general store, and a host of others, set out beautifully. It's Gippsland's best designed streetscape! My first visit there blew me away! Run by volunteers, too. You'll love it!

As for the racetrack, it's cheek by jowl with the town. Gippsland has some fine racecourses, though fewer, sadly, than in the old days. There's the Pakenham Racecourse (at Tynong!) and also Sale amongst the major ones, but they lack the homeliness of Moe. There's plenty of homeliness with the picnic racecourses like Buchan or Woolamai or Drouin, let alone Tambo Valley or Omeo. There are other fine courses, like Traralgon and Bairnsdale, while Stony Creek has its backers (note the pun). But for me, Moe takes the cake. The only complaint I've got is that the Club is too pussy-footed in its self-promotion. Consider this from the present website:

> *The Moe Racing Club is one of the best places to enjoy a great day out, whether on business or for a fun social event.*

Compare that with the 1921 style:

> *Best and most convenient course in Gippsland. Step out of the special train and you are in the Paddock. Moe is the garden of Victoria; the eyes of the world are on Yallourn, which is only four miles from here. This is going to be the greatest place Gippsland has ever seen. Don't be afraid of wet weather; in fact, it improves our track – it is a sandy heath, well –pressed, like a bowling green.*

No pussy-footing there!

Shakespeare asked the question, 'What's in a name?', and answered his own question, 'A rose by any other name would smell as sweet.' The question of their name is of great interest to several Gippsland towns. Churchill, for instance, once called 'Hazelwood', or Garfield, once 'Cannibal Creek Siding' or, right here, where we are now, Yallourn North, once 'Brown Coal Mine' and Newborough itself, once 'Moe East'. When I was young, it wasn't Moe East that sparked our interest so much as the Haunted Hills nearby. There are as many theories of the name as there are hills themselves. Most of the theories have to do with the strange rumblings and reverberations from below ground, caused, say some, by hollows formed by burnt-out coal seams or subterranean streams. Some time in the early twentieth century, the place was re-named Herne's Oak. Whoever thought of that name had a turn of literary knowledge. It comes from Shakespeare's play, *The Merry Wives of Windsor*, where there's a hunter called Herne, and the merry wives make play with Falstaff at a mysterious place named 'Herne's oak'. Now Shakespeare is transplanted to mid-Gippsland!

In the days when the Princes Highway passed right through the middle of Moe, where it crossed the railway line on that steep, curving bridge, we used to look out for the sign for Purvis Stores painted on the roof where no one could miss it. The Purvis story, with its signature motto, 'Purvis for Survis', is a romantic and historically important part of the old township of Moe. WA Purvis started his store in 1910, but it was his family, especially his widow, Alice, and his son, Jack, who made it a legend. The legend was one of honesty and fair dealing. During the Depression years, struggling families had their bills reduced or cancelled. Purvis Stores was highly successful as a business, and was given a huge lift by the population surge after the SEC began its work nearby. In the end, some thirteen branches were established, from Bairnsdale to Thorpdale. The name has gone from Moe, but the Purvis legend lives on. The business morphed into the Aussie Disposals Group.

When I was young, a lot of people called Yallourn, 'Yallern'. I think it might have been an attempt to make it sound more hoity-toity, in the same way that people used to say, 'Wongaratta' for 'Wangaratta', or 'Cres'ick' for 'Creswick. But the times are now too democratic for that sort of thing.

Yallourn North, originally Brown Coal Mine, was close to the Yallourn W power station and close, also, to the open cut. Too close, as it turned out. In 1950, some of the town's shops and houses found themselves on the brink of the pit when a landslide sent hundreds of thousands of tons of coal and overburden crashing down below. Two men leapt across the chasm to safety as the ground they were standing on disappeared under their feet. Bert Meadows' wheelbarrow was the only item lost, but all the shops and houses alongside had to be removed.

Slips of the coal face were not uncommon. In 1919, just when work on the brown coal was opening up, a slide buried the pay shed just when the men were being paid. £300 in notes and silver were buried under four feet of mud. The policeman on guard duty and the paymaster were unhurt, but it took a long time to dig out the cash. Who said there was no money in coal?

A series of events made life difficult in Brown Coal Mine in the early days. Many lived in tents and rough huts. In the 'twenties the miners went on strike. A bushfire in 1929 took hold in one of the mines. The heat was intense and people came from miles to see the brilliant spectacle. Then came the Depression. In 1934 the floods filled the open cut to the brim. It took twenty hours to fill and five months to empty, Kath Ringin tells us in her book, *The Old Brown Coal Mine*. Meanwhile, the health of the community was at times threatened by disease. Five children died of gastroenteritis in the summer of 1927-28.

Many of our country towns tell of a heroic medical man in the early times, and the great medical figure in Yallourn North was Dr James Andrew, who gave forty-five years of his life to the people of the district. You can see his desk and many of his possessions at Old Gippstown in Moe. Dr Andrew was a great friend of Frank Macfarlane Burnet. They used to go bushwalking together.

Percy Dicker was a missionary minister at Brown Coal Mine in the 'twenties. He worked amongst the huts and camps in those crude early days, working out of a tent himself, and eventually built St James' Church. He is well remembered. Many years later, in another place, he conducted my wedding. I know there were many heroic figures like Dr Andrew and Percy Dicker in the early history of 'the hill'.

Narracan Creek rises in the hills south of Moe, tumbles down on to the lowlands, then through the Moe Botanical Gardens and on to join the La Trobe River just north of the town. Most people regard it as the boundary between Moe and Newborough. A railway once ran from Moe, through Coalville to Narracan, and on to Thorpdale. There was coal at Coalville, not brown coal, but good black coal, as used in the steam engines at that time. The mines turned out to be disappointing, but the line continued to carry timber palings and farm produce from the rich soils round Thorpdale. That is until the line suffered the fate of so many of our small branch lines and went under.

Potatoes aside, there's a human product from up this way who has become very well known. One of the greatest of our high jumpers came from Narracan. Tim Forsyth was six foot six himself, but jumped higher than that to win bronze at the Barcelona Olympics when he was still eighteen. In fact he equalled the height of the winner, but was placed third on a countback. Altogether, he won a string of Olympic, Commonwealth Games, and World Championship medals, and was our National Champion six times during the 'nineties. You can't always rely on the newspapers to tell an accurate story, but the press report on Tim after he'd won his bronze in Barcelona rang true: *The eighteen-year-old high jumper with long hair, a pierced ear and a piece of well-chewed gum in his mouth would have been as comfortable among farmers from his Gippsland hometown as he was sitting with the world's best high jumpers*. Tim's best-ever jump was 2.36 metres, that is, in my language, seven foot, seven and a half inches. How anyone can jump that high is well over my head.

We end this section not with potato-diggers, but with pea-pickers. The author Eve Langley lived as a child at her mother's hotel in Crossover, north of Warragul. She always loved and romanticised Gippsland. Her book, *The Pea Pickers*, is "a raucous romp through the Victorian countryside", to use her own words. In the book, a train pulls into Moe station. Langley writes

> *At last, in the dry afternoon, we came to the town of Moe, which is Gippsland's outermost door* (this was the 1920s). *Ah, now we near our promised land. Up from the dust rose the station and on the coppery gravel platform stood an old Gippslander, tall, thin and long-whiskered; around his hat was a snake-skin, the small metallic scales gleaming and snake's eyes staring towards the low hills far in the distance".*

I must get down to the station to see if our long-whiskered friend is still there!

Morwell and Churchill

There are place-names in Gippsland that roll off the tongue, like 'Tarwin Lower' or 'Omeo' or 'Bete Belong'. Morwell is not one of those. Like 'Garfield' or 'Kongwak', its mellifluousness is not immediately apparent. Some say the name comes from the Gunaikurnai name for the local possum, but my own theory is that it's another of our towns named after a British counterpart, in this case Motherwell, in Scotland. The early settlers, being economical with their letters, simply omitted the middle part, and, hey presto, you have a name to puzzle future lexicographers.

Morwell does not always get a good press from those who don't know it well. This posting on the internet is a case in point: *Morwell has "a very eclectic mix of people"* (sounds suspicious), *and "as a place to live is what you make of it"* (is this a hidden message?). *"There are social issues here, but it can only improve"* (goodness gracious, what goes on there?). The posting ends, *"Go to Morwell for cheap housing and quite neighbours (sic)"*. Quite! Sounds like someone's out to give the place a dusting.

In reality, Morwell is a town with a distinctive and proud identity. The area was settled in the 1840s, which, it's hard to realise, is getting on for 200 years ago. It has watched its upstart neighbours, Moe and Traralgon, crowd it in on either side, yet it retains its own identity. It's true that developments over time have changed the nature of the place, so that if you conducted a word association test with the name, 'Morwell', most people would answer, "brown coal" or "Latrobe Valley" or "Princes Highway". But when you walk the streets and go into the shops and talk to the locals, you find a different Morwell.

We've known Morwell since we were knee-high to a grasshopper, as people used to say. Let's visit again with a more definite purpose: to unearth the real Morwell. A good place to start is the Rose Garden in the centre of town, set, not amongst sweet bucolic vistas as you might imagine from the name, but amongst asphalted streets and busy commercial premises. This may be a symbol of Morwell's character: something precious surrounded by materiality. Here in the Rose Garden are 400 varieties and 4,000 individual plants. They reach their peak in mid-November, when the International Rose Festival is held. Not just a Rose Festival, actually. You have live music and brass bands, light shows, and guided tours as well. The Festival even attracted the famous Costa from the ABC Gardening Show on one occasion

A further sign of the surrounding materiality can be seen from the Rose Garden – the empty smoke stacks of the now-defunct Hazelwood Power Station, just outside town. Before its de-commissioning in 2017, it produced 25% of Victoria's base-load electricity, but also 14% of the State's greenhouse gas emissions. The inside story of its closure is that an Australian reporter in Paris at the signing of the Paris Climate Agreement in December, 2015, privately asked the Head of the Engie Corporation, Isabelle Kocher, if she realised she owned the dirtiest power station in the world. Shocked, she investigated, discovered the truth, and, as a result, ordered its closure. It shows that the world is not yet governed by intractable market forces; there is room, still, for personal responses and action.

A hop, step and jump from the Rose garden is the Art Gallery. Art Galleries, like libraries, have transformed themselves in recent years. They used to be places that offered customers something which they could either like or not like, accept or not accept. But those passive days are gone. They're now places of personal exchange, where the exhibits and the staff take up an interactive relationship with the visitors. So we discovered we could have a guided tour of the Morwell Gallery; we could bring our children on the weekend for art activities; we could have a meal; we could become members. When we were there the main exhibition was by an interstate artist's part-art, part-sculpture, part-science display. Eclectic, I think you could say. It left us reeling, but then our taste in art was formed in a more orderly era.

However, the greatest art work in Morwell is not in the Gallery, but across the railway line in St Mary's Anglican Church. There the whole wall behind the altar – the reredos, I think is the term – is filled by a huge painting of the Ascension by Arthur Boyd, one of the greatest Australian artists of the twentieth century. It was placed originally in the church in Yallourn, but when that church was pulled down, together with the rest of the town, because of the coal deposits below it, the painting came to Morwell. They even designed the Morwell church to accommodate the painting. You should go and see it. It's awe-inspiring, as the church's blurb puts it.

But now to get into the shops and streets of Morwell. There is a barrier, however. A barrier in the form of the main Gippsland railway line which cuts the town in two. It's not a social divide; there's no social cachet in living north or south of the line. It's just a hugely inconvenient divide. To cross the line by car means a maybe ten-minute journey. Other towns suffer from the same problem, Drouin, Longwarry and Garfield, for instance, although Drouin and Longwarry have convenient crossings near the centre of town. Morwell is one of those which need quite a journey to cross the line by car.

Most of the shops are south of the line, but we found the streets there quite quiet for a town of 13,000 or so. The reason is not hard to find. A couple of kilometres out of town, cunningly placed between Morwell and Traralgon, is the Mid-Valley Shopping Centre. A lot of the shops and much of the money have migrated eastwards to Mid-Valley. You need a car to get there, of course, but everybody has a car these days! They don't, actually. Many residents don't have a car or don't have access to a car through the day. You can take a bus, but somehow catching a bus to go shopping is not something people are enthusiastic about. We heard some bitter words about the effect Mid-Valley has had on Morwell's CBD. As for Mid-Valley itself, opinion is divided. People like it or they hate it. As for us, the best thing is to say we like parts of it.

You could say that Morwell is the capital of the Latrobe Valley, if there were such a place. The Civic Centre of the City of Latrobe is here and local people are pleased about that. It's one in the eye for Traralgon, someone told us, revealing the feeling of rivalry that still goes on round here. The law courts are here. The airport is just out of Morwell. The headquarters of TAFE is in Morwell. The crematorium serving the whole of Gippsland is near town.

There's an air of uncertainty hanging over Morwell because of the rapid changeover from brown coal to renewables as a source of Victoria's power. It seems certain that in thirty years, and probably less, there will be no coal-fired power stations left in Gippsland. Some point to the possibilities that are opened up by the switch to greener energy. One of these pointers is the huge wind turbine farm proposed for Bass Strait which would provide hundreds of permanent jobs, as well as powering 1.2 million homes. Another is the coal-to-hydrogen project that is already underway at Loy Yang, at least at the pilot stage. There are environmental difficulties about that, however, such as the sequestration of carbon produced in the process. So uncertainty remains.

The atmosphere of uncertainty has other origins as well. There's the question of decommissioning existing plants and rehabilitating the mined areas. Many ask how the government will handle the need to re-train workers, or indeed how to deal with a likely rise in unemployment.

Alongside these aspects, there is the constant uneasiness about fire. In February, 2014, embers from a grass fire set the coal beds in the Hazelwood field alight. During the seven weeks and more that the fire burned, the people of nearby Morwell were subject to nauseous smoke, dust, and toxic carbon monoxide fumes. Illness and death rates rose during and after these weeks, and the company has been found guilty of a raft of offences. The people of the town have been very active in seeking redress.

Perhaps Morwell's greatest son is Lt-Gen Sir Stanley Savige. Savige was born here, in Tarwin Street, in 1890, although he did his schooling in Korumburra. Savige served in both World Wars. In the 1914-18 conflict, he performed heroically at Gallipoli and on the Western Front. After the War he was instrumental in founding Legacy Australia. He continued as a citizen soldier between the wars, then in World War 2 had a stellar career in both the Middle East and the Pacific theatres. 3,000 people attended his funeral in 1954. One speaker said, *"Sir Stanley's greatest virtue was humanity. He had great consideration for his troops. He thought they were there not just to be used, but to be helped"*. One of his greatest contributions as a soldier was his leadership in the 'Dunsterforce', a select group sent in 1918 to protect the Assyrian minority from slaughter at the hands of their sectarian enemies in the Middle East after the collapse of Russia. It is said that his personal intervention rescued 50,000 Assyrian people and perhaps saved the nation from extinction. His efforts were recognised at a ceremony at his grave-site in Boroondara Cemetery in 2006. As part of the same commemoration, the Mayor of Latrobe City, Lisa Price, unveiled a bronze bust of Sir Stanley in Morwell. The memorial stands in Legacy Place, between Commercial Road and Princes Drive.

Unlike Moe and Traralgon which have smaller towns and villages as satellites, Morwell is on its own. You could argue that Churchill is a satellite of Morwell, but it's really a major town in its own right, and the smaller towns around there are satellites of Churchill rather than Morwell.

Churchill is a planned town, like old Yallourn. The planners envisaged it as a place where people uprooted from Yallourn could come and live, as well as an overflow residential town for the whole of the region. Official estimates of many tens of thousands eventually living in Churchill were made, but, fortunately, "as the best laid schemes o' mice and men gang aft agley", so this one did also. Some four and a half thousand now live here.

The name, 'Churchill' comes from the great British statesman, of course. I remember the fruitless protests made by the locals when they lost their former name, 'Hazelwood'. In 1965, the bulldozers moved in and the construction of Housing Commission houses began. The first two families were the Arch and Ayers families. I came to know Peter and Margaret Arch in later years. Peter was the first church minister in Churchill, and is well-remembered for his contribution to just about every aspect of the developing town. Perhaps the Ayers were just as notable. Churchill the man is commemorated by a gigantic tower in the commercial centre which everyone takes to represent the great man's cigar. Alongside is a plaque showing Churchill's early settlers. Now there's an idea other towns could follow, but then Churchill is one place where its origins are within living memory.

Federation University has a campus at Churchill, with just about as many students as there are residents in the town. Some can take their courses online without even living in the country. In my day you went to lectures and then to tutorials where you were coached in small groups. Those days seem to be over. I suppose they know what they're doing! The university, however, is authentic in the sense that it grew from local grass roots. The old Yallourn Technical School became the Yallourn Technical College, which transitioned into the Gippsland Institute of Advanced Education. GIAE put itself under the wing of Monash University, Clayton, becoming known as Monash University College before becoming a full-blown Monash campus.

In 2013 and 2014, Monash seemed to tire of its country cousin, and to the intense displeasure of the locals put forward a plan not only to divest itself of its Churchill campus but to actually sell the site. A solution was eventually found. Ballarat University offered a marriage of equals, and a name was given to the new entity: Federation University. There are three things about the place that I particularly like. First, it's set in beautiful country (and in an attractive town); second, it has the excellent Centre for Gippsland Studies (though, regrettably, access to that was severely restricted in 2019); and thirdly, there's a golf course there, right on campus, where students can play for $10 a day and even borrow a set of clubs for nothing if they don't have any. What more could you ask?

We can't leave Churchill without touching on the bushfires of 2009. In early February of that year, a catastrophic heat wave swept across the state. The scorching temperatures were accompanied by violent winds and extremely low humidity. Dozens of fires broke out, over 2000 homes were lost, and 180 people died over the whole of Victoria. The Central Gippsland fires began when a Churchill man lit a blaze in a pine forest on the outskirts of the town on Saturday afternoon, 7 February, a day now known as Black

Saturday. The man was subsequently imprisoned for seventeen years. The fire swept southwards towards Yarram, then, when the wind swung to the south-west, towards Callignee, Koornalla, Traralgon South, Gormandale, and Willung South. The fire caused terrible destruction. In Callignee, for instance, almost all the sixty homes were destroyed. Eleven people died in this one fire.

It seems as though bushfires take on an evil intention and personality of their own. One perceptive observer put it this way:

> *A bush fire is not an orderly invader, but a guerrilla. It advances by rushes, by little venomous tongues of fire in the grass; it spreads by sparks burning leaves and bark. Its front is miles deep. It is here, it is there, like a swarm of venomous wasps. It shams dead and stabs you in the back. It encircles you so that there is no sure line of flight for its intended victims. It destroys bridges in your rear. It bars the road with blazing trees ...* (HG Wells, on a visit to Australia, 1949).

The area was at least spared the fires of 2019-20.

Nar Nar Goon, Tynong, and Garfield

Where does Gippsland begin? I remember the time we thought of Dandenong as the 'Gateway to Gippsland'. Then it became Pakenham. Now Pakenham is a suburb of Melbourne, there's no doubting, so we roll along to Nar Nar Goon before we can really breathe the pure air of Gippsland. The three towns, Nar Nar Goon, Tynong, and Garfield, have this in common, that they edge on to the Koo Wee Rup Swamp. So do Bunyip and Longwarry, of course, and, on the other side, Koo Wee Rup and Lang Lang. And there are the Swamp villages like Bayles and Catani. But we must not take too large a canvas or the particular characteristics of each place will be lost.

Nar Nar Goon began as Mount Ararat, a pastoral lease in the 1840s. Legend has it that Mount Ararat is where Noah's Ark touched firm ground after the Biblical Flood. Not this Mount Ararat, however, but the one in Turkey. We'd pass through Nar Nar Goon on the train when we were young, looking for the remains of the Ark, but to no avail. We knew we were in Nar Nar Goon because the warning bell at the railway crossing would sound. Children delight in marking their progress by regular remembrance points.

A lot of Irish migrants came here in the early days, making this a solidly Catholic district. The O'Briens were one of those early families. They built and ran the Limerick Arms Hotel, which did a roaring trade. In the days before churches were built, a priest would come to the Limerick Arms every six months, say Mass, and baptise the little ones. The Pitts, who became a highly-respected family in the district, were part of the O'Brien family. One of the O'Brien great-granddaughters, Kathleen Fitzpatrick, nee Pitt, has written about her childhood in Nar Nar Goon in her book, *Solid Bluestone Foundations*. I feel a connection here, because Kathleen Fitzpatrick taught me History at Melbourne University back in the Dark Ages.

Many people now think of Nar Nar Goon as the 'Town with the Murals'. I've seen murals on street buildings in many places all over Australia, but none as good as at Nar Nar Goon. There are so many and they're so consistently excellent, I can't begin to describe them. You can see them on the internet, but they deserve more than that. If you haven't seen them, go … soon! All the paintings were done by Andrew Rowe, a local artist and signwriter, about twenty years ago. He worked from photographs, so these murals have absolute authenticity regarding Nar Nar Goon in the 1920s. To add to the outdoor art work, the schoolchildren have put three panels of mosaic with aboriginal motifs on display in the park.

A little to the north of the town, on the other side of the freeway, is the Light Horse Museum. This is an eclectic, even quirky, collection of war memorabilia, with an emphasis on the materials of war, and especially the animals that were drawn into service. The owners have had their problems with local restrictive regulations, but have managed to hang on. I went there once with a U3A group when we were studying the First World War. We found it fascinating. Because it's a private collection, the owners fuss around and give you a lot more than your money's worth. Like the old times!

They had horse racing and trotting in Nar Nar Goon before the War, and after it, for a while. And car racing. I remember as a boy going to watch cars racing round a Nar Nar Goon paddock, though I can't think just where it was. My chief memory is of amazement with the passenger in each car who would hang out prostrate, inches from the ground, grasping on by their finger-tips, to balance the car as it took the bends at what seemed like a hundred kilometres an hour.

We've been dropping in to Maryknoll over the years. It's unique, for Gippsland at any rate - a planned settlement, rather reminiscent of 'New Australia', that idealistic venture when hundreds of intrepid Australians sailed to Paraguay to establish their own utopian society. In this case, at Maryknoll, the motivation was different. Maryknoll was born of the post-war emphasis in the Catholic Church on co-operative endeavour, hardy self-management, the celebration of family life and values, and the virtues of rural living, all bathed in the faith and community of the Church. Father Wilfred Pooley was the Founding Father. The 'settlers' had their small blocks of land and their modest cottages. They built their church and school and store; they established co-operative industries; they lived and worked and worshipped together. As the spirit of both church and society changed over the following decades, so the nature of the community changed. The Catholic element is now more dispersed, though none the less tangible, and the old and true Maryknollers still abide by the spirit of the foundation. This comes out in various ways. Vin Tyler was the village plumber, an original settler, who immersed himself in everything in Maryknoll for sixty years. When the time came for him to retire into Bunyip, the community gave him a grand farewell. That's the sort of thing that both honours and builds community.

We drive along the bottom road to Tynong. The Koo Wee Rup Swamp is on our right, the railway and fruitful green slopes on our left. Tynong must be the neatest town in Gippsland. Have they ever entered the Tidiest Town competition, we wonder. The houses are unpretentious and welcoming; the gardens are kept with a view to the pleasure of the resident, not to impress passers-by. No bustle. People live here because they like it, not because of work or shops or government services. I think I'd like to live here. One could be like W.B. Yeats ... "And I shall have some peace there. For peace comes dropping slow ..."

But there *are* things here that bring people in. In a radical moment, they decided to move the Pakenham Racecourse here to Tynong. Why didn't they re-name it, 'the Tynong Racecourse'? Unfair to

Tynong! I see the Garfield cricket team now uses the Tynong oval as their home ground. Same thing! Then there's the church and school. The Society of St Pius X in Australia, part of the Traditional Catholic Church, established a presence and a school – St Thomas Aquinas College - in Tynong. The Corpus Christi Parish is now a thriving congregation, while the school has some 300 students at all levels. Many parishioners and students travel from Melbourne suburbs, although quite a few families have moved to the district in order to be close to church and school.

Out on the highway, Gumbuya Park has changed itself into a ritzy theme park, with all the trappings of Queensland glamour. I suppose I'll get used to it, though it still strikes me as being brash, which is not the Gippsland way.

The past hasn't always been as congenial as the present. Life was uncertain. In the early days when doctors were few and far between a small boy from here stuck his hand into a hollow log and was bitten by a snake. He was taken to hospital in Melbourne by train, but died there.

Again, most people know of the 'Tynong murders', though they were committed many miles away. Some of the bodies were discovered at Tynong North, however, and the name, 'Tynong Murders' stuck. It's a pity. Tynong's not the place to associate with cold-blooded crime.

There's an excellent winery and eatery at Tynong North now, and also Peppermint Ridge Farm where you can find out about bush food, and there's a church youth camp as well. These places have been here for years. That's one thing about this part of the world. People don't come and go like they do elsewhere. They stay. The Weatherheads were pioneers of Tynong North, and they've stayed. I remember as a boy going to the Weatherheads' Cornucopia Museum. Max Weatherhead wrote a book about it – *From Bark Hut to Cornucopia Museum*. There's a working granite quarry just north of the highway. Down in Melbourne, the few people who know about Tynong know about it because the granite to build the Shrine of Remembrance came from here. Granite's the best kind of rock!

We're in Garfield now, having followed the railway from Tynong. Two or three minutes and we're there. There used to be apples on these hills to our left. These were sweet, natural apples, but were driven out of production by the hi-tech large-scale operators in other parts. Now the hills are grass, used for indeterminate purposes. On the other side of the railway line there are small holdings. 'Hobby farms' used to be the term, though they got a bad name because many were neglected and unsightly. We lose sight of the Swamp for a mile or two. This higher land has Mont Albert Road running through it and, if you follow that road along, you come to Governor's Hill, so named from when Governor Loch used to come here from Melbourne to shoot ducks before the Swamp was drained.

The town of Garfield migrated from further north when the railway line went through, and for a while kept its old name, 'Cannibal Creek Siding'. Cannibal Creek runs a few miles to the north, though how *that* got its name is a matter of conjecture. In 1881 the President of the United States, James Abram Garfield, was assassinated, and in his honour, the authorities in Melbourne bestowed his name on this little burg so far away. The town grew quickly. The Melbourne papers advertised land for sale. It was destined to be "the garden of Victoria". In the 1890s it was discovered that the soil was good for apples – the land north of the Swamp, of course. So orchards appeared, especially at Garfield North where the granitic soil was especially good for apples, or so it was claimed. Garfield North, supplying timber and apples, was an economic powerhouse!

To the south of the town, roads, straight as a dye, criss-crossed the Swamp, now drained. The Bunyip River that had previously lost itself in the morass of the Koo Wee Rup Swamp, was channelled into the Main Drain, all the way to the sea. Villages appeared. Vervale and Iona were satellites of Garfield, while, further out, places like Catani and Bayles looked more towards Lang Lang and Koo Wee Rup, and Modella was an out-station of Bunyip or Longwarry.

Iona and Garfield were particularly close. The hotel in Garfield to this day remains the Iona Hotel, and the Garfield football team was originally the Iona Stars. As a small boy I once went to a football match at Garfield and distinctly remember an old man walking up and down the boundary line shouting for 'Iona'. Iona was quite a place originally. In August, 1915, a fifteen-year-old girl, Elsie Clarke, wrote to the paper about living in Iona. "We live very near to the Post Office," she wrote, "and two stores and a blacksmith's shop and a creamery. ... The Iona school is a nice new one and has fifty children attending." She added a happy note: "The people here are very nice. They are always ready to do anything for us." It's still the same.

The locals fenced off a race-track just south of Garfield on the now-drained Swamp. The Iona Annual Carnival was held there annually. I looked at the programme for the 1916 carnival – horse races, boys and girls races, sheaf tossing, stepping the chain. The sheaf-tossing was a handicap. How do you handicap sheaf-tossing? About the same time as I saw the old man barracking for Iona, I saw a sheaf-tossing competition at the Garfield Football ground. Maybe it was the last one ever held anywhere in the world!

When war came, the Garfield races took on a patriotic colour. In 1915 a race day was held in support of the Belgians. There was intense fury at the invasion of little Belgium by the Kaiser's forces. However, things went badly wrong on the day. The promised special train from Melbourne failed to arrive and hardly any locals turned up. The crowd, such as it was, behaved badly. Tickets were passed "indiscriminately" over the fence that separated the members' enclosure from the hoi polloi. Only £20 was raised for Belgium.

Later on, during the next war, a racehorse named 'Garfield' gained some notoriety in the press. Its owner brought it from South Australia back to Victoria by train. However there was a ban on transporting racehorses on the railways, due to war priorities, so the enterprising owner put the nag down as a draught horse - which made it legal. Unfortunately for him, the ruse was discovered. The magistrate fined him £15.

Farmers in early times were always on the lookout for a new wonder crop. It reminds me of the crazes we've seen more recently, like ostriches and emus and paulownias. Farmers got enthusiastic about sugar beet at Garfield in the first decade of the twentieth century, and flax as well, although nothing permanent eventuated. But the one crop that stayed and stayed was potatoes. The rich Swamp soils rivalled the volcanic soils of Neerim and Thorpdale. In the mid-1920s they were sending out seventy to eighty thousand tons of potatoes each year from Garfield. To sell into a later market and thus gain a better price, some growers put their crop into deep pits, as with silage, but the higher price they hoped to get was mostly lost due to the shrinkage that occurred in the potatoes.

The industry has largely gone from round Garfield now, but in the decade after the Second War it was still flourishing. The railway trucks would be lined up at the Garfield siding, stories abounded about undersized spuds being placed in the bottom of the bags to trick the potato inspector, diggers became local heroes, travelling from farm to farm with their spud forks, while lesser mortals trailed after them picking up, filling the bags, each picker-up with a metal ring tied to their waist. If in doubt about the size of a spud, they would try to push it through the ring. If it went through, 'toss it out!'

The main street in Garfield is just as it was seventy years ago. It should have a heritage order placed on it as a piece of living history. Even the empty blocks back then are still empty blocks. It's one of the comforting things about Garfield that though people come and go the mood of the town stays the same. Garfield doesn't care what others think of it. It just carries on. It knows it's neither a big deal nor a little deal. But those who have spent their lives here love it deeply. And they don't forget the old times.

Neerim South

'I lift up my eyes to the hills', says the psalm. I'm in Neerim South looking at the hills now. Row after row of gum-grey hills stretching northwards to the Great Divide. Coleridge wrote of 'forests ancient as the hills, enfolding sunny spots of greenery'. He could have been standing here with me.

So Coleridge and the Psalmist and I are looking at the "great grey forests that know no change" (Banjo Paterson this time). Tom Griffiths wrote a book about these forests, *Forests of Ash*. He tells the story of Australia's giant eucalypt, the Mountain Ash, and of the indigenous people coming each season to harvest the forest products, and later the miners and sawmillers and then the permanent settlers. He tells of the conservationists' struggles to preserve the forests, and the life cycles and fire cycles of the forests over their thousands of years. He makes it an enthralling story. Something of that story has crept into the soul of this place.

The township of Neerim South lies in the foothills, but we get the feeling that the spirit of the place comes from those tranquil hills to the north rather than the bustling busyness of the south. Do others feel a lightening of the heart as they come towards town, catching on their left the deep gash of the Tarago River, then driving beneath the blue curves of the Neerim Bower sculpture, up the final hill, and into the main street? In an instant the road curves again and points into the mystery of 'further north'.

The way to experience the place is to walk it and smell it. I walked recently, leaving the town and heading northwards. This is what the text book would call 'intensively-cultivated land'. The first silage cut was being made. I couldn't see it, but the delicious smell was in the air. There were Ayrshires cropping the grass, though some, I saw, stick to their little Jerseys. Black Angus, too, and these others. Limousin, are they, or Murray Grey? We can't be sure. Alpacas also. They stare at us. Haughty things! Do they despise everything in the same way? The people who live here store up for winter just like the ants. There are enormous stacks of split firewood alongside the houses. Nobody could use all that wood in a dozen winters.

A log truck comes by. Such small logs. Do they have to harvest them at that age? Could they not let them grow into some sort of maturity and pride of life? Later we see some huge logs, also heading south, taking the fruits of the forest to the world of commerce and construction. Each log was just days ago a stately tree, a prince of the tribe 'Eucalyptus regnans', the tallest flowering plant in the world, and highest of all trees, except for those redwoods in California. But everything in America has to be bigger!

The bower bird sculpture is still in my mind. People round here find satin bower birds in their back garden. The male bird builds an elaborate bower like an open tunnel, and uses it like a theatre stage, performing his dance routine to attract the females. He gathers up anything he can find, flowers or feathers, berries, even glass and bits of plastic, especially if they're coloured blue. He does a crazy dance in front of the female, leaping about, flaring his wings and tail, making wheezing and whirring sounds. Suddenly he'll go into a trance, head down and eyes rolled back. The females, meanwhile, go round touring from one bower to another, watching these antics. Charles Darwin came to Australia in 1831 on the 'Beagle'. He was amazed at the architecture of these bowers and the rituals of these beautiful birds.

Back in the car, now. It's cooler by the time we reach Neerim Junction. Snow falls here not every winter, but often. I follow the sign to Glen Nayook, off to the left. The gully is rough and wet and slippery underfoot, the sun struggling to reach into the deep bottom. There are tree ferns everywhere, and granite boulders across the path, the rivulet flowing swiftly in little runs and sallies. Suddenly comes the riveting screech of a lyrebird. Then another calls higher up the hillside. The lyrebird sometimes mimics other birds and bush sounds like the thwack of an axe or bark flapping across a tree trunk, but the lyrebird's call is so penetrating there's no mistaking it.

Marjorie and Ralph Cornwall lived deep in the forest above Noojee. Ralph was one of the finest bushmen for miles around, while Marjorie came from England and seemed out of place walled up by the huge gums. But she loved it. Every morning she'd whistle up the lyrebirds and they'd come to her to be given tidbits for their breakfast.

Back on to the main road and down and down into the chasm which is the Latrobe River valley. Here the river glideth at his own sweet will, like Wordsworth's Thames, and the township of Noojee straggles along the curves of the valley. The first European in the district was Dick Belpoole, a loner, who worked his way through the bush, seeking his pot of gold. He was hard and tough and wiry, like the Man from Snowy River's pony, and had hair down to his waist. He let it out he'd discovered a rich vein of gold in the hills, but wouldn't say where. At last he relented, and promised to tell a young chap his secret. Exhausted – he was eighty-seven – he crawled into bed, saying, 'Tomorrow, I'll show you', but he died during the night.

Noojee was burnt out in 1926, and again in 1939, on Friday, thirteenth of January, Black Friday. The temperature was said to be 114 degrees at ten o'clock in the morning. Gladys McIntosh was the postmistress. She stayed at her post until the last moment, locked the valuables in the safe, and took to the river. "After the fire had passed, we got out of the river and I walked down the hot road to see the ruins of the main street," she writes casually. She'd used the phones to save many lives. Now Noojee is rebuilt, and the people and the fire brigade prepare themselves against the possibility of another fire.

Here, the Latrobe River is fresh and clear and strong. Like many of us, it loses much of its vigour as it goes coursing onwards. Agatha Christie came here on a world tour in 1922. She arrived from Warragul on the train, stayed the night, and visited the timber camps up in the hills. One of the tourist pamphlets about Noojee shows a pretty girl sitting on a rock in the river, holding a book and looking up at the tree ferns on either side. We can't see her this morning. Perhaps she's gone to the Ada Tree or the Toorongo Falls with the tourists.

She's not at the Trestle Bridge, either. But many other people are. The bridge is huge – a curved hundred metres sprint along the top and higher than a cricket pitch is long, a marvel of bush engineering. There were seven bridges like this in the roaring days of timber, connecting Noojee with Warragul. They disappeared one by one, mostly in mysterious circumstances. Only this one remains, and it's here not to carry trains across as in the old days, but to commemorate the old timers and to bring the tourists.

Thirty years before the railway actually came, a previous generation had thought of bringing the iron rails here, not from Warragul, but through from Yarra Junction. There was a vigorous campaign launched to move the government to action. Mr Petschack was one of those who campaigned. He had to cart his pigs to market by horseback. He'd put two pigs in separate bags, tie the bags together, hoist them on to the pommel of his saddle, one on each side, and take them to market that way. Poor horse! Poor pigs! Poor Mr Petschack.

From the trestle bridge, you can look across to Boys Camp Road on the other side of the river. In the Great Depression, groups of thirty lads at a time were brought up - three months at a time - from Melbourne to be trained for forest jobs. Where are they now? Did some stay on and settle? Or did they drift back to the City? I'm thinking of a day long ago when I walked the road, past this trestle bridge, to raise money for a good cause. From Icy Creek to Buln Buln I walked, and here at Noojee the children from the school came out to walk with me. Nice kids. Mrs Blacker was the teacher.

You can take a back road out of Noojee which loops back to Neerim. Or you can branch off and get to the Hawthorn Bridge at Neerim East. I remember the road winding down to this quaint crossing of the Latrobe River. There was that typical smell of the bush coming from the dusty road and the rank growth of the river bed. Families would camp here, and optimists pan for gold. But there's a new bridge now, high above the river, all concrete and metal. The romance is gone. Ah well, it's supposed to make things better for the firefighters.

Further down the river is Forest Edge, where a church organisation has built an adventure camp. *"Just ninety minutes east of Melbourne, you can escape to your own river valley, where rich farming lands, quiet rivers, lush fern gullies, tall old growth forests, and majestic mountains come together to frame this uniquely beautiful 120 acre property*", I read in their blurb. I'll have to get them to work on the back cover of this book!

The visitor has to come to terms with the multiplicity of Neerims. It's as if the god of place-names had sprinkled the name all over this part of Gippsland like pepper from a pepper pot. There's Neerim itself (a few houses here, a cemetery, and a showground), Neerim Junction (a shop and petrol station and public hall – the third hall, the previous two having burnt down), Neerim North (once a school and hall here, both gone), Neerim East (a 'locality', as they say), and Neerim South (the centre of civilisation). There was gold at Neerim East at one time, a spur of the rich Walhalla goldfield. In the 1890s the Miners League at Neerim was active and militant. But it wasn't all mining. Mr Mapleson of Neerim East was having a commodious dwelling house erected on his farm. "Mr Mapleson, senr, has a splendid herd of milking cows, thirty-one in number, in first-class condition," the report went on. I think he might need more than thirty-one cows to make a living these days, even if they were in first-class condition!

The smiling landscape hereabout belies a tragic past. The old papers tell of accident after accident in the timber mills and along the tramlines that snaked into the mountains, bringing in the logs. Many men, mostly young and now forgotten, lost their lives. The mills are a story in themselves – little communities of men, women, and children spending their years in lonely isolation. Sister May, a deaconess, travelled from camp to camp bringing companionship to the women and enlightenment to the children. She deserves a statue if anyone does. The women were the real heroes. Take Elizabeth Mitchell who brought her first baby home from Warragul in 1929 by bus to Noojee, then on top of the logs on a timber truck to Loch Valley.

The tragedy of fire has dominated the mood and history of these parts. Time and again the red devil has scorched the countryside as if to mock the puny efforts of the human interlopers. 1898, 1926, 1939, and 2009 were the worst years. Heroic tales are told. Put yourself in the place of Mr and Mrs Holt at Neerim East in January, 1898, with their six children, the youngest four weeks old. The whole township of Neerim East was to be destroyed that day. *'The atmosphere became so dark that the people could not see each other more than a few yards away, and in the roaring of the fire could not hear each other's voices'*. The mother took the children into some clear ground beside the house, lay them on the ground, covering them with sacks, while the oldest boy dashed water on them. The father dug a shallow hole for the baby, who promptly went to sleep amidst the roar of the fire and the crashing of the surrounding trees. All survived.

Motorists coming through from the south may be headed towards Powelltown and the Yarra Valley further on. If so, they might make a detour to see the Ada tree, some twenty-five kilometres from Noojee. It's one of the State's tallest trees, a mountain ash, thought to be getting on for 300 years old, and seventy-six metres tall. Thick, too. It took ten of my outstretched arm lengths to go round it. The country through here was completely burnt out in 1983 – a blackened desert – but within a few years it had returned to its old glory. A eucalypt forest regenerates after fire more swiftly than any other type of forest in the world.

On the other hand, our motorist – and this is more likely – may turn north-east and head on to Mount Baw Baw. They'll pass the turn-off to the Toorongo Falls on their left, and continue on to Vesper, Icy Creek, then Tanjil Bren. This is bracing country, but folk who live in harsh climates tend to stay where they are. Begone the temptations of the warm south! The road up to Mount Baw Baw is winding and steep. Just the sort of road for the rally car enthusiasts. Cyclists too. The Warragul Cycling Club runs the Baw Baw Classic – from Warragul to Baw Baw Village - here every year, the most gruelling road race in the State. One of the women contestants described her feelings:

> *The real battle is between you and the mountain. During the last 4km my quads and left foot began to cramp and I was relegated to climbing in the saddle, repeatedly counting to*

100, just to concentrate on something else. I "sprinted" the last 500m to the finish to be 2nd placed C grade woman ... Mt Baw Baw and I are at peace with each other once more ... until next time.

They talk about a white season and a green season at Baw Baw. It's the closest downhill skiing resort to Melbourne. The other perhaps better-known resorts have more snow, but are further away from Melbourne and less chummy, or so I've heard. Besides downhill, you can do cross-country, tobogganing and snow-boarding at Baw Baw. Or just enjoy the fun park. In the green season there are wildflowers and nature trails. One favourite trail is from Mount Baw Baw to Mount St Gwinear, summer or winter. I walked it once ... then headed back to the temptations of the warm south!

Omeo

As I came over Livingstone

The day was like a flame,

But suddenly I saw below,

Far and far and far below,

The shining roofs of Omeo,

And said its singing name. *

I'm looking at a sepia photograph at this moment. It shows a straggling stringybark in the foreground, an old settler's cottage hard against it, the shining roofs of Omeo town in the middle distance, and Mount Livingstone looming in bulky majesty in the distance. The first sighting of Omeo by the white newcomers, however, was from the other way, from the north, in 1834, at the time when there was no building, no home, no outbuilding, no structure of any kind in what is now the State of Victoria. Stanley Porteous has imagined for us, in *Providence Ponds*, what that first sighting might have been like:

> *The creek valleys narrowed, the forests closed in, until suddenly the Omeo basin fairly burst upon us – an open treeless plain, encircled by a rim of mountains ... But it was not the mountains that made the scene notable. It was rather*

that the Omeo plain, because of the absence of trees, was an oasis in reverse, a spot of space in a sea of forest.

The first squatting run, Omeo Station, was actually at Benambra. In those early years, the settlers looked northwards to the Monaro rather than southward as we naturally do today.

The peace of the valley was shattered in 1852 when gold was found in Livingstone Creek to the west of Omeo. Everyone was looking for gold at that time. It was only months since Hargraves had found gold at Ophir near Orange. Gold, which meant nothing to the first people of our nation, was the cup of desire to the 'civilised' ones who followed. That 'civilisation' in the Omeo Valley was marked by violence and lawlessness. The first magistrate to be appointed, Thomas Alexander Browne, believed the Omeo goldfields to be "the roughest and toughest in Australia". He was a good judge. Later, he wrote a famous book under the pen-name Rolf Boldrewood, *Robbery under Arms*. Many structures from early Omeo remain, most notably the 1893 Court House, which, together with the Golden Age Hotel, makes up the pair of most distinctive buildings in town.

The aboriginal inhabitants of the Omeo district were very different from those further south. The Yaitmathang people related well to the Monaro tribes, but were on hostile terms with the Gunaikurnai to the south. When European settlement of the high country occurred, the relationship between blacks and whites was very harmonious. It is indicative of this good feeling that Europeans chose to retain aboriginal place names rather than impose European names as happened further south. Ruth Lawrence has detailed these things in a fascinating article in the book, *Earth and Industry: Stories from Gippsland.* Aborigines willingly guided the first settlers and gold-seekers through the difficult mountain country, using their own trails. Indeed, many of their tracks form the road system in use today. Aborigines were employed by white settlers, chiefly as horsemen. When needed, they helped the police as trackers. In one celebrated case, when two miners murdered a shopkeeper, Cornelius Green, on his way to Sale with gold, two aboriginal men followed their tracks for fifty kilometres through very rough country before finding them. One was hiding up a tree!

Sadly, the newcomers learned nothing from the native people about sustainable food production. In particular, Lawrence details the Europeans' use of fire, burning large swathes of country, as opposed to the aborigines' localised fire-stick, cool-burning farming techniques. Edward McNamara, an early settler, records that "the blacks were not only frightened of bushfires lit by white men, but protested that their hunting grounds were being ruined". In spring, the Yaitmathang, in company with other friendly tribes, made their annual trek to the alpine regions to feast on the bogong moth. The balanced diet of the natives – mammals, reptiles, birds, fish and insects, together with the roots and leaves of various plants contrasted with the unhealthy 'beef, damper and tea' diet of the whites!

I'm very fond of Omeo. Who couldn't be? The folk take their colourful history in their stride. When I was visiting there regularly some years ago, I met some of the old pioneers. People at Omeo seem to live to a great age, though I don't know that that is borne out in the statistics. Their own personal history and the history of their town was of no great moment to them. It's an old-fashioned attitude and very mature. They've lived through tough times. Their isolation didn't worry them. The 1939 fires were very bad here, but 'that's what you expect' was their attitude. The fires struck again in 2020. The town was evacuated, many by helicopter, but most residents chose to stay. The local minister with her two girls was ordered to board the helicopter. The sky pilot piloted through the skies! She was back within a couple of days and spent months of exhausting work amongst the traumatised people of the district.

It's quite a shock to realise that when you drive from Bruthen up to Omeo, you're actually crossing the Great Dividing Range. The water that flows through Omeo in the Livingstone Creek ends up in the Murray-Darling Basin, not in Bass Strait. The Tambo River rises on the southern side of the Divide and flows through many of our towns – Swifts Creek, Ensay, Tambo Crossing, Bruthen and Swan Reach. Normally placid in its lower reaches, in its upper reaches it is a different kettle of turbulent water.

The poet Frank Williamson caught the spirit of the Tambo better than anyone else. Williamson was a relief teacher and taught in a number of our Gippsland schools. Some of you may remember his poems in the old School Readers. His best-known poem, 'A Magpie's Song', has some very evocative lines about the Tambo Valley:

> *Oh, I love to be by Bindi, where the fragrant pastures are,*
> *And the Tambo to his bosom takes the trembling Evening Star,*
> *Just to hear the magpie's warble in the blue gums on the hill,*
> *When the frail green flower of twilight in the sky is lingering still,*
> *Calling, calling, calling to the abdicating day:*
> *Oh, it fills my heart with music as I loiter on my way!*

My feelings towards Swifts Creek have been governed since near birth by a faded photo showing my mother standing outside the home of the Huttons at Swifts Creek in 1921. She had gone there straight after arriving as a migrant from England to be a governess to the Hutton children. There are bare hills in the background and forlorn domestic animals (and children) lying around. I believe there are still Huttons in East Gippsland. I've since found that Swifts Creek is much more animated than the photo indicates.

The backbone to the town over the last half of the twentieth century was Ezard's timber mill. The old mills of the high country are bathed in a romantic pathos. Helen Martin, Linda Barraclough and others have told the story of Ezard's mill and helped to keep alive the legends surrounding it. There's a large sub-culture of interest in the early timber days, and you can glimpse something of it in the deep pockets of the internet.

One of the continuing features of Gippsland is that things do not continue. Other parts of Victoria have long-settled industries that provide an overall sense of permanency. Gippsland is different. Gold was our economic backbone, then it virtually disappeared. Timber became a mainstay; now it is in serious decline. The power industry based on coal provided a huge economic stimulus; now it seems to be in its death-throes. Thus we have boom periods and downturns, an inflow and outflow of population, as well as considerable movement of people within the region. The effect of these things put together is that there is an ill-defined sense of Gippsland being on edge, of being unsure where we are heading. This applies to Swifts Creek as much as to the Latrobe Valley.

South from Swifts Creek there's a rest stop known as the Connor's Hill Lookout. The mountains stand in the distance, cleared hills in the foreground, and a tubular steel interpretation of the scene 'in real time' in front of you. Barry Heard wrote a book called *The View from Connor's Hill*. Earlier he'd written *Well Done, Those*

Men about his life as a Vietnam War conscript and afterwards. Then he sat down and wrote this 'Connor's Hill' book telling what went beforehand – his coming to this outlandish place as a boy from the city and being gradually enchanted by his new surroundings. It's a familiar story. A young teacher is posted to a country school, marries a local farmer, and settles down here for life. A young engineer comes to Gippsland for a short stint and never leaves. A green-change city evacuee discovers a place in the Gippsland bush and finds their Shangri-La. Retirees find a place in Gippsland and wonder why they didn't make the break years earlier. Barry Heard wrote a third book, *Tag*, about a Gippslander and his experiences in the First World War. He has brought home the dreadfulness of war and helped to reveal Gippsland to us all.

Ensay is a tiny island in the Outer Hebrides. No one has lived there since 1930. The population of our Ensay has fallen also, though not so dramatically. Most of the public services have gone. Not the hotel, though you have to turn off the main road to find it. I think of Ensay with some sadness. Our friends there built up a fine flock of sheep over generations – our friends' generations, not the sheep's. Then Ovine Johne's Disease struck and the flock was compulsorily destroyed. Lock, stock and barrel. It was heart-breaking for them and others in the same position.

From Omeo on, there are three roads – west to Dinner Plain, Mount Hotham and Wangaratta, north to Mitta Mitta and Albury, and north-east to Benambra and Corryong. The state of these roads is a principal topic of conversation - and part of the psyche of this high country. The factors at play are rain, snow, fire, where the road gang is at any moment, and the state of your tyres.

On the Benambra road, you first come to Hinnomunjie, where a patch of fertile soil accumulated in long-gone ages. The first station was established here by Edward Crooke. Now Hinnomunjie is known for its calf sales and its picnic races – and for its beautiful hand-hewn timber bridge over the Mitta Mitta River.

Benambra is also famous for its calf sales. The young beasts develop sturdy frames in this high country, but they need to be grown out and fattened in the sweeter country lower down. Each year, before the first cold winds of winter, buyers fill their order books at the annual sales in March. The top sellers often have the Pendergast brand. John Pendergast, generations ago, established Omeo Station. It was 1835, which makes Benambra an equal claimant - with Melbourne and Portland - to the title of the first settlement in what was to become Victoria sixteen years later. Now the town, as far as buildings go, is a shadow of its former self, but the old spirit remains. That spirit was tested in 2007, when the football team, unable to make up the numbers, merged with rivals, Omeo. A new jumper was designed, white snowy peaks set against a blue sky – or is that the blue water of Lake Omeo?

When you get to Anglers Rest on the Albury road – actually the Omeo Highway – you're entering the Alpine National Park. Anglers Rest is prettily nestled into the countryside –a bend in the road, the bubbling Cobungra River alongside, and a friendly bridge across. People come from all around to fish for trout. The ABC had a programme called 'A River Somewhere' some years ago. One of the episodes was set here, on the Cobungra River. Tom Gleisner and Rob Sitch came to fish the Cobungra. The commentary is hilarious ... and beautifully descriptive:

> *The mountains and the valleys appear to wake up softly, slowly, in some sort of natural order. The blanket of frost begins to lift, and the dew that coats every blade of grass (and the shoes you left out last night) sparkles briefly as if signalling its departure, and the light doesn't arrive in these valleys; it sneaks in. We're always talking about the light up in these mountains and we're not sure what it is – the clear water, the rocks, the way the eucalypts filter the light, or just the purity of the air - but at certain times of the day the light up here becomes positively incandescent. It's as if everything's on fire and the river is burning with sunlight.*

The Alpine National Park is a naturalist's wonderland. Some of the vegetation is extremely fragile. Take the sphagnum moss, which is like a sponge and can hold twenty times its weight in water. In the dry seasons it releases this water which keeps the mountain streams running and other plant forms alive. The moss can be damaged by feral animals - horses, cattle and pigs. I once wrote a book, '*Wild Beauty*', about a girl and a horse from up here. It shows a good deal of sympathy for the brumbies in the Park. I rather regret that now!

Further on, you come to one of the most tranquil spots in all Gippsland – the Glen Wills cemetery. Once the scene of a bustling town in the swinging days of gold, Glen Wills is now a wilderness … except for the graves of the ninety-seven people buried here between 1894 and 1920. Forty of those were infants. In recent years the cemetery has been put in order and become a place of beauty, with crosses placed in the clear spaces between the gums.

The third road out of Omeo is the one most travelled – to Dinner Plain and beyond. Dinner Plain is a new town. There was nothing here (except nature!) until the 1980s. The development conformed to strict rules. No building could be higher than the gum trees, for instance. There's a distinctive style in the design of houses and lodges, using, principally, stone, timber, and corrugated iron. I first saw Dinner Plain when I rode through on the Great Victorian Bike Ride. Luckily, we were going downhill, towards Omeo.

* RH Croll, in *By-Products: A Book of Verse*.

Orbost

The very first time I came to Orbost, I was met by three stockmen on horseback, whips in hand, riding down the main street. Ever since then, over many visits, I've carried this picture in my mind. Is Orbost still the outback town that first image suggested to me? Over the years I've pondered the question. The answer, I believe, is that the stockman and his horse are no longer representative of the town, but local people still keep a wistful spot in their remembrance banks for those former times.

They maintain properly their wide main street (wide enough to handle large mobs of cattle in the droving days); they are proud of their fine old public buildings and their classic hotels; and most importantly for me, they keep the history and tourism of the town tied together in the tourist centre, a log cabin wonderfully placed as you come into town. The log cabin is A1 genuine. It was built further out in the bush in the 1870s and later moved in here. You can get all your tourist information, then browse through the historical displays, all in the one place. They're very keen on their history, these people of Orbost. There's a strong feeling of closeness in the town, and the people who were raised here and moved to other parts of Gippsland have hung on to this feeling.

In recent visits I've come seeking the spirit of Grace Jennings Carmichael, the 'sweet singer of Orbost'. Grace grew up on a property near the town managed by her stepfather. She began to write winsome verses about the sights and sounds and scents of the bush, sitting amongst the gums as she wrote, and hiding her notebooks in a hollow tree, because at home they didn't approve of her 'scribbling':

> *Each soaring eucalypt, lifted high*
> *The wandering wind receives.*
> *I watch the great boughs drawn against the sky,*
> *Laden with trembling leaves.*
> *A soft, harmonious music, full and rare,*
> *Murmurs the boughs along –*
> *The voice of Nature's God is solemn there,*
> *In that deep undersong.*

The Bairnsdale Advertiser was the first to publish her work, and soon she was published all over Australia and rubbing shoulders with the literary giants of the 1890s. She left Orbost for Melbourne when she was twenty, and after her marriage to an Englishman moved to England. There things began to go wrong. Her family appears to have cut her off, and she died in a workhouse in 1904 at the age of thirty-seven. Two children died before she did, and the others – three boys – stayed on in the workhouse until they were rescued by a group of Victorian supporters and brought to Australia. They lived as adoptees in private homes with the name, 'Carmichael'. Does anyone know what happened to them? Poor Grace! From the soaring eucalypts of Orbost to the foul workshops of the Old Country. She was commemorated at the Orbost Back-To in 1937, when a bronze panel was placed for her and a photograph hung in the State School.

About the time of Grace's death, a duo of talented writers and poets was emerging, also in Orbost. These were the sisters Hilda Temple Kerr and Mabel Stewart Temple, whose parents, George and Mary Temple, ran the store in Orbost opposite the Post Office for long years. Hilda married James Kerr, who was the doctor in town – the only doctor for thirty years. He roved far and wide in the bush country all around in the heroic manner of those days. You'll find the graves of all these people in the cemetery here.

A friend of mine, years ago, driving back round the coast to his home in Melbourne after working away from his family for some months, came to the Snowy River. He was suddenly seized with a little tenderness, so he stopped at the Post Office in Orbost and sent a telegram to his wife to tell her he was at last nearing home. In a fit of light-heartedness, he signed it, 'The Man from Snowy River', and handed it across the counter. The Post Office man read the name at the bottom and shook his head. 'You're the fifth one today!' he muttered.

The people of Orbost have known hard times, none so critical as the disastrous floods of 1934. They were bad everywhere in Gippsland, but nowhere as catastrophic as here. The Bete Belong levee, built at a cost of £21,000, was ripped away. The railway bridge collapsed. The highway bridge was washed away. The new bridge upcountry at McKillop's Crossing, so new it hadn't been officially opened, became a mass of shapeless steel and concrete, "like a tiny twisted toy". Crops of beans and maize, ready for the picking, pastures, cattle, fences, all went downstream in a torrent of death and destruction.

In Melbourne, even in nearby towns in Gippsland, no one knew of the plight of the people of Orbost. All means of communication had been severed - until Mr Birkett, a young postal clerk, set off with a companion to drive to Bombala in New South Wales, a hundred miles away, but the closest reachable place with telephone communication. It was a nightmare drive, through gales and storms, across flooded creeks. But they got there and alerted the authorities of the Orbost disaster. Then the rescuing started. A team from Lakes Entrance brought a sea skiff and a surf boat to Newmerella by road, then set about rescuing dozens of people. Eleven pea-pickers who'd spent the night on their boss's roof fending off huge logs intent on crushing the place to matchwood were saved. Two adults and a girl sought sanctuary from the ten-foot torrent on top of a huge stump. They were rescued by a young man in a flat-bottomed boat.

Perhaps the most terrifying experience was that of two couples, together with two infants. Their houses were swept away, and they sought safety in a partly-constructed house nearby. They climbed into the gap between the roof timbers and the ceiling, crouching on doors they'd placed on the bare rafters. During the night the water crept higher and higher, while the wind and rain poured through the gaps in the roof. They spent the night in mortal terror until rescued the next morning. But no lives were lost! Marlo, downstream, was luckier. The force of the rushing water smashed away the sandbar, so the furious water was able to flood out to sea rather than spread over the land.

The old railway bridge at Orbost is one of the most obvious and interesting man-made structures on the Princes Highway all the way from Sale to the Border. Now there's a move to restore it. It looks very buckled and forlorn, but it's structurally sound. Not that they want it to carry trains again. It's planned to be the starting point for the East Gippsland Rail Trail, an outstanding feature that will bring fame and fortune to the town.

Country towns are very resilient. Orbost has been in economic decline for some years, and now bushfire has added another dimension. Orbost was directly impacted by the 2020 fires like so much of our eastern Gippsland territory. During the height of the fire attack, the town played a vital role as the Control Centre for the whole fire-fighting operation as well as being the principal relief centre. Before the fires, the government, the Shire and the Orbost business community had been working to revitalise the town. Their task will be more difficult, but at least both federal and state governments are now committed to the relief of rural areas. Perhaps the coronavirus experience will make city folk more open to rural living. If only town dwellers could understand the advantages of life in the country, they'd come and revitalise rural towns - and themselves!

Marlo is only a short drive from Orbost, but has a quite different feel to it. There's a smack in the air as you come into town, and people talk about fishing and boats and the weather. Marlo gets the prize for the best-named street in Gippsland. Holy Nelly Lane is named after an early pub licensee who used the words, 'Holy Nelly!' as her stock exclamation. Better than some things I've heard in my day!

In 1890, a paddle steamer, the 'Curlip', was built at Richardson's sawmill at Tabbara on the Brodribb River. It was a beautiful boat, made even more beautiful by its name. The indigenous people used the name, 'Curlip', for this part of the country. The boat was forty-eight feet long, and fat in the beam, with a mere two-foot draft, which was vital as she could get over the Snowy River bar and meet the ketches which brought supplies from the passing coastal steamers – and take off local produce, especially maize. In calm water, the Curlip could tow five barges behind her. The paddle steamers were an integral part of the economic development of the region. They contributed to the social life of the place, too. Things like Sunday School picnics were held on the Curlip, and I've seen a great photo of a High Tea being held aboard. The Curlip served the Snowy for thirty years until she was swept downstream in a flood and smashed to pieces in the Marlo surf. A year or two ago they built a replica to sail as a pleasure boat on the Gippsland Lakes. Not quite the same, but a nice nod to history.

Recently, we drove on from Marlo to Cape Conran. It was forty years since our last visit, and our consuming memory was of the beautiful shells we'd gathered on the beach. Yes, here they were, these delicate shells - great-grandchildren of the ones we discovered here ages ago. We gathered them and held them to our ear, though there was no need of an artificial tuning-in to the sound of the surf. It was there beside us in actuality. That vast curving stretch of sand was just the same. You can walk for three or four days, over a hundred kilometres, along the coastal walk that begins here. We camped here once, in a tent. Today's campers can do it in great comfort in the cabins or even the Lodge, but you need to book a long way ahead if it's school holidays. Several bushfires in the last two or three years have struck hard at Cape Conran, but by March, 2020, much of the foreshore had been re-opened, if not the nature reserve.

Coming from the west, you come into Orbost through Newmerella. We have a friend who was brought up here, and we've been hearing for years that Newmerella is the choicest place in Gippsland. I daren't disagree. However, I know of another town with almost the same name. Numerella is on the road between Cooma and Canberra, where the Numerella River winds its way between sandy banks, very like the Snowy here. There's a famous old song about the other Numerella. It starts,

> *There's a pretty little valley on the Eumerella shore*
> *Where I've lingered many happy hours away ...*

Someone should write a song about our Gippsland Newmerella. At least, we know how to spell it!

Orbost is on the Snowy River, of course, but when you head north along the Bonang Road you're following the Brodribb River, more or less. Occasionally we choose to go this way, crossing the New South Wales border near Delegate and continuing on to Bombala and so to Canberra. This is deep forest country and has been a battleground between loggers and environmentalists. At Goongerah, about fifty kilometres north of Orbost, there's a lively organisation called the Goongerah Environment Centre Office (GECO), which stoutly waves the environmentalist flag. Goongerah was horribly impacted by fire in the recent holocaust, and the Centre is desperately working to rehabilitate wildlife in the surrounding territory. The school in Goongerah offers to take students through from Prep to Year 8, but the last time I checked there were only five students. Will it stay open?

When last in Bonang, we saw evidence of the 2014 bushfire which swept through here. In 2020, fire struck again. The marks will be here for years to come. On the Bonang Road, we were keeping our eyes open for the Snowy River Bandit. Alan Torney, an escapee from a mental home in New South Wales, hid out in these parts just after the start of the Second World War. He had a gun and would demand clothing and food from householders and travellers. I don't think he meant any real harm.

From this road you can access both the Errinundra National Park and the Snowy River National Park, though there are probably better ways in to those by starting somewhere else, as the Irishman would tell you. Bendoc is quite a substantial village with a mixed grazing and gold-mining heritage. Many people miss it because they stay on the Bonang Highway or else they seek other pleasures to the west, pleasures like Tubbutt and McKillop's Bridge.

Tubbutt Station goes back to the earliest days of settlement in Gippsland. The author, Henry Kingsley, is thought to have visited here in the 1850s. His description of the cattle station in his book, *The Recollections of Geoffrey Hamlyn*, fits Tubbutt Station exactly. Louis Buvelot painted the homestead in the 1870s. I can't find where the painting is now, but probably in England. It was sold at auction in London in 2007 for £26,900.

Farmers round here have many difficulties to deal with. One of them is the problem of wild dogs. Most of the locals favour aerial baiting as the primary weapon, although there's a counter-argument about the collateral damage to native species. Like most things in life, there's something to be said on both sides.

On this last trip, we hurried on to McKillop's Bridge as we wanted to re-live the memory of a meeting we had in the middle of the bridge thirty years ago. We found things had changed! There's a more-than-decent campsite there now. Many people use it as a base camp for rafting or canoeing the Snowy. As for the bridge itself, it's "one of the most spectacular bridges in the world" according to one admirer. A quarter of a kilometre across and rearing high above the surging river below. We walked across the bridge last time we were here (everybody does!) Half way over we met a languorous fox soft-footing it towards us. We all stopped, looked at each other, then the fearless fox gently turned and ambled back the way he had come. There should be a sign on that bridge: 'Give Way to Foxes'.

Phillip Island

Eleven thousand people live on Phillip Island. Three and a half million visitors come each year. 9,500 every day, on average. How do they cope? Most visitors come to see the penguins on a day trip and leave each night, which makes it easier. There are 32,000 penguins at Phillip Island. I won't do the Maths there, but it's easy to see how the little creatures need to be guarded against packs of marauding visitors. They are. Going to see the penguins is rather like going to a drill camp. There's a sergeant-major who tells you what to do at every turn.

These penguins are Little Penguins, the smallest of all penguin species. They stand at 33 cm tall and weigh about one kilogram. They're blue and white in colour. 80% of their lives are spent in the ocean, feeding, sometimes for weeks on end. They come back to their burrows to rest, to breed, and to raise their chicks. Penguins often mate for life, but not always. The divorce rate, where a female will go off to find a new mate, is hard to tell, but is somewhere between 18% and 40% - about the same as humans. 30% of first marriages in Australia end in divorce (60% for second marriages). Fifty years ago there were ten penguin colonies on Phillip Island. Now there is only one, but the numbers there have increased from 12,000 to the present number over these years; it seems that preservation programs are working.

One of my friends grew up on the Island, went away for forty or fifty years, then came back to live there again. She tells me that when she was a girl in the 'fifties, there was no 'Penguin Parade' as we know it, nothing at the Nobbies except the cliffs, the sea and the seals. She used to go where the barricades are now, sit on the bare cliff top and watch the seals – or the penguins - with no-one around at all. Gone are those careless barefoot days!

To come back to how the Islanders cope with the crowds. My expert witness just mentioned says the locals adopt a siege mentality. They know 'the season' is from Christmas to Easter, so they bunker down in the knowledge that their present travail will soon be ended. Meanwhile they develop a camaraderie in the face of the enemy. It sounds rather like the spirit that developed in the prisoner-of-war camps. Meanwhile the natives are keenly aware that the visitors bring lots of spondulicks with them. So it's a give-and-take relationship.

My friend's father had a dairy farm on the island and grew chicory as well. That was a common pattern. Chicory was always a subsidiary crop. Chicory is a root crop, very like sugar beet. The leaves can be used as a salad dish, but the chicory here was grown for the roots. It was hard work: the roots had to be dug, carted to the nearest kiln, washed, and sliced. The chicory was then taken by conveyor belt to an upper level, spread out on a grill, and dried by means of a slow fire beneath, having to be constantly turned in the process. Chicory is used in a variety of food substances but principally as a coffee substitute. It's better for you than coffee; there's no caffeine in it, for a start. Chicory was grown on Phillip Island for a hundred years, but the industry died out in the 1980s. Some kilns remain, and the fashion is to convert them into chic residences.

I'm struck by the number of Historical Societies in Gippsland. Almost every town has one. The Phillip Island and District Historical Society is particularly active. Mind you, there's a lot of history over there! The Bunurong/Boonwurrung clan of the Kulin Nation was here for ages untold. In 1798 came George Bass in his whaleboat, followed by James Grant in 1801. Grant cleared a patch of land on Churchill Island and planted field crops and vegetables. He then sailed away, leaving the foodstuffs to be a pleasant surprise for Lt John Murray when he came to the same spot ten months later. The corn was as high as a kangaroo's eye.

Churchill Island is an island abutting the Island. It's a beautiful piece of land. James Grant thought it a veritable Eden:

> *'I was anxious to mark my predilection for this spot on account of its beautiful situation, insomuch that I scarcely know a place that I should sooner call mine than this little island.'*

Over the years, Churchill Island came into private possession and passed through several hands until the Victorian government bought it in 1976. Samuel Amess and his family held the island from 1872 until 1929. Amess built the homestead, established a herd of highland cattle (still there, though not direct descendants), and planted trees, now monsters. He also planted in the garden (also still there) a cannon from the famous Confederate American warship, *'CSS Shenandoah'*. This has been held to be an amazing thing. The *Shenandoah* was one of the most celebrated vessels of all time. During the American Civil War, she captured dozens of Union vessels around the world in an effort to destroy the North's economy. How did this cannon come to be on Churchill Island? The answer, still faithfully retailed, is that the *Shenandoah* was in Melbourne for provisioning and refitting during its piratical raids on enemy shipping. That's certainly true. The captain and crew were received as heroes, and as a thanksgiving for his warm reception, the captain, James Waddell, presented the cannon to Samuel Amess, who was Mayor of Melbourne. Amess subsequently installed it in his garden on Churchill Island. You probably have heard this story. Sorry, I have to upset your apple cart. It's not true. It's been proved conclusively that the cannon could not possibly have come from the *Shenandoah*. But be sure to visit Amess House and read the plaque alongside the cannon, with the (false) claim as to its origin.

On Phillip Island itself, if you're so inclined, you can amuse yourself in a hundred different ways. You can play golf on a nine-hole course or watch the pelicans being fed (that's at San Remo, actually) or visit a chocolate factory. You can get lost in the Maze or go to the Vietnam Veterans Museum. You can see koalas or penguins or seals, or go on a cruise. You can eat or drink or swim or learn to surf or fish.

Cowes has one of Gippsland's premier thoroughfares. You drive across the island with a mounting sense of expectation. Where is the sea? When will we get to Cowes? Then you roll into Thompson Avenue, with its double avenue of cypresses, the neon signs, the enticing notices on the off-streets, all the while the roadway falling gently away to the foreshore, jetty and beach. I find it an exhilarating experience each time I go. And where in Gippsland can you find a north-facing sea-front? Nowhere but here. "O for a beaker full of the warm North", John Keats would have said if he'd been here. Nowadays you can have your beaker at any one of the numerous hostelries and hotels along the Esplanade.

The good thing is that Cowes hasn't become a glamour resort, as you find elsewhere. The hotels are relatively modest and stand cheek by jowl with other modest places. Walking east along the Esplanade, for instance, you pass the Continental Guest House on your right. Here's where Gregory Peck, Fred Astaire and Tony Perkins stayed in 1959 for the shooting of 'On the Beach'. (Ava Gardner was at the Sunseeker in Settlement Road). But across the road from the Continental is Erewhon Point with its picnic tables and swings, and room for all to frolic. Cowes is for all sorts. That's a large part of its charm.

The Islanders are a close community and they like to keep alive their stories from the past. One of those stories is of Florence Oswin Roberts' koala. If you continue eastwards along the Esplanade and then along Lovers Lane, you come to Edward's Tree, which stands in memory of this koala. 'Broadwater', one of the Island's stately homes and guest houses, once stood here. A long list of famous people stayed beneath its roof, people like Prime Minister Stanley Melbourne Bruce, Mary Grant Bruce and Crosbie Morrison. In 1940, Broadwater was owned by Mrs Oswin Roberts. A fire swept through the island and many of the koalas were killed, others injured. Mrs Oswin Roberts took many of the injured koalas into the house, placed them in individual hammocks, and nursed them back to health.

One of them, Edward, became her favourite. It used to ride on her shoulder like Long John Silver's parrot. It slept in a cot and sat in a high chair at family meals. It climbed this very tree. Mrs Oswin Roberts was issued with a Wildlife Keepers certificate to enable her to keep Edward as a private possession. Edward died in 1944. His stuffed body is on display at the Historical Society's museum, while Edward's Tree still stands for all to remember him by. *[Footnote. Edward was actually a female.]*

We think of the coastline of Phillip Island in benign terms, with mental images of penguins, seals, and soft sand. However, this coast can become a savage beast. Many vessels have come to grief here. The worst disaster occurred in 1934, a time of storm and flood. The '*TSS Coramba*', sailing from Portland bound for Melbourne at the height of the storm sank in Bass Strait near Phillip Island. Wreckage washed ashore on the island; some of it has been put on display by the Historical Society. Seventeen crewmen died.

Earlier, in 1906, one of the biggest vessels on the Australian coast, the '*SS Speke*', struck the reef at Kitty Miller Bay not far from the Nobbies. One of the crew drowned. What remains of the wreck still lies, a rusting hulk, on the reef. It's a tourist attraction. Again, some items from the wreck are housed at the Museum, while the ship's bell is now at the Uniting Church at the corner of Chapel Street and Warley Avenue. It has its own bell tower and calls the people to worship every Sunday.

Ventnor is westward of Cowes, a town in its own right. I remember staying at Ventnor one summer and watching the shearwaters (mutton-birds) coming in at dusk from feeding out at sea. These birds are wonderful flyers with their extremely long wing-span, but they're terrible at taking off and worse at landing. They hit the ground hard. I expected them to do themselves a damage. The adult birds head off each April to their summer feeding grounds in the northern Pacific, in the Bering Sea and along the Kamchatka

Peninsula, 15,000 kilometres away. The chicks are left behind, but a few weeks later, with their feathers grown, they follow their parents. How do they know where to go? Instinct is a marvellous thing! These chicks often have great difficulty in getting off the ground, and many of them are confused by man-made objects such as street lights. Large numbers are attracted by the lights on the San Remo Bridge and crash on to the road. Teams of volunteers rescue them there and on many of the Island roads. For a few nights while the migration is at its height, the Bridge lights are turned off.

At the western end of the Ventnor settlement is McHaffie's Point, sometimes known as Grossard's Point. John Daniel McHaffie was the original landholder here, and William Philip Grossard, a retired ship's captain, was his guest. The year was 1868. Grossard loaded a gun for another guest, Frederick Sheppard Grimwade, which accidentally discharged, killing Grossard. The man lived long enough to forgive Grimwade and to say "he did not know Grimwade was such a muff with a gun or he would never have trusted him with it". His grave stands alone near the cliff-top beneath a large cypress and is sometimes referred to as 'the lonely grave'. It's quite a tourist attraction.

The Grand Prix circuit is also in Ventnor. It's a very busy business. There were thirteen major events listed in the Events calendar for 2020. The hottest tickets are the Superbike World Championship round in late February, the Australian Superbike Championship in early October, and the Australian Motorcycle Grand Prix, also in October. In between the major events, they fit in sessions where you can take your own bike or car and give it a spin on the famous circuit, imagining you're Jack Brabham or Mick Doohan. Outside the Visitors Centre just as you come on to the Island there are busts on pedestals of our three greatest riders of the modern era, Casey Stoner, Mick Doohan and Wayne Gardner. Their fame is set in concrete.

In the same place you'll find a plaque recording the Melbourne Cup win of the local horse, Wollomai, in 1875. The horse was owned and bred by Captain John Cleeland from Wollomai House on the Island and ridden by canny Scottish jockey, Bob Batty. To get to Flemington, the horse was swum across the channel to San Remo and then walked to Flemington.

Bushwalkers head to Cape Woolamai (notice the different spelling). You should take a walk in the Fauna Reserve on the Cape. You can easily get as far as the Pinnacles and then perhaps on to the point itself, the Beacon, the highest point on the Island. There are other walks too. It's a forgotten corner of Phillip Island.

The Island connects to the mainland via the concrete bridge over The Narrows. The crossing was originally made by ferry. A suspension bridge was built in 1940, and then the present structure in 1969. The site was first called Griffiths Point; it developed as a port for sending black coal, farm produce and wattle bark to

Melbourne. The change of name to San Remo was made in 1888 as a manoeuvre to attract tourists. San Remo remains a tourist town but has a solid feel more akin to an inland town. Over the last fifteen years trials have been going on to harness the tidal power running through the Narrows. Power has been fed into the national grid, and no harmful effects on aquatic life have been reported.

A memorial cairn stands on the foreshore dedicated to those who have lost their lives in the fishing industry. An anchor is beside it, and the names of the men are listed. A poem has been placed there, which closes with these words:

> *Down to the sea in ships they go, these chosen men of steel,*
> *Though mist and foam and North West wind is founding at the keel.*
> *So sail they must each crispy morn, away from trees and sod;*
> *The sea may own their wind burned flesh, but their souls belong to God.*

Rosedale

The most eye-catching object in Rosedale is the full-size statue of the race horse, Patrobas, winner of the 1915 Melbourne Cup. It's a fine piece of work. Patrobas was owned by Mrs Edith Widdis from Nambrok Homestead. She was the first woman to own a Melbourne Cup winner, and at a time when, as a woman she was not eligible to enter the Victorian Racing Club's precincts at Flemington. Her racing colours were pink! Patrobas' win was no flash in the pan. In an amazing few weeks, he won the Caulfield Guineas, the Victoria Derby, and the Melbourne Cup. The next year, Edith's husband, John's, horse, Shepherd King, came second in the Cup. Bragging rights to Mrs Widdis! It's constantly claimed that Patrobas is the only Gippsland winner of the Cup. That's contestable. Wollomai from Phillip Island won in 1875, and I've written about him earlier. It depends on whether you think Phillip Island is part of Gippsland. Most of us do. The Rosedale race course is now the Rosedale Speedway. In 2017, the Andrews family placed a plaque alongside Patrobas's statue in honour of the old Rosedale race course. The Andrews family was intimately associated with the course. Kevin Andrews, MP, used to call the races here before he took on a larger calling.

The Widdises are a famous Gippsland family and Nambrok a famous Gippsland estate. The story begins with John King who took up this land in the 1860s and employed William Allen to build a grand home. More about William Allen below. King was the son of Admiral Philip Parker King and grandson of Philip Gidley King, third Governor of New South Wales. The place eventually passed to the Widdises and from them to the McGaurans. John McGauran was a hotelier with interests throughout Gippsland and in the City. His sons, Peter and John, were both members of Federal parliament. The property is actually on the market at the time of writing. The National Trust lists Nambrok Homestead. Its description is a little beyond me, but you might appreciate it: It is "an eclectic derivation of the Dutch and North Italian Renaissance fused with the Lombardic Romanesque". In more homely terms, it is a beautiful and perfectly preserved place.

There are many interesting tales of old Rosedale. William Hobson was born at Kilmany Park in 1856. He was a marvellous concertina player, and once, in Melbourne to deliver a mob of cattle, he saw a street musician doing his poor best. Hobson took over his instrument and played so well that a crowd assembled and threw in a small fortune for the bemused busker.

Blind Joe was a shepherd on one of the early runs in the Rosedale area. He is said to have been Chinese and blind in one eye. People once referred to the place that became Rosedale as 'Blind Joe's Hut'. He is commemorated by Blind Joe's Creek you drive over on the highway and also by Blind Joe's Rest Area beside the highway on the western edge of Rosedale. We call in there sometimes to renew our acquaintance with our favourite Gippsland tree, a scraggly grey gum watching sentinel there.

The entire district was convulsed in 1868 by the disappearance of Mrs Ross, wife of the local saddler, who left her home in Rosedale and wandered into the dense bush. She was never seen again. How many stories like this have we heard over the years? There are many secrets locked away in the Gippsland bush.

A more recent story is of the man who used to run the Rosedale tip in the 1980s. These were the days when people used to be able to take away 'treasures' from the tip; visiting was like going to an op shop now. This caretaker used to gather discarded items and make them up into art works. People came from far and near to see them.

Rosedale is fortunate in that it has kept most of its old public buildings. Doubly fortunate that most of them were built by the same man, William Allen. As well as Rosedale Homestead, he built the Rosedale Hotel, the Exchange Hotel, the Mechanics Institute, the first school, and the Presbyterian, Catholic, and Anglican churches. His obituary in the Gippsland Times in 1924 gives a classic account of one of our builders of Gippsland:

> *... Mr William Allen a fine old pioneer [died] at the great age of 95 years. He was born in London ... and arrived in Australia in 1852 with his wife and carried on his trade as a brickmaker and builder at Flemington ... In 1858 he came to Rosedale for the express purpose of building the*

> *Rosedale Hotel, and has lived there ever since. ... He came by schooner to Port Albert, thence by bullock wagon to Rosedale. At that time there was a camp of blacks at Rosedale, and ... he and others had to guard [the hotel] with guns at night from attacks by the natives.*

William Allen also built the Rosedale Tannery for Paul Cansick. We used to hear a lot about the Rosedale tannery. It was the biggest employer in Rosedale for many years. 200 worked here at one stage in the 1990s. Now it is no more, but the building has had a reincarnation. A firm making cables and wires has relocated from Sydney under the General-Managership of Alf Chown, originally a Gippslander. Chown is very experienced in the field of establishing industries in new locations, and has made some interesting comments about rural manufacturing. He says, '*Everywhere I have been around the world, the best factories have been in rural areas ... I think that's something Australia's got wrong – manufacturing has tended to congregate on the edge of metropolitan areas, and struggle with expensive rents. That's why we are moving from Sydney to Rosedale – it makes great business sense.*' I couldn't agree more. We need to get away from our citicentrism.

My eye always falls on the Catholic Church as I drive by. It's dedicated to St Rose of Lima, a sixteenth-seventeenth century saint who lived, as you might imagine, in Peru. If you happen to have some Peruvian banknotes, you'll find her image on one of them.

There are only three churches in the land dedicated to St Rose, one in South Australia, one in New South Wales, and our one in Rosedale. I've tried and failed to find why the dedication is to this faraway saint. I can only presume it was thought right to have Rose for Rosedale. Rosedale Parish is one of the few larger towns of Gippsland not to have its own primary school.

Rosedale has from the first been surrounded by large pastoral properties. It isn't surprising. We're in East Gippsland here, open plains country, settled very early by squatters who took up vast acreages.

I believe there's a change in the atmosphere as soon as you leave Rosedale, heading east. You leave the town, cross the Latrobe, wind up the hill, then, as you swing right, the plains begin. This is East Gippsland. Those lines from Banjo Paterson always come to my mind (for me, they're the finest lines ever to flow from an Australian pen):

> *And he sees the vision splendid of the sunlit plains extended*
> *And at night the wondrous glory of the everlasting stars.*

One of those old properties is Holey Plain. Most people immediately think of the grand red-brick building with its splendid tower. The Curlewis brothers took up the original lease and later sold to Edward Crooke. The Crookes have been there ever since. The house was built with bricks made on the property in the late 1880s. The Holey Plains State Park (some people like to pluralise the name) was opened in 1977. It has over 10,000 hectares of undulating, sandy country with very diverse plants and many native animal and bird species.

Linda Barraclough has told the story of the Holey Plain 'bushranger', George de Thouars, who held up the homestead (the original one, not the present mansion) and everyone in it. His was a singularly inept crime, occasioned not by premeditation but through a surge of quick temper. He was, however, handed a stiff fifteen-year sentence. Public sympathy was with him and he was released after serving about half that time

I know Kilmany Park better. It's now a 'Bed and Breakfast, Conference, Function, and Reception Centre'. Gosh! I knew it in earlier and simpler days, when a church group called 'Fusion' was quartered here. Before then it was a Boys' Home for over fifty years, run by the Presbyterian Church. In those times, there was a mania for institutions. 'Put people into large buildings away from everyday life' was the overriding principle. Nowadays we feign to know better. William Pearson was the original owner of Kilmany Park. He took up the run in 1841, very early by Gippsland standards. A Scot and former seaman, he was elected to the Victorian parliament, but had many other interests. His racehorses won hundreds of races, while he was the chief investor in the lucrative Long Tunnel Extended gold mine in Walhalla from which huge profits flowed into his pockets. Pearson had a pack of hounds and hunted kangaroos and wild dogs. While travelling on the Old Sale Road he once threw a bottle of brandy into the creek, giving Brandy Creek, near Warragul, its name. Or so it's said! Pearson's reputation with aboriginal people was not so kindly.

Willung is not a place of wealthy squatters and large acreages, but of homely small settlers with a wealth of community feeling. It has always been so. I checked the old newspapers for references to the township, and found this entry for May, 1945, which I thought illustrated life in our small rural communities wonderfully well:

> *A successful dance and euchre was held recently, a profit of £10/2/0 being made for Red Cross. Music was supplied by the Victory Orchestra. Mrs. E.M. Young was the winner of the fat lamb donated by Mrs. N. Farley. Mrs. Farrar was the winner of the gent's euchre, and Mrs. A Young the lady's. Five guineas was obtained at auction for a fat lamb donated by Mrs. P. MacReadie. ... Red Cross Sunday was observed with a service by Mr. Buchanan. ... Willung ladies conducted afternoon tea at the Gippsland Hospital on May 11 and with collections £10/10/0 was handed in.*

It's not a misprint. When there weren't enough men, the ladies made up the gents' numbers!

Kilmany township is no doubt a good place to live, but its reputation comes mostly from its Tip. 'Transfer Station' is the proper name. If you haven't called in lately, you should do so. They seem to like visitors. It's remarkably hi-tech; technology is working its way even into the most isolated of places! You can buy soil conditioner there, and timber. There's even a Tip Shop, selling things like bikes, tables and chairs.

In this connection, I find there's a movement called 'Women against Waste', whose aim is to "make it easier for women to share quality unwanted personal and household items, keep stuff out of landfill, & money in pockets". They have a secretariat in Paynesville, while more than eighty women came to 'events' in Warragul and Bairnsdale in 2019. They can do anything. It seems to me that a quick fix to Australia's problems would be to appoint these women to replace our Federal government!

North from Rosedale, we're in plains country. The story of land settlement here is of large runs being taken up by squatters, and, later, attempts made to break up the large holdings and put smallholders on the land. The selection acts of the 1870s were the first step, followed by the government acquiring land for closer settlement. This movement accelerated after the First World War, and again after the Second War. 138 soldier settlers, for instance, were put on small blocks on these plains after 1945, with the provision of irrigation water from Glenmaggie Weir a vital part of the planning. Dairying took the place of grazing, and public facilities grew in Nambrok and Denison. In more recent years, there has been some aggregation of farms and so the population has fallen. As a sign of this, the Nambrok and Denison schools merged in 1994.

Many of the irrigated farms now have their paddocks laser-graded. In this process, a tractor tows a laser-guided box blade over the surface, cutting high spots and filling depressions. The result is that with flood irrigation, less water is required and pasture or crop growth is better controlled. Dairying has become very high-tech. With larger farms, modern milking systems, computerised recording of breeding and culling, for example, the computer has become a necessary adjunct to successful farming. My regret is that whereas we could always make jokes about the old milking sheds, there's not so much fun in computers and lasers.

The first explorers reported finding open grasslands here, and that is a tribute to aboriginal land practices. Their slow mosaic burning kept the land open for grass to grow and game to feed upon. The newcomers were blind to all this. In his journal, McMillan wrote of his feelings as he entered what was for him a new Eden:

> *I keenly felt that I had a noble and glorious task to perform, and that I was only an instrument at the hands of the Almighty to accomplish it. Here was a country, capable of supporting all my starving countrymen, lying dormant ...*

We bridle at such a statement today. McMillan was oblivious to the thousands of years of settlement and civilisation that had existed in these lands. To him they were an open canvas; in fact the indigenous inhabitants made up a rich tapestry of life. We might give Bruce Pascoe (in *Dark Emu*) the right of reply:

> *It is clear from the journals of the explorers that few were in Australia to marvel at a new civilisation; they were here to replace it. Most were simply describing a landscape from which settlers could profit. ... Invaders like to kill the original owners of the soil they intend to plunder, but, even better than that, they like to humiliate them. Once that hard work is over, their grandsons rewrite the history of the renamed land and paint their grandfathers as benevolent visionaries.*

Such thoughts are far from the traveller's mind as they drive through Rosedale. That coffee shop on the highway is more on their mind. Or perhaps they're thinking of Patrobas and the Cup, or looking for the stop-over on the Latrobe River just around the bend. This is the way of the world ... but perhaps a few moments' reflection would not be out of place.

Sale

Sale is one of Gippsland's three cities. Some say a city has to have a cathedral. Sale has two. Some say a city has to have walls and gates. Not in Australia. Some say a city has to be of a certain size. Not so. Officially, in Australia, a town has to have at least 1000 inhabitants. There is no such requirement for a city. I know Sale has a Town Crier, though I doubt that is a necessary appointment for a city. On the weight of evidence, we'll allow Sale its city status!

There is no capital of Gippsland because Gippsland is not a specified political region. But if we were to ask people in the street what is the capital of Gippsland most would say that Sale is. Why? Well, Sale has audaciously proclaimed itself as the capital of Gippsland, and that goes a long way. It is the centre of the Catholic and Anglican churches, although the Catholic Bishop has now gone off to Warragul to live. It has a number of State and Federal administrative offices. And, historically, Sale has been the main centre of pastoral and business development at least for the eastern parts. So we'll also accept the acknowledgement of Sale as the unofficial capital of Gippsland.

I'm struck by a certain feeling of reverence whenever I'm in Sale. It's like the respect you have for a benign elderly uncle. A little tired, respectable, predictable. Tree-lined streets, nineteenth-century buildings, and gentle traffic all add to the impression. Proud peacocks take their lordly path through the Botanic Gardens. It seems somewhat out of character that Sale was the nerve-centre for that slick American oil producer, Esso, until recently ... or that on the edge of town is one of the nation's major defence installations in the RAAF air base. It's more in line with one's expectations that Sale was in the past an important port on the Gippsland Lakes system. Gracious steamers came and went, bringing an air of Savannah and the Deep South of USA straight out of 'Gone with the Wind'.

The Port of Sale is the city's central focus. In Gippsland, only Lakes Entrance can match it. It's an artificial port, actually. The railway from Melbourne, that great shaper of Gippsland towns, came to Sale in 1879, but no further at that time. To link the railhead with the Gippsland Lakes required the digging of a mile-and-a half canal from Sale to just below where the Thomson and Latrobe Rivers meet. From there it was plain sailing to Lake Wellington and on to the whole of the Lakes system. The era of Lakes navigation had begun. To allow for both river traffic and road traffic, rather than build a fixed bridge over the river, they built a swing bridge. It's a low road bridge, but whenever a boat appears, you swing the bridge around ninety degrees, so that boats can get through – on both sides! Percy Grainger's father was the designer.

That's just the beginning with the Port of Sale. Alongside it is the Wellington Centre which has the Library, the Art Gallery (how good are our regional art galleries!) and the Visitor Centre. The

Council Chamber is here, too. Alongside is the Wedge, a centre for the performing arts and all kinds of theatre shows, and also film. And a fine restaurant. It's a superb place. In Gippsland, only the Arts Centre in Warragul can hold a candle to the Wedge.

Many Gippsland towns can thank one or two outstanding citizens for building community assets and community spirit. John Leslie was one such person. A grand old Sale name. There's hardly one of Sale's community organisations that he wasn't actively involved in. The arts received his special benevolence. The main theatre in the Performing Arts Centre is named in his honour.

Sale, as elsewhere (except, say, for Yallourn) had humble beginnings. We read of the squatters who took up runs round Sale and tend to overlook the harsh conditions they lived under in the earliest times. Take Francis Hales' experience for example. He visited all the runs from Traralgon to Bairnsdale in 1848. Staying at William Montgomery's The Heart Station, which included Flooding Creek, the present Sale, the rain came through the bark roof of the homestead on to his bed. Later he visited Dr Ewing, Flooding Creek's first doctor, in his "miserable wattle and daub hut".

The people at Flooding Creek suffered from having the Great Morass on the southern side of the settlement. Parson Bean, travelling through in 1849, wrote:

> *As to Flooding Creek, it is too near the morass to be healthy, they say, and I think probably the water is bad, being either procurable in the neighbourhood out of the morass or the dirty pools in the Creek, or else from the River Thompson, at some two miles distance ... If the Government and inhabitants could spend some £3,000 on a causeway across the Morass ... and establish proper licensed punts on the Latrobe and Thompson Rivers, convenient to Flooding Creek township – its position as a centrical point for the whole district would be indisputable.*

The morass has now been tamed. Controlled water areas and wetlands occupy the place. A difficulty has been turned into a benefit. Sale has indeed become a centrical point for the whole district! Still, there are those who claim that the country around the city, on the western approach especially, is so prone to flooding that in an emergency, the evacuation of Sale would be fraught with difficulty. Our Gippsland experience with the 2019-20 fires makes this a telling observation. Sale might one day again become Flooding Creek!

It's easy think of Sale as a city of institutions – hospital, schools, churches, government instrumentalities, nursing homes, and the like. One of these institutions stands out – the prison. For many years the high basalt walls of Sale Prison gave a forbidding greeting to people as they drove into the town. In the days when I had a bit to do with the place, it was a protection prison, which meant it was for men who, elsewhere, were likely to be set upon by other inmates because of their particular record or previous occupation. There was a mild attempt to ameliorate the men's conditions. A couple of devoted women ran the school. One man was learning all he could about Venezuela; there was no extradition treaty with Australia at that time, he told me.

Now the walls are gone, and the prison has been moved out to Fulham and become a general prison, though there remains a protection unit there. Officially, it's the Fulham Correctional Centre, a medium security prison, and can hold nearly 1000 men. It's run by a private enterprise firm. I've lost touch with it, but I do know about the great work being done by volunteer organisations like Kairos Prison Ministry that cares for inmates and their families. And it's good to know that 30 per cent of the prison work force is made up of women. That's bound to have a beneficial effect on the men.

On the softer side, Mary Grant Bruce was born in Sale, at Woondella Park on the Maffra Road, and lived there until she was eighteen. Her books evoke the bush humour and melodrama of the time, all carrying dashing pictures of young women on horseback on their covers. The first was *A Little Bush Maid*, and this was followed by the *Billabong* series. The heroine is Norah Linton, and we follow her adventures in several volumes as she grows up into womanhood. To give a taste of the series, we could take this summary of *Norah of Billabong,* published in 1913, from the Mary Grant Bruce Family Trust:

> *With a night in the city behind them, a pantomime, and distributing gifts at the Children's Hospital, Norah returns to Billabong for the holidays with a school friend after a whole year away at bothersome boarding school. The family settles back into their station life, cattle mustering, dealing with a snake bite, a maliciously lit bushfire that destroys their house, rescuing a stolen child, and the shenanigans of her brother, Jim, and his friend, Wally.*

How young people of those times would thrill to these adventures!

Time now to take a drive out of Sale and down towards the coast. We follow the South Gippsland Highway past the Sale Wetlands (featuring a wonderful long duckboard), over the swing bridge, to Longford. Longford, named after an obscure Irish gent, not the film actor and director, has about a thousand residents, most using the sleepy place as a dormitory from their work in Sale. The vast plant that supplies Victoria with its gas is here. The gas is piped directly here from the off-shore rigs to be cleaned and processed. In 1998 a terrible explosion killed two workers and started a fire that lasted for four days. It cut off the State's gas supply for nearly three weeks - an early reminder of the vulnerability of our power supplies.

Bypassing the Golf Club, just off the road, we leave the Loch Sport road on our left (that can come later) and instead head to the coastal town of Seaspray. Before the development of Golden Beach, Paradise Beach, and Loch Sport, this was Sale's favourite watering hole, and still is for many. Families from Sale and further afield would come to Seaspray every summer; they'd never dream of going anywhere else.

I've had the chance to read through some old copies of the Gippsland Times about Seaspray. They refer to duck shooting and rabbit trapping here as well as fishing. Sports days were held on ANA Day (now Australia Day) and Fancy Dress dances during the season. Tents covered the foreshore and the dunes. The Briagolong cricket team came down every year to play the locals, but the summer holiday tennis tournament was the hottest ticket in town. There were drawbacks – firstly, the wind which never seemed to stop blowing, and, secondly, the mosquitos, which should be in the Guinness Book of Records for their size. It's not just at Seaspray. You find these things right along the coast. But along the Ninety-Mile beach they take some beating.

I was amused by this anecdote from the Gippsland Times in 1937:

> *One of our visitors, Mrs. W. McDonald, has a great regard for Seaspray, for her first trip to this one-time isolated spot was when pioneer Buckley was at Prospect [the original name for Seaspray]. At a much later period Mrs. McDonald*

visited the Old Country, and when staying at St. Ives, a Cornwall man said that she should see the beach there before her return to Australia. He impressed on her its beauties and pointed out with much delight, that it was three miles in length. Mrs. McDonald was not going to let the man from Cornwall have it all his own way, and informed him that they had a beach in Gippsland ninety miles in length. "Oh yes," he replied, "you Australians always go one better than the Americans with their tall stories."

The coastal road – Shoreline Drive – takes us along the sea front, except that we can't see the sea because of the dunes for a good part of the way. We pass The Honeysuckles. People have been camping and living here where the land broadens out for 150 years. We continue with ocean on one side and lake on the other to Golden Beach and Paradise Beach. Longford gas workers, Sale commuters, retired folk and holiday makers make up the bulk of the population. In the early days, people came down here and built shacks on crown land without any licence to do so. They had a great time, but officialdom necessarily caught up with them. The wreck of the *Trinculo* lies rusting in the sand, like a whale's backbone. It's hard to imagine from this rusting hulk the terror of the wreck and then the bravery that brought all safely to land in 1879.

And so to Loch Sport. This whole coastline is vulnerable to coastal erosion. The landforms are fragile. The Ninety-Mile Beach is, after all, in technical language, "an elongate accumulation of sand initiated by waves, sand transport and vegetation growth". It's a highly dynamic natural construction. The threat to it has been accurately measured. The sea level has risen twenty centimetres in the last century, and is currently rising at three millimetres a year. The changing climate brings not only these rising sea levels, but also more frequent storms (which means the beaches have less time to recover from each storm) and also more powerful waves. Without doubt regulations controlling everyday life and activity will become stricter in the future along this coastline.

Loch Sport itself has become very well established. You find here all the trappings of town life you find elsewhere in Gippsland. There is a strong feeling of community togetherness. It comes from several factors: the unique location, the rare combination of old and new, the story of the town's development still ringing in the ears, and the low-key lifestyle of the residents.

On the return journey we take the inland road from Golden Point through Dutson Downs. There's a good news story in Dutson - the Soil and Organic Recycling Facility (SORF). In a few words, this plant takes thousands of tons of commercial waste products, food, green waste, and sewerage from Gippsland and parts of Melbourne and converts it to compost. They'll take contaminated soil from petrol stations. Even the used oil from your fish-and-chip shop is likely to end up here. The compost is used on the farm alongside. The grass is very green!

Further on and away to our right is The Heart Morass, well-known to generations of Gippsland duck-shooters. There's a success story here, too. Less than twenty years ago, this land was degraded and desiccated. With the combined actions of the West Gippsland Catchment and Management Authority and a number of other groups, it's been restored to something like its former beauty. The process has involved purchasing additional land, planting trees, shrubs and grasses, controlling invasive weeds, raising water levels, and removing carp, which has caused much damage here and elsewhere in Gippsland.

We end up in Sale drinking coffee in the Mall, with the Clocktower alongside. That's a good place to conclude. The original Clocktower was part of the Post Office, built in 1884. When that building was pulled down, the clock itself and other parts of the tower were made part of the present structure. So it's a mixture of old and new. Rather like Sale itself!

Stratford

With Stratford, we're in the heart of old Gippsland. William O'Dell Raymond is said to have built the first house in the province here in 1842. Fortunately, Raymond was a copious writer of letters and reports and has left excellent descriptions of the earliest Gippsland days. It's clear that after Strzelecki's reports of his explorations in Gippsland, the stock route from Monaro through the mountains became a regular 'Collins Street'! Three weeks after reading Strzelecki's report, Raymond had 8,000 sheep on the road. He established his run, 'Stratford', on the banks of the Avon River (the aborigines' name for the river was 'Dooyeedang').The town grew in importance as a trading centre and fording place on the route between Port Albert and Omeo.

Today, Stratford lies between the larger centres of Sale and Bairnsdale. There was a move some years ago to call this area 'Central Gippsland'. Geographically, that was a sound enough proposition. Bairnsdale is roughly half-way between Nar Nar Goon and Mallacoota, Gippsland's virtual extremities. But the suggestion didn't accord with grassroots sentiment. To bona fide Gippslanders, East Gippsland has always begun at Sale and extended eastwards. If you want to use the term, 'Central Gippsland', apply it to the Latrobe Valley region, but best not use it at all.

Stratford and district is replete with aboriginal associations. In 2010 an Act of the Victorian Parliament established aboriginal land rights to crown land in a huge area of Gippsland extending from Warragul to the Snowy River. The practical outcome was that ten significant areas were placed under Gunaikurnai ownership but under joint managership between the Gunaikurnai people and the government. The Knob Reserve at Stratford is one of those ten reserves. It commands a key position on the bluff above the river. Over many centuries the Knob was a gathering place of five Gunaikurnai clans. Here they would periodically come together to establish and maintain clan relations, feast together, trade, and conduct ceremonies. The marks of their presence can be seen – instrument-sharpening grooves in the rocks and scarred trees. Happily, the Knob still functions in much the same way. Many groups use it; visitors come here; people mingle for mutual enjoyment.

The Knob is one of the way-stations on the Bataluk Cultural Trail. 'Bataluk' is the word for 'lizard', and the Bataluk Trail winds its way across Gippsland in the manner and pattern of a lizard, from Won Wron in the west to Cape Conran in the east, linking places of particular cultural significance for the Gunaikurnai people. There are eleven featured spots along the course of the Trail – the White Woman's Waterhole, the Sale Common Reserve, the Knob Reserve, Ramahyuck Cemetery, the Den of Nargun, the Krowathunkooloong Keeping Place in Bairnsdale, Howitt Park in Bairnsdale, Legend Rock at Metung, the Buchan Caves, the Burnt Bridge Reserve, and Salmon Rock at Cape Conran. The

Krowathunkooloong Keeping Place is the main centre and has a large collection of aboriginal art and artifacts.

Near the mouth of the Avon, where it's joined by the Perry River, at Boney Point, the first large massacre of aborigines in Gippsland took place, in 1840. It followed the spearing of cattle and several attacks on settlers. Like later massacres, there is little direct evidence of it. Events were hushed up. After the Myall Lakes massacre two years earlier, seven white men were hanged for murder, so it is understandable that the perpetrators at Boney Point should have kept their silence. Some who were in the district at that time or shortly afterwards made comments on the widespread slaughter of aborigines. One of them, Henry Meyrick, wrote in a private letter to his family in England:

> *The blacks are very quiet here now, poor wretches. No wild beast of the forest was ever hunted down with such unsparing perseverance as they. Men, women, and children are shot whenever they can be met with ... I have protested against it at every station I have been in Gippsland, in the strongest language, but these things are kept very secret as the penalty would certainly be hanging.*

There are many groups in Gippsland working towards reconciliation with aboriginal people. My belief is that reconciliation can be authentic only when 'white people' acknowledge with a due sense of remorse the evil things that were wrought upon the First Settlers of our nation in times gone by.

Some miles south of Stratford, on the banks of the Avon, the Moravians established a mission station in the 1860s. The superintendent, Frederick Hagenaeur, was a harsh man, unlike his opposite number at the Lake Tyers Mission, John Bulmer, who identified deeply with his charges and was referred to as 'God's Good Man'. At Ramahyuck, Hagenaeur would not allow any expressions of native culture, such as corroborees, and native languages were banned.

The Avon River was named first (after a river in Scotland), and the name of the town, 'Stratford', followed. The Shakespeare connection was further established when O'Dell Raymond built the first hotel here and named it the 'Shakespeare'. There's been a Shakespeare Festival held annually since 1989. All sorts of things happen. I remember rather uncomfortably the time when I gave a talk here as part of the Festival, dressed as William Shakespeare himself! I'm older and wiser now. The Courthouse Theatre, "the beating, beautiful entertainment heart of Stratford", as one person describes it, has put on a Shakespeare play. Unfortunately, the Courthouse Theatre has recently been sold, and its future is uncertain. There are Stratfords in England, USA, Canada, and New Zealand, as well as our own Stratford. They have regular gatherings. In 2013 and again in 2018 they descended on Stratford,

Victoria, 3862, and some Stratford folk have been to the Sister Cities gatherings elsewhere. There's now a Shakespeare-themed Arts Walk in Stratford, featuring a mix of artistic interpretations and impressions over a mile and a half. I walked it with a mate. We called ourselves the Two Gentleman of Verona.

The most notable landmark in Stratford is the railway bridge over the Avon River. The river here is mostly a mild lamb, meekly limping along the sandy bed of the river, but it can become a roaring lion. Such a time was April, 1990, when flood water came pouring down from the northern mountains. Boisdale was inundated, while at Stratford, the water crest was threatening to spill over the railway bridge. The same thing happened in June, 2007. The Bureau of Meteorology calls them 'one in a hundred years' floods, although in these days of more extreme weather events, I think they need to shorten their expectations.

The old railway bridge has been part of the Gippsland scene for almost 140 years and in 2018 had a Heritage Order placed on it. However, a new rail bridge is being built to replace the old one. Trains gliding over it will be faster and smoother and safer, and Apex Park is to receive a make-over as part of the project as well.

East Gippsland is noted for its many fine old homes. Strathfieldsaye at Perry Bridge is one of these, the original home of William O'Dell Raymond. You can see the pit-sawn timber and hand-made bricks. The old outbuildings also remain in place. Those old squattages were really small towns, providing everything needed for a large number of employees. The gardens include some magnificent trees. One of the old trees – a giant redgum – is known as the Navigation tree. It could be seen from out on Lake Wellington and sailors would set their course by it. The property was in the hands of the Disher family for over a hundred years, until it was bequeathed to the University of Melbourne in 1976. The University has handed it over again, to the Australian Landscape Trust.

The Forest Redgum does very well on the plains north of Stratford. If you drive out on the Briagolong road, you go through the Briagolong Forest Redgum Reserve. At Briagolong you can take a signposted walk through the forest. It's not a forest as we usually imagine it. The trees grow in open formation and the undercover is a mixture of native perennial tussock grasses and other tough grass species, as well as wildflowers like native daisies, lilies and orchids. You can find the same type of country in the Stratford Highway Park and the Fernbank Recreation Reserve. Along the walking track through the Forest at Briagolong you might see brushtail possums, sugar gliders, echidnas, kangaroos, blue-tongue lizards, and red-bellied black snakes.

In the earliest days, Briagolong grew hops and tobacco. They had a factory making cigars. The redgums were chopped down to make blocks to pave Melbourne streets. The yellow stringybarks became flooring for Australia House in London. The Briagolong Mechanics

Institute is built of local redgum. As time passed, Briagolong became renowned for its alternative lifestyles. The residents were progressive, even daring. They built mud-brick houses before they were in vogue. They planted vineyards. They flaunted their culture. I remember one place, its name in bold letters – *Bringyagrogolong*.

Once described as a "bite-sized country village", Briagolong now has over a thousand residents. That's more than Fish Creek or Bruthen or Toora, twice as big as Omeo or Thorpdale. Not that Briagolong has become middle-class respectable, but it may be heading that way. The old pub is still there. It's been going since 1880. Does the Briagolong Bush Band still perform there? They were all the rage twenty and thirty years ago. No show was worth going to unless the Briag Bush Band was to play.

Briagolong has had many notable residents. Perhaps the most famous was Edward Bennett, who lived to be 108 years old and died in 1943. In his younger days, he knew the Kelly family. "There was a lot of cattle-duffing going on at that time," he said when speaking at his 100th birthday party, "and the Kellys were blamed for a lot they did not do." He should know! Ned Kelly was "a decent young man. I always felt sorry he ever went bushranging," he said. Edward Bennett remains a legend, and there are plenty of Bennetts still around. The man had sixty-three grandchildren at the time of his death, and eighty great-grandchildren. I can add another story about him. Unpublished, but I can vouch for its authenticity. I was told by a funeral director who was there. When he was 107, one of his sons died, aged in his 'seventies. At the funeral Mr Bennett stood at the graveside, shook his head, and turned to the person alongside him. "I knew I'd never rear that boy," he said.

Beyond Briagolong we come to Stockdale and then Glenaladale. The original Glenaladale Station was run by Angus McLean and his brother. The McLeans were a notable Gippsland family. Angus wrote books about life in the early days, while his nephew, Allan, became Premier of Victoria. The quiet calm of Glenaladale was broken in 2018 when a mineral sands company proposed to open a mine at the Fingerboards, claiming it could be one of the world's major producers of zircon, ilmenite, rutile, and rare earths. There is strong opposition, reminiscent of the reaction to the proposal to establish a vast granite quarry hard against Mount Cannibal in West Gippsland. The Fingerboards is the junction of the Fernbank, Lindenow and Dargo roads. It's been a focal point for generations and part of the folk lore of the district.

Taking the Dargo road, we skirt the Mitchell River National Park, unless we turn off to visit the Den of Nargun. This a place of deep significance for the Koories, specially the womenfolk. The Nargun, in dreamtime story is a half-human beast dwelling in the cave behind a deep pool on Woolshed Creek. There are walking tracks there and views over the Mitchell River. Close to this spot, in the hotel on the Iguana River, Angus McMillan breathed his last. He was crushed when a pack-horse fell on him while he was in the last stages of constructing the now-famed McMillan's Track from Omeo to Woods Point.

Dargo is famous for its walnuts. The walnuts are still there, and about a hundred residents. The main features of the town are the hall, the store and the hotel, the latter with its name brandished in huge letters on the roof. Tourists now outnumber the locals, which probably means more money comes into the town than goes out of it. That's called running a surplus. Tell the Federal Treasurer!

Beyond here are the Dargo High Plains, renowned in song and story. 'Rolf Boldrewood' described them in one of his novels:

> *Far as eye can reach, a verdurous plain extends – a mountain park, in truth, it may be called, differing from almost any other such formation in Australia. Three thousand feet above the sea, a sheet of snow in the midwinter, it is a prairie waving with giant grasses when remorseless suns are scorching the heart of the continent into barrenness.*

Wonnangatta Station on the High Plains was reputedly the most isolated homestead in Victoria. Now there's only a scattering of stones marking where it stood. It was burnt down, accidentally, by bushwalkers in 1957. The Bryce family ran the property for decades up to 1914. Two years later the unsolved Wonnangatta double murder was committed, when the new station manager and his cook were killed in circumstances that seized the nation's morbid attention. The Guy family took over the lease from the 'thirties through to the 'sixties. I knew Arthur and Agnes Guy later in their life when they had retired into Maffra. Arthur was regarded as one of the finest of Gippsland bushmen. I've heard many stories about his exploits and unerring instincts in the bush.

There's high romance in the stories of the high country. Over at Briagolong, one of the great bushmen was Bill Gillio. His name's written all over the early years of exploration and derring-do in the mountain country from the 1920s onwards. Grazing cattle in the high plains, building log cabins in the snow country, cutting a track into Tarli Karng, conducting horseback tours – it was all in his day's work. There's a photo of him at the Moroka Hut, together with Andy Estoppey, Clive Hodge, and Jack Treasure. What great high-country names! There'll never be their like again. Those days have been magnificently researched and recorded by some fine local historians, like Linda Barraclough. The Stratford Historical Society has produced some splendid material on the early days of the district. I'm hugely impressed and grateful to them and to similar local history groups around Gippsland.

Trafalgar and Yarragon

It's hard to realise it, but of the three towns alongside one another – Yarragon, Trafalgar, and Moe – it was Trafalgar that was cock of the walk right up until the Second World War. In the 1930s, Trafalgar's population was half as big again as Moe's. Yarragon was smaller than Trafalgar, but still larger than Moe.

In a roundabout way, Trafalgar borrowed its name from Yarragon. Yarragon was originally called Waterloo, so when Trafalgar came into existence they could think only that if Waterloo could be named after a famous British land victory, they could name themselves after a famous British naval victory. In those days, the British connection was revered and commemorated. These days we're more likely to brand places with an aboriginal name. Right and proper, too.

At the same time Trafalgar and Yarragon were forming into tiny settlements, Melbourne, so close by, was a bustling metropolis, an international city, while, to the east, Sale was a prosperous, well-established town, with cathedrals, banks, and thriving businesses. West Gippsland was so late in being developed because of the terrain - the dense forest and huge swamps. Between Yarragon and Trafalgar and continuing further east lay the Moe Swamp. The Moe River and Shady Creek drained into a morass covered with reeds and bordered by ti-tree. The reclamation work started in 1888, ten years after the railway came through, and, once again, Carlo Catani, was in charge of the scheme. Twenty-seven lateral drains were constructed, feeding into the main drain, which was the course of the Moe River. On the Willow Grove Road just out of Trafalgar, there's a monument to Catani's work, featuring an embossed portrait and an honour roll of the first selectors. Carlo looks out with a satisfied look on his face over the smiling farmland that he brought into being. With the railway in place and the swamp cleared, Trafalgar and Yarragon began to go ahead. By 1911, there were 1285 people in Trafalgar and 989 in Yarragon.

I believe it's because of its late development – and also because settlement was by small farmers – that West Gippsland is a relatively egalitarian community. There is no wealthy land-holding class, or, to the extent that there is, they have no power politically or in society. There's another side of that coin. Because of the struggle settlers had in establishing themselves, such wealth that was generated was spread over the whole community rather than accumulating in a few hands and being available for larger-scale development. Some have gone further and suggested that this background of hardship and struggle has brought about a less generous attitude in the community as a whole. If this ever was the case, I think it's rapidly disappearing.

Yarragon has the disadvantage of having the highway run through the middle of town, though the commercial development is on the service road, which takes the edge off that inexpediency. The town has gone out of its way to present itself as a place for a stop-over. The advertisers tell us it is 'delightful' or even 'quaint'. It's a 'hidden gem' and is referred to as the 'Village'. All these things are true enough, even if you have the feeling as you wander the streets that you're in a movie set. Writing in another place, I once described Yarragon in lighter vein in these words:

> *Yarragon's the place that everyone takes their visitors to. When you get there you meet all your friends who are taking their visitors there also. So does anyone actually live there? Or is it just a town of visitors? No, there are people who live in Yarragon. I know two of them ... You can walk to the shops. It's got a market once a month ... There's an art gallery in the railway station. Now, that's cute. Though you've got other art galleries if you don't fancy that one. I don't know if they made them do it but most of the shops are the same yellowy-brown colour, so when you think of Yarragon you've got a colour pattern in your head. There aren't too many places like that ...*

Two items that catch your eye as you drive through Yarragon are the Steam Engine and the Rotunda, both beautiful in their own way. The steam engine in glistening black bears the number K183, but there's something of a fraud here, because it's actually engine K162. These K-class engines, K183 in particular, worked their way round these parts from 1922 right through to 1982. If you ever travelled by train from Warragul to Noojee, you were probably taken by one of the K-class engines.

The rotunda is in high-classical form. When the yarn-bombing craze was in full flight some years ago, Judy Bennett organised a lot of people to knit squares which were sewn together to make a huge 'beanie' for the rotunda, which was ceremoniously placed in position. I was there at the hoisting. The beanie was later disassembled into small squares once again. I was rather cut up about that.

Despite Yarragon's charms, it's time to head south through the green uplands of the Strzeleckis to the Mount Worth State Park. Mount Worth itself – the bump in the Strzeleckis we see from all over the place – is not part of the Park, but is private property. The people most associated with that land have been the Hayes and Worth families. The original Hayes was a doctor who used to be in partnership with the renowned Dr Trumpy in Warragul. The Worths are still well represented in the Warragul community.

The State Park came into being through pressure from the Warragul Field Naturalists Club and the Shire of Warragul. Various titles were bought up until the park reached its present configuration. It's just over a thousand hectares in size, and although there have been recent plantings and regrowth, you can get a good idea here of what the pre-settlement Strzeleckis were like There are many tracks to walk on, picnic facilities, and relics of the timber mills that tore down most of the majestic trees to feed their rapacious maw. There are native creatures galore – tawny frogmouths above the ground, tiger snakes on the ground, and giant earthworms below the ground. The Friends of Mount Worth do great work in maintaining and improving the Park. The last time I was there I couldn't find a place to park the car. A local church group was holding its annual outing!

The Battle of Trafalgar was fought on 21 October, 1805. The French and Spanish fleet was en route to take control of the English Channel preparatory to an invasion of England, rather like the Spanish Armada a couple of hundred years before. But the British fleet under Nelson met them off Cape Trafalgar and blew them out of the water. Nelson disregarded accepted naval strategy. Instead of standing off and bombarding the enemy, he formed his ships into two columns and charged straight at them. They won, but Nelson himself lost. As everyone knows, he was shot by a French marksman and died on the deck of the *Victory*. Admiral Cuthbert Collingwood was Nelson's second-in-command. There's a place named after him, too.

The town kicks up its heels every October when the Battle of Trafalgar Festival comes round. And the battle is well-commemorated in the naming of Trafalgar's streets. We have Nelson Road, Victory Court, Neptune Lane (at the Battle of Trafalgar, the *Neptune* was under the command of Captain Thomas Fremantle), and - rather cheekily - Lady Hamilton Lane. Lady

Hamilton was Nelson's mistress. The two government schools feature an idealised galleon on their school crests. The main street, however, Contingent Street, was, I suspect, named for the Victorian Contingent that fought in the Boer War.

On the outskirts of Trafalgar there are three 'top-of-the-class' features that many in the town know little about. The first is the adventure park on Cemetery Hill. (It's a very fine cemetery, too, giving its residents a great view over the sparkling farmland down below). The adventure park is known as the Summit. It's one of the best in the land. Huge numbers of children and youth groups go there to have fun swinging from high wires and crawling through mud. They love it. Develops the character – for those who survive!

The second is the Uralla nature reserve to the south of the town. It's not big, but it's a small world in its own. One minute you're in dry sclerophyll forest, the next you're on a boardwalk amidst the fern gullies. You can park your car there, have a picnic, and take any one of a number of walks, but there are no toilets. 'Toilets are available in Trafalgar, 2.5 km away', the guide book tells you. Very helpful!

The third of these relatively unheralded features is the golf course, on Gibson Road to the north of the town. Some say it's one of the finest courses in Gippsland. I've played here quite a few times. It's hilly but the fairways are wide and you don't lose too many balls.

There's one monster hole on the second nine. Take a packed lunch before starting!

If you leave the golf course, turn into Wheelbarrow Road (!), then north into Willow Grove Road, you'll eventually come to Willow Grove itself. It's another pleasant and well-knit community, though most of the people go elsewhere to work. I know it best through coming along Old Sale Road, so my impression is of a lot of bushland round about, though if you come the more common route, from Trafalgar or Moe, you'll appreciate more the farmland that lies around the town. On the town's doorstep is Blue Rock Lake, or Blue Rock Dam, as most people say. It's quite new, finished in 1984, and supplies the Latrobe Valley with water. It's a popular place for boating and picnicking, though it's most famous for its fishing. Bass is the prize variety, though my fisher-friends tell me that it's not easy going, because the bass like to moon around in the fallen trees and logs near the top end of the lake, so you can lose both your line and your fish if you don't take care. Everybody remembers the tragedy of little Jaidyn Leskie's body being found here, now over twenty years ago, and the public grief that occasioned. The mystery has never been solved.

Further on is Hill End, where timber millers and dairy farmers have struggled over the years. The town was devastated by the Black Friday bushfires in 1939, though there is little evidence of that now. There are not many towns like this where the main street is an avenue of ninety-foot grey gums close in on both sides. Sensibly, Hill End has combined with Willow Grove to form their football/netball team.

Further up the road is Fumina South, now a shadow of its former self. It's described in one place as "an isolated pocket", but the few people who live there might have some words to say about that. Beyond Fumina South you get to Icy Creek, where you can turn left to Noojee or right to Tanjil Bren and Mount Baw Baw. I've driven down this road from Noojee to Willow Grove a couple of times. The air was clear and there was a cold sharpness to the landscape. I can't think of any other road in Gippsland quite like it.

I re-connected with Narracan quite recently. It was after the heavy rains of February, 2020. The water was gushing over the Falls in a three-pronged avalanche, brown as the chocolate soils it flows through, carrying away the rich topsoil to deposit it further downstream. In the Falls Reserve, a plaque stands in honour of the early settlers, notably the Savige family. It was placed there by "their proud descendants". Long may we also remember them! On the far side of Narracan, a winery has been established. The grapes stand out amongst the acres of potatoes.

The railway from Moe up to Thorpdale once ran through here. A glance at the old newspapers shows that Narracan was once a lively and extensive community, but only a shadow of its former glory remains. The advent of the motor car, together with the lure of life in the big smoke – or, at least, bigger smokes – has brought about the winding down of many of our towns. Narracan is still a good place to live. Many of the old family names remain.

Thorpdale is a lot more than a pub, but many people think of the pub when they think of Thorpdale. It was burnt down in 2017, a fire in which the very popular publican, John Bantock died, but was re-opened in 2019. It does dominate the town by its location in the main street if for no other reason. It may not be exactly a bustling town, but Thorpdale always gives the impression of purposeful activity. There's a bakery, a school and kindergarten, several churches, the CFA depot, sports facilities, and businesses linked to trucking, especially of potatoes.

You can't miss the potatoes. Before you hit the town, you see the rolling red-soil hills and all the signs of an intensive potato industry. The welcome sign at the entry to town, proclaims, *Welcome to Thorpdale, Heart of Potato Country*. You're likely to follow one of the potato trucks as you leave town. Every second year, the Thorpdale Potato Festival brings in ten thousand or more people. There are many imaginative events, the best, to my mind, being the 'Hessians on the Field'. It's a great thing that such a small town can put on such a major event. It speaks volumes about town spirit. The most famous name associated with the Festival and with Thorpdale potatoes in general is Val Murphy. She was virtually Thorpdale's

Potato Ambassador to the World. She passed away in 2019 and was given a huge funeral from the Uniting Church in Thorpdale.

The road from Trafalgar up to Thorpdale continues on to Mirboo North. It's a great road to drive, in the daytime at any rate. Wombats and other nocturnal creatures make night driving hazardous. On the way you pass close to the site of 'the world's tallest tree'. You can take that claim with a grain of salt, actually. There's a sign by the roadside to direct you to the spot, and a plaque has been placed at the actual site. The plaque records that the tree was chopped down in 1884, and officially measured by a government surveyor. It stood 375 feet high, 114.3 metres. That's a deal further than a 100-metres running track! I can't say I was particularly thrilled when I stood there. The word is that it was chopped down so it could be measured. That's like the story of the farmer who put a hole in his tank so he could measure how much water was in it.

Traralgon

I lived in Traralgon for a year. It was in the early 'eighties, when Loy Yang was being built. Now it's an aging power plant and people are talking about how long it will go on, same as me, I suppose!

People who don't live there, when they think of Traralgon, think 'Latrobe Valley', and that's unfair on the town because Traralgon's a lot more than Latrobe Valley and brown coal and carbon emissions.

A town grew up here on the sweet waters of Traralgon Creek in the 1860s. Well, that's when the Post Office came, and historians usually measure the origins of a town by when the first Post Office was built. But there were settlers here for twenty years before that – after Strzelecki came through from Mount Kosciusko, discovering and naming places left, right and centre – and the aboriginal people of the Gunaikurnai tribe for aeons before that. The early settlers named the town from the aboriginal language, but they got it wrong, and nobody seems to know what the name, 'Traralgon' derives from in the old language.

They put up some fine public buildings in the early days, but later generations pulled them down, mostly. When will we learn? One of the early buildings that did survive was the Post Office, and it's now the most handsome building in town. It replaced the original one in 1886. When you walk along the street now, you see people sitting on the seats outside the Post Office, and you can see at once the harmony between the building and the people who live in Traralgon. That's what fine old buildings do - they make people feel restful and at home.

I wonder if Sir Frank McFarlane Burnet sat on one of the seats outside the Post Office. I look for him there every time I go past. Mac Burnet, as he was known to his friends, lived here in Traralgon for the first ten years of his life and went to school here. He was the second oldest of seven children, but didn't have a particularly happy childhood, not because of Traralgon, but because he didn't like his father very much, and his mother couldn't give him much attention because one of his younger sisters was quite severely disabled. Outstanding people often have a difficult childhood. Perhaps it's because they need to prove themselves, whereas those who are more content as children tend to just go with the flow, so stay with the herd throughout their lives.

Anyhow, Sir Frank was an outstanding scientist in the field of immunology, chiefly. We all live safer and healthier lives because of him. He was Australian of the Year, won the Nobel Prize, and was a Knight of the Order of Australia. There have been only fifteen Knights of the Order of Australia, and two of those are Prince Philip and Prince Charles, and they don't really count. What I like best is that Sir Frank did nearly all his work in Melbourne at Melbourne

University and the Walter and Eliza Hall Institute. No brain drain there!

I seem to be dwelling on Macfarlane Burnet, but I must add one more thing that took my fancy. I recently came across a letter he wrote to his fiancée when he was twenty-seven. He was in the depths of a London winter and she was in sparkling summer, visiting the Burnet family in Traralgon. The letter brings both him and his old town into personal focus:

> *Traralgons a pleasant spot isn't it and for all its untidiness the house and grounds are rather nice. Didn't you like the view up to the Callignee hills along the creek? I'm looking forward to a wander around Traralgon with you Linda. It's a particularly attractive place to me from the fact that I left it when I was 10 or 11 and didn't return for 10 or 12 years then only occasionally so that all my memories are the romantic ones of a small boy not overgrown with those of growing up. ... I'd love to show you where I once caught an eel in my hand where I used to catch mussels by pushing a reed into their open mouths in the mud of the creek bottom.*

It's comforting to know that even Nobel Prize winners may not be on top of their punctuation! And do the small boys in Traralgon still catch eels in the muddy creek bottom?

I once asked a group of people from Traralgon if they knew of any famous people from their home town. It wasn't necessarily a statistically valid survey, but, from memory, out of ten people, two said McFarlane Burnet, one said Peter Siddle, and one said Michael Voss. For the uninitiated, Peter Siddle is an Australian cricketer who has taken 200 Test wickets and Michael Voss played football with Brisbane. Peter Siddle is a vegan and eats fifteen bananas a day. Some say he does that to make the ball bend. He was born in Traralgon, but grew up in Morwell. Michael Voss was born in Traralgon, but grew up in Orbost. I think it's legitimate to claim them both for Traralgon.

I remember when I lived here that we had a long drive to the railway station – across the line and about half a kilometre further on. About twenty years ago, they did a brilliant thing. They built a new station on the other side of the tracks, and, hey presto, there it was on the highway, right in the middle of town, really. It's part of a shopping complex, so you can do your shopping while you're waiting to meet the train. I had a coffee there not long ago, waiting for a train. There's a roundabout at Traralgon so they can turn the engines round. When the steam train A2 986 came from Melbourne to Warragul a while ago, it had to go all the way on to Traralgon to turn around.

Many people drive out to the Loy Yang Power Station just to marvel at the place. They've got places where you can have a close look. Coal goes in one end and electricity comes out the other. It sounds simple, but it takes all those machines and all those wires to do it. The chimneys are a quarter of a kilometre high! Think of the men who built them. Not for me, thanks!

The road goes on through the Strzeleckis to Yarram, but if you turn off before Loy Yang you get to Traralgon South and Callignee. It's very pretty country, and a lot of people build their houses to take in the view. The fires raced through here in 2009, and, sadly, several people died. One man lost his home a few days after he'd finished building it. It had taken him two years to build. Undaunted, he set straight in to build again, this time making it as fireproof as human ingenuity could make it, recycling as much as he could from his first home. It's called the Bushfire House; I remember seeing something about it on TV. The blackened trees stand on all sides, but the green shoots are everywhere. They're a sign of the spirit of the people not to be overwhelmed by their tragedies.

I know the northern side of Traralgon better than the Strzeleckis side. Driving out from town heading for Glengarry you cross the Latrobe River that we first met at Noojee. Since then it's done its work in the power stations and now flows rather the worse for wear out onto these flatter regions. If you had your bike, you could ride out to Glengarry on the rail trail. You'd think that Glengarry would be like a suburb of Traralgon, being so close, but, in fact, it's one of the proudest and most independent places I know. It used to be called Eaglehawk and then La Trobe (watch the spelling, please – two words), but when the railway came through they went for

'Glengarry', which Angus McMillan had used for the Latrobe River. So the names were turned around. The river Glengarry became the La Trobe, and the township La Trobe became Glengarry.

A lot of people drive right past the town without seeing it at all. What a pity! There are several beautiful old homes and public buildings in Glengarry, and some very handsome trees. And the town is nicely laid out. A developer wants to put in a huge subdivision here in Glengarry, though the locals are fighting against it. The blocks are too small, they say. How is it that these developers have the first say in land development proposals? Any development should be worked through with Council while it's still on the drawing boards, it seems to me. As it is, the locals – and the Council - are always on the back foot. More regulation, less free market, I say, and we'd all be happier.

The Glengarry Hall is superb. It became very run down, but a few years ago the people here had a drive to restore it. They got financial help from different sources, but it's a good story of local voluntary endeavour. The Anglican Church was built by John King on his own land, but was later moved into the town. It's built from local red gum. When the flu epidemic struck after the First World War, the services were held on the grass outside the church to lessen the chance of infection. Every Anzac Day, they used to cart the organ up to the War Memorial for the services there. The old butter factory still stands. For a while after it closed it was used to make wine for the Narkoojee Winery. A lot of people who come this way these days are headed for the good food and wine at Narkoojee at Glengarry West. The name comes from the aboriginal word for 'place of flowers'.

On to Toongabbie. Sounds Scottish, but you'd be barking up the wrong thistle. The other Toongabbie, the one in New South Wales, one of the earliest settlements on the continent, is an aboriginal name, or that's what Governor Phillip heard when he asked. This Toongabbie has a superb turf cricket pitch, which seems out of place for a little place like this, but all the more credit to the people who keep it up. In the old days, Toongabbie was a jumping-off place for the gold fields of Walhalla. They could get supplies to Toongabbie by road and later rail, but it was work for mules and pack-horses from there on over the rough tracks into Walhalla.

The man who found gold at Walhalla was an ex-convict, Ned Stringer. Poor old Ned made no money from his discoveries, and died soon afterwards here in Toongabbie. There's a memorial to him in the town with a very imaginative inscription: *'Here lies he who sought the Midas seam, where Valkyries played hosts beside his crystal stream in the valley of the ghosts.'* In Norse mythology, the valkyries were female figures who chose those who were to die in battle and those who would live. They brought those who die in battle to the hall of the slain, Valhalla, ruled over by the god Odin.

Very poetic, though I doubt old Ned would understand the reference.

Across to Tyers, which is about as far from Traralgon as Glengarry is. This is more of a dormitory town for its big neighbour, and it's got fewer shops and services than Glengarry or Toongabbie. But there's one thing they're very proud of, and that's that one of Australia's most important naturalists lived right here in the town. Over seventy years, living quietly in her lovely garden, Jean Galbraith wrote beautifully and tenderly about the things about her. I've seen the notebooks she kept when she was just a girl, where, at thirteen, she wrote pieces like this:

> *After we left the road the ground was almost purple with pink bells, the two species growing together all very beautiful. It was broken everywhere with clustering bushes of small leaved parrot pea. The heath itself is a broad stretch of white, broken by a very narrow winding path of White titree and great masses of White Heath while the pink and white velvet flowers (Styphelia) grow in beautiful sheets.*

Meredith Fletcher has written a book about Jean Galbraith, *Writer in a Valley*. You should read it. When Jean was still at school, she rejected the offer to finish her schooling in Melbourne. She said she would only be half a person in the city. Well said! Miss Galbraith went on to become one of Australia's most influential botanists and writers on native plants and gardens. In some of her writings she used the pen name, 'Correa', and since I learned this I've planted correas and come to love them. You try it. They do well in Gippsland!

Back now to Traralgon. The first settler here was Edward Hobson. He was commemorated in recent times by a psychiatric hospital on the southern edge of the town. That was broken up with the trend towards de-institutionalising, and they have a psychiatric ward in the new hospital instead. The new hospital – the Latrobe Valley Hospital - was built on the main road between Traralgon and Morwell. The old building was pulled down and houses built where babies were once born and surgeons did their work. The new hospital is so big you need a bicycle to get around the long curving corridors.

The Latrobe Valley Hospital employs hundreds of men and women, but it's the paper pulp mill out of town at Maryvale that has been the big economic driver of Traralgon. It exports huge amounts of paper products. You see the long trains taking them down to the docks in Melbourne. In 2015 they started recycling waste paper and cardboard. I suppose you've got to balance the harm done to our native forests by logging against the good the mill does through its recycling. But there's no gainsaying the contribution the mill has made to Traralgon and the wider region. There are 900 workers on site and another 2300 are in flow-on employment because of the mill. $450 million flows into the Gippsland economy every year through the Maryvale mill.

Traralgon was home to a remarkable father-and-daughter team of civic officials. Walter West was Secretary of Traralgon Shire for ages and a Member of State Parliament in the 'twenties. But he was outshone by the community service of his daughter, Eva. Eva West was one of the first female accountants in Victoria. She was in private practice in Traralgon before joining the Shire Council, rising to become a long-serving Shire Secretary like her father.

Miss West was a member of more than twenty local voluntary organisations, though her main passion was for the welfare of girls. She had a lot to do with the Girl Guides and also with St Anne's School in Sale. The government recognised her work with the award of an MBE. In 2018, her name was posthumously added to the Victorian Honour Roll of Women. The Latrobe City Council offers a scholarship in her name, worth $3000, for girls who want to study business and accounting at university. Maybe there'll be a statue of her in the main street one day.

Walhalla

One of my treasured possessions is a booklet called *The Switzerland of Australia: Views of early Walhalla and district*. It's a reprint of the original 1910 publication. There are dozens of superb photographs and paintings of the town when it was a seething beehive of industry, where thousands laboured and lazed, lived and loved, most of them in the noonday of their lives.

The rise and fall of Walhalla can be briefly told. Ned Stringer and his three companions found the first traces of gold in what is now Stringer's Creek in 1862. A rush began, but the alluvial gold was soon exhausted. Deep lead mining began the next year after John Hinchcliffe noted an outcrop of auriferous deposits on the near-vertical hill above the creek. The most famous of the many companies that exploited the hidden wealth were the 'Empress', the 'Walhalla' (this is where the town got its name), the 'Long Tunnel' and the 'Long Tunnel Extended'. Cohen's Reef became the richest gold reef in Victoria. The Long Tunnel mine reached 3,675 feet into the bowels of the earth (that's 1.12 kilometres), and at that point the miners were actually three-quarters of a kilometre below sea level – in Walhalla!

Walhalla was in its heyday in the first decade of last century. The *Cyclopedia of Victoria* published this description of the town in 1903. It's reprinted in my little booklet:

The township is situated in the bend of a narrow valley, and the feet of the circumscribing mountains on either side approach each other so closely as to leave just space enough for a brawling stream to delve its channel in, with here and there an occasional widening out of the valley just sufficient in area to afford room enough for the erection of quartz-crushing mills, stores, cottages, three places of worship, a State School, a couple of banks, half a dozen hotels, a Mechanics Institute, three halls, and the public offices incidental to a municipal township which is the chief place of a shire covering an area of 409 square miles, and containing a population of about 3,500 souls, of whom nearly six-sevenths are concentrated in the town itself, the only other places in the shire being the small townships of Aberfeldy, Bluejacket, Donnelly, and Toombon.

I wish you could see my prized booklet. Some of the photos and paintings pull at the heartstrings. There's one of a boy about ten years old, on his pony, delivering milk from his home in Moondarra to Walhalla. He's leading a pack-horse with two cans of milk strapped either side. He did this every morning before school. Probably milked the cows as well! Another shows the funeral procession of a prospector. His coffin is strapped in ungainly fashion to the side of another pack-horse, being led by the funeral director on his horse. There are no mourners. Another photo is of Walhalla's 'Mountaineer Brass Band' – nearly thirty of them in their crisp new uniforms. They used to play in the rotunda on Saturday evenings for the late-night shoppers. Another shows five locked cases of gold stacked on the footpath outside the Bank of Victoria, about to be placed in the four-horse wagon to be taken down to Moe. The police guard on their mounts are at the ready. And on the much-celebrated cricket ground there stands Warwick Armstrong, Australia's test captain, at first slip, arms folded, even as the bowler delivers the ball. He's never going to take that catch!

Walhalla folded almost as quickly as it grew. In 1911 the Long Tunnel Extended mine closed – just the year after the railway reached Walhalla! In 1914, the Long Tunnel itself shut down. The newspaper followed. Public offices shut their doors. Houses were removed to other locations. Some were burnt down for the insurance. Fire destroyed some of the remaining buildings. Floods ruined others. In 1954 the last train left for Moe. The school lingered on until 1965.

The latest census records twenty permanent residents, although many more come at weekends, and thousands of tourists each year. Many are attracted by the chance to tour the Long Tunnel Extended mine, others by the restored railway that runs from Walhalla to Thomson station through the Stringer's Creek gorge. Thompson Station is where the line crosses the Thompson River. You can scramble deep down into the gully and take a photo of the train, high up, crossing the bridge. They've done the tourist thing well, those Wallhallorans! We like to take our English visitors there, but try to avoid the weekends and holidays!

Walhalla is not the end of the road. If you're game enough and have the right vehicle, you can get up along the east bank of the Thomson Dam to what is known as the Toombon Historical Area, along Donnelly's Creek Road. People do live here, and others come to take in the historical features. There are ghost mining towns like Toombon itself, Goonan's, and Jorgensen. If you stick close to the Dam, you get to Aberfeldy. On the way you pass Kitty Cane's grave. It's said that Kitty owned a sly-grog tavern here in the 1860s. When she died, her customers began to carry her the many miles to the Aberfeldy cemetery. She weighed twenty-two stone, however, and it was too much for the pack-horses and the grog-affected bearers. So they buried her here. It's a lovely spot. I'm sure she'd like it.

At Aberfeldy we're in seriously cold country – 1060 metres above sea level, as compared with Walhalla 360 metres. It's another gold rush town, now greatly diminished. A fire that started at Aberfeldy in 2013 caused much anguish. It resulted in a man's death as far away as Seaton and destroyed twenty-two homes. The cemetery here has been lovingly cared for. In fact, if you want to appreciate the history – and the beauty – of this district, you could well make a tour of the cemeteries. The Cemetery Trust at Aberfeldy also looks after the cemeteries and burial grounds at Toombon,

Donnelly's Creek, and Edwards Reef. They are all beautiful places. In 2007, fire swept through Toombon and Edwards Reef. Because the covering scrub and litter was removed, the unmarked graves in both these burial grounds could be discerned. Now, with the help of some 4-Wheel Drive clubs, they have been marked out with white stones, set amongst the open bushland. It is a very moving experience to walk through these places

Pushing on, you can get to Matlock and Woods Point. The gold relic towns of Jericho, Red Jacket, and Blue Jacket are off the track. I have done this road in a 2-wheel-drive car, but don't recommend it. It's doubtful if we're still in Gippsland, anyway. We've come to the Shire of Mansfield and the Electorate of Indi. Matlock has fallen away to near-zero population, while Woods Point is a shadow of its old self. The northward-flowing Goulburn River flows through Woods Point. We're definitely beyond our Gippsland limits!

Heading back from Walhalla, we're in more familiar territory. Rawson is close to where the road from Moe turns off eastwards towards Walhalla. That junction is Parker's Corner. If you claim to know anything at all about this part of the world, you'll let 'Parker's Corner' slip from your tongue without explanation, and everyone will understand that you're fair dinkum! Rawson is like Yallourn in being a town planned from the beginning, though on a much smaller scale. The town was constructed from 1977 onwards to house workers on the Thomson Dam. This is one of the biggest infrastructure items ever undertaken in Victoria. It accounts for 60% of Melbourne's water capacity. Water from here flows to the Silvan Reservoir for distribution to the suburbs. The Dam has had its highs and lows. During the Millennium drought, it fell to 16% capacity. In 1992, 1993, and 1996, it was full, though that was partly because water was sourced from elsewhere to allow the Thomson to fill up.

Rawson has become a permanent settlement. The hostel buildings left from the workers' accommodation have been well put to use. 'Rawson Village' offers accommodation for small and large groups as well as families. Church groups use it, as do university groups, and sports groups. Some organisations have conferences here. Up to 300 at one time can be catered for. There are onsite activities like a ropes course and climbing wall, and outside attractions too, such as canoeing, mountain biking, and tours of Walhalla. It sounds like a scaled down version of a Billy Butlin holiday camp!

Erica is a timber town. In January, 1939 it suffered badly from the fires that swept across southern Australia. The town was ringed by disaster for days before the fatal Black Friday. I've been reading the telegrams received by the Age on 14 January that year. They make horrific reading:

> *1.50 p.m. Erica now menaced on all sides by 50 miles' hour gale; temperature 103; all available men fighting onrushing flames ... situation looks desperate many places; women*

and children leaving mills in attempt to reach safety. 2.30 p.m. ... people close to town have left; heat terrific and wind fierce ... train from Moe not through; this message written by lamplight so black here owing dense smoke. 3.05 p.m. lurid glare all directions ... believed 25 Greeks trapped at White Hills; no news other mills ... reported P.O. at Moondarra burning; Ingram's mill property burned; all people at Tyers Junction safe, where all are in river; 3.50 p.m. ... flames now on top of town from west; 4.39 p.m. women and children have been sent from town to ploughed clearing half mile from township; terrific gale blowing, intense heat. 5 p.m. ... now every man for himself; all praying.

The town survived. We speak glibly of the events of that time, and casually mention the death toll. However, reading these telegrams makes us realise what it was like for people to live through those terrifying times. Think of the people making decisions; think of the mental damage to people; think of the individual acts of bravery, now passed into the shadows of history.

Nowadays people who go to Erica have other things on their mind. They're on their way to the snow fields to the north or to the mountain bike trails close to the town. The Australian Four Day Enduro motorcycle championship was held at Erica in 1987 and was due to return there in May, 2020, coronavirus pandemic permitting. With the approval of DELWP and Parks Victoria, the event is held along trails in the State forest. Erica is also the nerve centre of the Country Fire Authority in this district. New and expanded facilities were built for them some few years ago. And there is an Erica SES unit based in Rawson.

The store is the centre of activity in Erica. You can stock up with snow gear, including wheel chains, as you pass through. People talk about the meals at the hotel. They have a hot rock menu, which means you can have your rump steak cooked on granite rocks. No fats or oils. Every last bite is as hot as the first. Or so they say. However, one of the most delightful places in Erica is the cemetery. Hidden away in the forest just south of the town, it's the perfect place to take a rest if you're passing through – a short rest or a long one.

Erica is named from Mount Erica, and Mount Erica is named from the native flower. Most people call it heath. The pink heath, *epacris impressa*, is Victoria's floral emblem. Our heaths appear shyly in the bush in winter and lighten up the bush with their pink or white or red bells hanging demurely towards the ground. There are also several introduced species of erica that are environmental weeds. If left, they will form into clumps and cover the ground, killing off more delicate species like some of our orchids. This is a threat in scattered parts of Gippsland, particularly in the west.

There's a track to the top of Mount Erica, though you get the best views by following the track a little further on. You can drive up the mountain as far as the Mushroom Rocks. If you haven't been to the Mushroom Rocks, you must go. They're in my Top Ten of Gippsland experiences – huge rounded granite boulders, clustered together, looking not unlike a herd of sleeping elephants. They stand silently and eerily in the bush. I keep expecting them to wake up and silently go stalking off down the slope. You might have seen photos of them. Nothing, however, can match being there amongst them.

At Tyers Junction you'll find a scout camp, Caringal, very well equipped and open for anyone to visit or camp. It's a stunning place on the Tyers River. For the stout-hearted and strong-booted, you can walk in from the main road. The beauty of this is that you're walking along a rail trail, though this is no ordinary rail trail. It's one of the old tram tracks that wound its way through the forest bringing logs down to the Walhalla - Moe train line in pre-war days. In your imagination you can hear the bullocky's cries and curses as he urges his team along with its heavy load. It would be only in your imagination, because this line was actually served by a small steam locomotive operating on a 2'6" gauge!

In 2017, an elderly woman camping at Caringal lost her way in the bush. She was found the next day by search parties including a Bush Search and Rescue team. BSAR is a volunteer organisation that has been involved in a number of searches in our high country. Praise be to them … and the Police and SES. They are our security blankets.

Moondarra is closer to civilisation, if you define civilisation as supermarkets and steakhouses. Moondarra is listed as a "locality", though it has had its glory days. It's best known in connection with the Moondarra Reservoir and State Park. The Moondarra Dam was completed in the early 'sixties. It's a smaller cousin to Blue Rock Dam on the other side of the range; Blue Rock contains nearly seven times as much water. Blue Rock is on the Tanjil River while the Moondarra Dam is on the Tyers. The township of Gould was covered by the waters of the Moondarra Reservoir. There was once a school and a hall and railway stop here, though the town was rather a spent force at the time it was flooded. The Moondarra State Park was proclaimed in 1986. You can drive in, and most days you'll have the place to yourself. One visitor said it felt like you were in your own private garden, but with someone else to do the work.

Warragul

Two or three years ago, someone wrote about the town of Warragul:

> *One of the best things about Warragul is its shape. You can hold it sideways and you've got these wavy up-hill and down-hill contours. You can look down on it and it puffs out equally in all directions like a nice bulgy cauliflower from Lean and Green. There's a nice balance between the two sides of the railway line, north and south. And above all, the streets go in interesting lines.*

Despite the flippant language, these things are largely true. Warragul is a compact town. There's no part of it where you feel you're out in the boondocks, and this promotes a feeling of community togetherness. It's a hilly town, and as a result most people have some sort of elevated view over the town and perhaps out to the Strzeleckis or to the mountains to the north. Unlike several towns on the main line, Warragul is not divided by the railway; three crossings within the town make it easy to get around, and there's no obvious social cachet according to whether you live north or south of the railway. And the layout of the central shopping area is visually pleasing. It really is a shopping *centre*.

Warragul is shaking itself free from its rural beginnings, though the process has not been easy. The disused butter factory close to the centre of town remains an eyesore, while the saleyards, also quite close in, are sentenced to be closed down in the near future. This has occasioned much angst. The saleyards are redolent of an era close to the hearts of most of us. To many they bring back memories of the Thursday market day in olden times when people came into town in their trucks or their jinkers, the women to shop and the men to stand around at the cattle yards in solid male companionship. Large numbers of cattle still pass through the yards. However the die is cast. New yards are planned for Longwarry, alongside the highway, where business will be done more efficiently, but at some cost to human wellbeing.

Like so many of our Gippsland towns, Warragul is growing at a fearful rate. People complain that good farming land is being eaten up and that the infrastructure needed to properly cater for the population growth is not being developed.

There are two ways to look at these problems. The first is to look beyond our own scene. We can't avoid the surge in development. We all benefit from the economic growth of the State of Victoria, which is the basis of the splurge in population. Melbourne grows by 1500 people every week, and the government actively pushes people to the regional areas for the good of the whole state. Yet it's a pity to give up our rich red soil to housing estates. I suppose this has been in process since the first subdivisions were made over a hundred years ago. And as someone from Warragul said to me,

'There seems to be a lot of good farming land still there'. At least we're more sensitive than we once were about preserving wooded and wet areas, and I think the Shire Councils here and elsewhere are now more alert to environmental issues. The question more is whether the State protocols our Shire Councils have to work under are sufficiently protective of the best interests of the community. We need to keep working at it!

Perhaps the best feature of Warragul is Civic Park. Originally the park was on the southern side of the railway, alongside Hazel Creek. Carlo Catani, the man who was in charge of draining the Koo Wee Rup Swamp, helped plan the gardens there. However, the site was always too low-lying, so in the 1920s the Shire wisely sold the land and bought ten acres between Albert and Clifford Streets. It's a perfect site, close to the town and next to the Arts Centre. The tree plantings and open space have been kept in balance. Every time I go there I see people enjoying it, and the children's playground is superb. I know two people who said they'd come to live in Warragul because of the Park.

Once a month a market is held in Civic Park – a produce market all year round and an arts market during the six warmer months. I don't know why they can't have the arts market outdoors all year round. Perhaps arty people are more susceptible to the cold. Community markets have become part and parcel of local life. I'm sure it's the same all over Gippsland, but within a stone's throw of Warragul, there are markets at Drouin, Rokeby, Jindivick, Noojee, Hill End, Longwarry, and Yarragon. Warragul's and Drouin's are on the same day! You may pay more than at Coles or Woolworths – or even Aldi's – but you get things straight from the grower, hormone free, and you get to meet the grower into the bargain. As for the arts market, the stall-holders are allowed to sell only their own creations. Meeting the maker is half the fun.

Another fairly recent development in town life is the proliferation of opportunity shops. In Warragul there are now six that I can think of. In England they call them charity shops, but in hard-headed Australia we're more interested in the bargains we can get than the charity we might be supporting. Hence the name they get here. The prices they ask are ridiculously low – and even so they have half-price sales every now and then. Once you step inside, it's hard to resist the 'opportunities'. They come at you in all sorts of ways. The best sign I've seen went like this:

> *The item you saw today*
> *And want to think about tonight*
> *Will be sold later today*
> *To the people who saw it yesterday*
> *And thought about it last night!*

Speaking of proliferation, the next award goes to the coffee shops, with hairdressers close behind. I heard a theory recently that, just as in the old days there would be a pub every fifteen miles because that's how far a horse and dray could travel in a day, so now there's a coffee shop every hundred yards because that's how far a man (or woman) can travel on one cup of coffee. Might be something in it. As for hairdressers, at least I can see some logic in their being so thick on the ground. I read that on average a woman has her hair done every six weeks. In Warragul there are, let's say, 5000 women, grown women. That means that, with each salon open for thirty days in a six-week period, the number of women needing their hair done each day is 166.66 repeated. With emphasis on the repeated. You can carry on with your own calculations after that, but it adds up to an awful lot of hairdressers being needed. If there's a downturn in the economy, Warragul will be very hard hit. But not the opportunity shops!

Warragul won the Victorian Premier Town award covering the period 1970-73. That award has now morphed into the Tidy Towns awards. In the early days, the Tidy Town awards had to do with things like litter collection, but now they lean more towards environmental matters and sustainable practices. Since the start of these awards in 1983 only three Gippsland towns have won - Maffra in 1989, Lakes Entrance in 1995, and Moe in 2008, and none of these went on to win the national award. My take on these awards is that the winning towns deserve huge accolades, but they may not reflect the ongoing tidiness and sustainability of these places, but rather the enormous campaigns that have been mounted to work towards and win the title. That comes from real local spirit, however, which is the more important aspect of the process.

Warragul has a host of things to brag about, like Farm World at Lardner Park, and Flavorite's huge glass-houses producing tomatoes, capsicums, cucumbers and eggplant, the biggest such plant in Australia. Then there's the Two Towns Trail between Warragul and Drouin, the Linear Trail along Hazel Creek, the readily-available health facilities, the new mega shopping precinct on the edge of town, the wide spread of schooling opportunities, the Warragul Show, the sporting facilities, the shows put on at the newly-refurbished Arts Centre, and the old streetscape of Queen Street (with a fine statue of Lionel Rose in the park opposite).

But there are two things that people who live here most value. The first is the beauty of the countryside – the rounded green hills and the fine vistas of distant mountain scenery. The second is much more practical. It is easy to get to Melbourne either by the duplicated freeway into the heart of town or the hourly train service to and from the city ... and nearly everyone needs to go to Melbourne from time to time.

Nilma was originally called Bloomfield. As with Warragul, the railway brought it into existence. It now lives in the shadow of Warragul, but has its own long history. The great founding industry of Bloomfield was timber. Timber, urgently needed for building the city of Melbourne during the boom period of the 1880s, was carted to Bloomfield railway station for transport to the metropolis. The mills then were built in the bush, close to the stands of timber. The milled timber was brought to the railway in horse-drawn tram wagons. Mike McCarthy has written about these things in his book, *Settlers and Sawmillers*. In one of his maps, you can see the network of tram tracks spidering in from the bush to the Bloomfield railway station during the 1880s. Other towns on the railway line, Warragul amongst them, acted similarly as feeders for the shipment of timber.

Many of Nilma's old buildings have now gone. In the age of the motor car, the proximity to Warragul proved too much. The butter factory went ages ago. The railway station was closed in 1950; the old churches have been closed; the Post Office is gone; the hall and some houses were pulled down when the highway was widened. Of the public buildings, only the school still flourishes.

The historic land routes through Gippsland all run east and west. The first and most important of them was the Old Sale Road. It still exists, though wrongly sign-posted in parts and a shadow of what it once was. Before the advent of the railway, it was the principal land route into Gippsland for passengers and goods. Cattle, sheep, and horses were driven along it. Bush pubs beaded it together. The settlements of Brandy Creek and Buln Buln lie on the old road.

In the 1870s Brandy Creek was 'no mean city', with stores, post office, hotels, churches, banks, and settlers' cottages. The reports of the grand future opening up spread around the globe. Brigham Young, the leader of the Mormon Church, wrote from Salt Lake City enquiring about the possibilities of settling his family there. But the grand future evaporated when the railway came through five miles to the south. Brandy Creek remains a quiet hideaway, much loved by its ninety-six inhabitants.

Buln Buln has 550 residents. Its history is similar to that of Brandy Creek. Flourishing in the pre-railway days, it lost out to the railway towns, and now remains a quiet residential outpost of Warragul. It has grown partly because Warragul folk who thought they were being crowded out moved out to the quieter backwaters of Buln Buln. Some thought it too quiet and moved back into town. There was a joke going the rounds at one time that the furniture removalists of Warragul spent half their time moving people out to Buln Buln, and the other half bringing them back in. The last store closed some twenty years ago, but there's a church and a football ground. The town fields football, netball, and cricket teams. And the school has 180 students, some of them from beyond the town. 'Buln Buln' means 'lyrebird' or 'place of the lyrebird.', but the only lyrebirds to be seen there now are on the school logo.

Buln Buln East is a distinct locality further to the east along Old Sale Road. It once had a church, school, and tennis court, but all have passed into memory. However, a local body of enthusiasts helps to keep alive a feeling of community togetherness.

Further from Warragul lie Rokeby and Crossover, both on the main road from Warragul to Noojee and Mount Baw Baw. Rokeby's monthly market attracts hundreds of followers, many from Warragul and Drouin. It takes place on the Rokeby Common, one of only three commons I know of in Gippsland. Here at Rokeby a rail trail begins, running all the way to Neerim, following the track of the railway that once ran from Warragul to Noojee. The trail passes by a unique architectural structure, the Rokeby Trestle Bridge, which once carried trains forty metres over a deep fern gully. A local group is working hard to restore it.

Crossover is now less of a settlement than Rokeby, but in 'the roaring days' it was the scene of mighty gold works. The Happy-Go-Lucky mine first mined gold here in 1868. Soon 300 miners were working the reef, both quartz and alluvial workings. There was money made at Crossover, but it was never the Eldorado the first miners were hoping for. Some colour still shows up in the area, and I myself have come across a few grains out at Buln Buln East. Some of the old-timers tell me they've made handy pocket money in the same area.

There are other satellite towns to Warragul on the other side of the line. Well, perhaps not towns. More 'localities', though 500 people are listed as living at 'Ellinbank and Environs'. There's a public hall, a church, a school, and a football ground … and a huge Dairy Research Institute. They Institute has 500 cows in their own herd, so they should know what they're talking about. Much of their work centres on pasture improvement and animal nutrition. The institute contributes a good deal to the local economy, but keeps a low profile in the community.

According to the census, there are forty-seven families in Cloverlea, and sixty-five private dwellings. Seems they spread themselves well out there. Cloverlea, like Ellinbank, is very pleasantly placed in the lower foothills of the Strzeleckis. The school here was shut down some years ago. The children have the option of travelling to Ellinbank or Bona Vista, or further afield to Darnum, Nilma, or Warragul. Beyond Ellinbank and Cloverlea, we're getting into the Strzelecki hill country. It was said about these parts that the cows had two legs longer than the other two … or were they talking about the people from up there?

Wilson's Promontory

Is this really part of Gippsland? I thought Gippsland was rolling hills and green valleys. But here we have the smack of the surf and the salt wind and rocky headlands. The rest of the Province has been tamed and tidied, but we're looking at a raw and ancient landscape. We wouldn't be surprised to see a group of the first inhabitants step from the scrub, the men holding their spears and the women their fire sticks and grinding tools.

This is Bunurong territory, though it's often spelt in other ways, mostly 'Boon wurrung'. They were part of the Kulin nation, and roved over these southern shores for thousands of years. They had a sophisticated legal and regulatory system, and entered into guarded treaties of understanding and trade with their neighbours, though this sometimes spilled over into warfare. I've heard it argued that these people were amongst the most technologically efficient people on the earth's surface, because their use of resources was perfectly balanced with the resources available to them. They practised sustainability naturally and unconsciously, while we stick our necks in the sand and pretend we can go on in the same old destructive way, raiding the non-renewable resources of our finite earth.

George Bass, with six others, sailed past the Promontory in a whaleboat ten years after the first British settlement in Sydney, and noted the 'high hummocky land'. He reached Western Port, turned back, and put into Sealers Cove. This was the first official landing on the Promontory, although there were almost certainly sealers camped here beforehand, and American whalers, too.

The first detailed charts of the Promontory were made by Captain James Grant in the *Lady Nelson* shortly afterwards. Of the three great names in the story of Bass Strait exploration - Bass, Matthew Flinders, and James Grant - only Grant had a happy ending. Bass turned to trading and sailed off to South America. His ship was lost with all hands. Flinders was detained in Mauritius by the French for over six years, and died soon after he got back home. Grant, however, completed his service in the British navy and died at a respectable age. He was in the colony for only twelve months.

There is some uncertainty about the naming of the Promontory. The most likely is that it was named for Thomas Wilson, a London trader who was well-known to Matthew Flinders. Wilson conducted some trade with New South Wales, but never came here.

But I don't want to speak only of the people. It's the land that captures the imagination, though there's a harmony between land and people here at the Prom that's achieved perhaps more than anywhere else in Gippsland. I suppose that's made easier by the fact that the only place you could call a settlement is Tidal River, and that's more a base for tourist activity than a town in its own right. The Promontory is now a reserve, 50,000 hectares in size. That's nearly 200 square miles for us old timers.

Bass, as we mentioned, saw 'high hummocky land' here. A hundred years later, and a bit more, Nathan Spielvogel came to teach at Foster. In his book, *The Gumsucker at Home*, he wrote, 'Looking south I saw Wilson's Promontory like a crouching lion, far more imposing than Gibraltar'. There are no lions in the Park, but you'll find kangaroos, wombats, emus, and echidnas, land birds like rosellas, and sea birds of many kinds. And penguins, though you'll need to go out in a boat to one of the small islands off-shore to get your best view of them. On the beaches, you need to watch out for the hooded plovers. They scrape their nests in the sand above the high tide mark. They have problems enough with feral cats and dogs and foxes, without human agencies as well. In spring, native flowers sprinkle the scene with colour – orchids and wattle, for instance – and flowering shrubs like mangrove and coast banksias and, my favourite, correas. Those who know the water more than the land would want to add the variety and beauty of the life you find beneath the waves. There's a separate Marine Park here that goes for miles along the coast. It's about one-third as big as the National Park itself.

Fire is always a threat to the Prom. The biggest and most recent fire started on the eighth of February, 2009, which Victorians will quickly identify as the day after Black Saturday. It began with a lightning strike and burned out half the Park. Tidal River was saved, just! The Australian bush regenerates amazingly quickly, and so it was here. The Park is almost back to what it was. And you can't burn the rocks and the beaches!

People who know the Prom well will return again and again to their favourite spot. Some go for the seclusion of Whisky Bay, and many go on from there to Picnic Bay. Children like to have fun in the rock pools. You get the combination of river and beach at Darby Beach. You can surf at Norman Beach, and catch some stunning mountain views as well. But most people, especially first-comers, head for Squeaky Beach. They play around the boulders and scrape their thongs on the white sand to catch the squeaks. I'm always amused and impressed by the way particular places grab hold of different people. I had a friend who came to the Promontory every summer of his adult life, where he'd sit beside Squeaky Beach and read Daphne du Maurier's *Rebecca* from beginning to end. We all need our rituals!

Oberon was King of the Fairies, and Titania was the Queen. Most people know about them through Shakespeare's *A Midsummer Night's Dream*. They fight a lot, and at one stage, Oberon gets Puck to give Titania a magic dose so that when she wakes up she will fall in love with the first thing she sees. He then arranges for that to be a donkey! Well, I've asked everyone who might know how it is that Oberon (Mount Oberon and Oberon Bay) and Titania (Titania Creek) are commemorated here at the Prom, and no one can tell me! Sure, Wilsons Promontory is a magical place, but rather too much made of earthy things like rocks and sand to be the stuff of dreams or elfin imagination. Did the early settlers, as they eked out their difficult existence, have Shakespeare in their minds all along?

Everybody wants to climb Mount Oberon, and it's not difficult to do. From the car park, you can be at the summit in an hour, and back in less. But you'll spend more time at the summit, blown away, if not by the wind, by the views. The islets off the coast look like slumbering whales, and are they the outer islands of the Furneaux Group in the distance? The Furneaux Islands are part of Tasmanian territory.

Wilsons Promontory is the southernmost place on the Australian mainland, and the lighthouse (or, officially, the 'lightstation') is the southernmost point of the Promontory. It's a wild romantic place because of its superb location and stunning vistas, but also because it's so isolated. You have to leave the motor in the car park and walk – for two days, for many people - to get there. Then you walk back again, though you can stay in one of the cottages alongside the lighthouse if you book ahead. While most Victorians were going mad about gold in the 1850s, convicts were building this lighthouse. They didn't have to go far for the raw material. They found a vein of beautiful stone amongst the bulbous granite tors which are scattered around like giants' marbles. It's an interesting reflection to put alongside each other the brutal convict system on one hand and the natural things of this place on the other, and the resulting construction of a building of beauty and utility.

A friend of mine came from these parts – Fish Creek, actually. His name was Terry Synan, and he made a special study of the Promontory during the Second World War. I've been reading his material. Hundreds of Australian and New Zealand commandos were trained at the Prom during the earlier years of the War. They made a significant contribution in the Pacific Theatre. The isolation and challenging terrain made it an ideal location for training. Today's idyllic places, like Lilli Pilli Gully and Tidal River and the Lighthouse area were then centres of tough military exercises. The concrete blockhouse they built is now an observation place for looking out over the Strait.

Many of these men were fated to fall captive to Japanese forces. In June, 1942, over 1000 prisoners-of-war were being transported to a base internment camp on the vessel Montevideo Maru when it was torpedoed by an American ship unaware that prisoners-of-war were on board. All the men died, including 133 of the former Wilsons Promontory commandos.

But the Prom played a wider role than training the commandos. Early in the War, a Signal Station was set up alongside the lighthouse. It played a key role in seaward defences at a time when German raiders were laying mines and sinking shipping along the strategic Bass Strait sea route. Later in the war, a highly-sophisticated radar installation was established here. Others were at Gabo Island, Metung and Cape Otway. Meanwhile, at nearby Yanakie, an aerodrome was built, like the ones at Mallacoota and Bairnsdale, to guard our shores.

Back to Fish Creek. Some people call it the Gateway to the Prom, but I like to think of it as a town in its own right and with its own special character. It's become a hub of communal and artistic activity. A couple of years ago I arrived in town one Saturday morning to find the streets crowded with laughing and chattering people. It was one of the happiest scenes I've ever come across. It turned out that I'd landed in the middle of a festival they share with neighbouring Foster. No parochialism here! They have a Tea Cosy Festival in May each year! The town itself has got a lot going for it. Those who speed by towards the Prom miss it by a whisker. How many treats we miss out on in the hurry and scurry of modern life because we haven't got the time to turn aside! The Fish Creek pub is a revelation. Built in 1939 out of the ashes of the former building (how many of our Gippsland pubs *haven't* been burned down?!), it's totally Art Deco, with a huge sculpted fish fixed on the roof and hanging out over the street. What a hoot! It's the work of Colin Suggett, who hails from Venus Bay along the coast a bit.

South of Fish Creek, on the road to the Promontory National Park, lies the small township of Yanakie. Here the land narrows before widening into the Promontory itself. Yanakie is on the eastern side of the isthmus and Sandy Point on the western. Yanakie offers attractions in its own right – fishing, boating, and even camp drafting in season – but makes much of its location a mile or two before you enter the Park. There are a number of accommodation options here, and you can stock up with food and fill up with petrol before entering the wilderness. The last glimpse of civilisation! You can see the Toora Wind Farm from Yanakie, just in case the natural world proves too much altogether!

If we follow the coast westward from the Promontory, we come to the deep indentation of Waratah Bay, and then Cape Liptrap juts out into Bass Strait like a miniature Wilson's Promontory. Waratah Bay is fringed with wide, sandy beaches. The shellfish here were a major food source for the aboriginal people. Middens still to be seen attest to that. Some are shown to be 6,000 years old.

Waratah Bay is named after a vessel, the *Waratah*, which put in here to effect some repairs. This was not the famous *SS Waratah*, which disappeared between Australia and South Africa without trace with 211 people on board in 1909 – one of the great tragedies of the seas – but a previous and much smaller vessel that put in here in 1850 to repair a damaged rudder. Waratah Bay, the town, is maybe unique in that it's a town without shops. What peace! By comparison, Sandy Point is quite a metropolis. The population of three or four hundred blows up like a balloon in holiday times when all the holiday homes, otherwise empty, come to life.

Windsurfers come from all over the world to Sandy Point to ride the winds on Shallow Inlet. It's not actually 'windsurfing' they're after, but 'speed sailing'! I don't claim to know much about this sport, so I'll let these enthusiasts explain it for you:

> *As storm fronts race through Bass Strait, they get compressed against the Wilson's Promontory hills causing them to accelerate across the spit, creating a laminar air flow. This produces the cleanest wind at the water's surface, without any chop. With the right gear and experience, 40 knots of board speed can be had in 30 knots of wind*

Walkerville and Walkerville South complete the trilogy of small holiday townships fronting Waratah Bay. You walk from one to the other over a high, windy bluff. These cliffs are made of limestone and were once mined intensively. At the peak of production in the 1890s eighty men were employed and a busy settlement grew up, all to be abandoned when production ceased in 1926. Quicklime was produced in the six kilns, while the stone itself, for building, was also shipped out from the jetty. The ruins here are a reminder of Gippsland's largely-forgotten coastal industrial history.

Walkerville is hard up against Cape Liptrap. Cape Liptrap is the second-southernmost point on the Australian mainland, next, of course, to Wilson's Promontory, but further south than Cape Otway. The lighthouse on the Cape was built in 1913, much too late to prevent the wreck of the *Nautilus* in 1856. The *Nautilus* was wrecked here when it ran on to the sandy shore. Three crewmen walked to Port Albert to report the wreck, arriving in a parlous state, and were at first taken to be escaped convicts from Van Diemen's Land. The captain had stayed at the wreck with the one passenger. They were eventually reached by a rescue vessel. The wreck was covered up by the shifting sand and lay forgotten – for sixty years - until 2015, when a storm uncovered it. Some nautical archeological studies were swiftly conducted, revealing her to have been a two-masted schooner.

The Cape Liptrap Coastal Park runs westwards from the Cape. You can camp at the Bear Gully (koala bears?) camping ground and take the twenty-kilometre hike along the Cape Liptrap coastal walk. It sticks close to the water against high limestone cliffs, black in colour where air pollution has dissolved the lime to create a hard gypsum crust covering the softer limestone. If you do take the walk, be warned: in places it's right on the waterfront. You may be stranded at high tide!

Wonthaggi

I don't think the people of Wonthaggi see themselves as I see them. They think of themselves as ordinary Gippslanders, but from my point of view, Wonthaggi is unique amongst our Gippsland towns. No other town has the same mix of location, history, tragedy, government involvement, and recent development as Wonthaggi has. I'll try to unravel these elements.

It's a great place to have a town – close to the sea so you've got beaches and camping places on hand, and the celebrated moderating effect of the ocean, so it's warmer in winter and cooler in summer. Besides that, you can get to Wilson's Promontory in one direction and Phillip Island in the other without too much trouble, and yet you're not on a main highway, so you don't get the through-traffic that is bothersome in other towns. I like the way the streets are laid out in the middle of town. It reminds me of Warragul. Anything to avoid a single linear string of shops. Next time you're in town, call in at the tourist information place. There's an excellent art gallery there as well. It gets my vote as the best tourist information centre in Gippsland.

In a way, Wonthaggi is a planned town, not unlike Yallourn or Rawson. There were people living here in the late nineteenth century, but when the State government opened the Coal Mine in 1909, Wonthaggi as a place name and as a town was born. Up till then the Victorian Railways brought their coal – black coal - from

New South Wales. In 1909, a long strike occurred on the NSW fields, which meant that our railway system was on the verge of collapse, and that would have meant disaster for the State. So the black coal of this area, which had been mined in a spasmodic way for decades, was hurriedly opened up and hugely expanded. Men came from all over Australia to find work here, but most were from Britain. It was mining in the classic British manner – poppet-heads, deep shafts, long lateral tunnels, pit ponies, and canaries to gauge the health of the underground atmosphere.

There's quite a story to the beginnings of the South Gippsland coal mines. William Hovell of Hume and Hovell fame had much earlier noticed some coal at Cape Paterson, but that was never followed up. However, when Victoria separated from New South Wales in 1851, the government was keen to have its own coal supply. Accordingly, they offered a prize of £1000 to anyone who could prove a commercial field in Victoria. Richard Davis, a Cape Paterson man, dug up fifty pounds weight of the 'black gold', put it in a sack, and carried it on his back to Melbourne. It took twelve years before his reward was paid, but at least he was given interest on the capital!

The coal mine remained a State enterprise rather than a private enterprise, which is another connection with Yallourn. But the government was not necessarily a better master. Conditions remained very difficult, and accidents occurred far too often.

Eighty men died in accidents over the course of the fifty-nine years of the mine's operation. The worst disaster was in 1937, when a match lit by one of the men underground caused an explosion in Shaft 20 that killed all thirteen men there. All were married and most had come from Britain. There was continual industrial strife in the mine. The militancy of the Wonthaggi miners helped bring about better conditions in mines across the whole of Australia.

Today, if you're looking for reminders of the coal-mining days you don't have far to go. In the middle of town stands the Workmen's Club, a direct descendant of the Club formed in 1911 by the miners, though it has had several incarnations due to the frequency with which it was burnt down. The present building has you walking into a foyer which is a reproduction of a poppet-head and proceeding through an entrance set up just as the mine shaft entrances were. As reproductions go, these are as authentic as you can get, though you're conscious of the rattle of poker machines not far away.

The story of the Wonthaggi Coalmine stirs the blood. There's something romantic, yet infinitely tragic, about the whole enterprise. The miners themselves and their families then and later have glossed over the deep hurts they have carried in the way those who suffer have done since the world began. But the reality is conveyed in many forms, not least by Andrew Reeves in his book, *Up from the Underworld*. The artist, Noel Counihan, came to live with the miners and went into the pits. "I crawled wherever they crawled." he wrote. "The length of timber needed to prop up the ground, we'd call the roof, were only eighteen inches long". Counihan did a series of compelling drawings and linocuts that tell of the miners' unyielding determination and bitter experience that no words could equal. Yet alongside their pain went a superb spirit of togetherness that their Union managed to catch and contain. Some of Counihan's linocuts are in Andrew Reeves' book.

The great observer of the Australian way of life, Wendy Lowenstein, wrote a book about the struggles of the Wonthaggi coalminers, *Dead Men Don't Dig Coal*. It was the basis for the film, *Strikebound*, made in 1984. Earlier, in 1934, another great Australian, Jack O'Hagan, the man who wrote 'On the Road to Gundagai', wrote the song, 'There's a Part of my Heart in Wonthaggi'. Leigh Moran sings it:

> *There's a part of my heart in Wonthaggi,*
> *And it's calling me, calling me, home.*
> *Skies are blue, hearts are true, in Wonthaggi,*
> *And when I get back there no more I'll roam.*
> *When I walk down the street, all my pals I will greet*
> *On that same old corner where we used to meet.*
> *There's a part of my heart in Wonthaggi*
> *And it's calling me, calling me, home.*

Maybe that same old corner was outside the Wonthaggi Hotel where they've put up the jawbones of a huge whale that was washed up on the beach in 1923. Opposite, in the park, from the mine tower that's been erected there, the blast of the old mine whistle is heard at twelve o'clock each day. That whistle used to control the lives not only of the mine workers but of the whole town. When I was there just a few months ago, a woman near me turned round viciously as the blast sounded, and swore. 'Bloody stupid!' she yelled. Some people have no soul!

They do serve water in the bar of the Workmen's Club if you ask for it, but if it's water you're after, you need to drive out a few kilometres to the Desalination Plant, where you can have 150 billion litres of drinking water each year if you're really dry. Wonthaggi is seldom out of the news – ABC TV gives you the weather for the town each day for a start – but the Desal Plant put Wonthaggi in the national headlines for years on end. It began when someone in the government noticed that Victoria's reserve water supplies had fallen from 97.8 per cent capacity in 1983 to 28.7 per cent in 2007, and that our warming climate boded ill for the future. It seems that nothing makes a government less popular than a shortage of water, not even a shortage of beer, so the plans for this Desal Plant were put in train. It's finished up nestling into the coastal strip there so that you hardly see it, and there are trails and wetlands surrounding it.

Unluckily for the government, the rains came before the project was finished, and our storages filled up once more, so that the completed water factory was something of a white elephant, worse even than the pink variety that sometimes appear in the Workmen's Club. It costs every Victorian, man, woman, and child, twenty-one cents a day just to maintain the operation in stand-by mode. Nevertheless, it's good to think that we've got this plant set aside for a rainy day! And climate change isn't going away. The wind farm almost alongside the Desalination Plant is a reminder of that.

One of the unfortunate but unavoidable truths of country towns is that locals who come to fame seem to live out their lives in pastures far distant. I'd like to put a stop to that. It could be done by government decree (everyone declared to be famous must return to the town of their origin on reaching the age of fifty) or by economic pressure (every famous person is relieved of paying income tax if they return to their home town). A list of famous Wonthaggians, not drawn up by me but by someone with an eye to more recent times, includes Jarryd Blair and Trent West, footballers, Darren Berry and Ian Harvey, cricketers, while on the less physical side of fame, there are James Mollison, AO, who was Director of both the National Gallery of Australia and the National Gallery of Victoria, James Phelan, who writes thrillers and Young Adult books equally prolifically, and Angus McLaren, best known to TV audiences as Nathan in 'Packed to the Rafters'.

Wonthaggi goes in for big things – coal mines, wind farms, desalination plants – and on my recent visit, for the next big thing I headed out to the RACV resort, not at Wonthaggi, but at Inverloch, which is either an outlier of Wonthaggi or a fiercely independent town in its own right, depending on who you're speaking to. I can't help seeing the resort as an outlandish monster invading this primeval place. Where our indigenous forebears combed the inlets and beaches for their fare, visitors now sip their lattes served on a tray. It's one of our modern problems: how to balance giving people the chance to enjoy our superb wildernesses on one hand and preserving them and their native creatures from spoliation on the other. Suffice it to say that other places, in the Northern Territory and Queensland, have done it better than we have in Victoria.

Inverloch itself is a pretty seaside town. If you picked it up and put it on the east coast of England it wouldn't be out of place. Or maybe on the west coast of Scotland, for that's where the place got its name. Lochinver in Scotland became Inverloch in Victoria, presumably because on the underside of the world you have to turn the place names round the other way to keep the world in balance.

The first place to go to in Inverloch is the Shell Museum, where they also keep dinosaur bits and pieces. The first dinosaur bone to be discovered in Australia was found at Eagle's Nest near here more than 100 years ago, and they're still turning up. Two schoolboys found a Qantassaurus claw in 2015. The Dinosaur Dreaming project, however, has been moved from Inverloch to the Otways. I guess that's because the last dinosaur in these parts was heading west when last spotted.

The name, 'A'Beckett' is found throughout Victoria and especially Gippsland. The clan developed from Sir Thomas A'Beckett, who was Chief Justice of Victoria. One of them, a grandson of Sir Thomas, played Test cricket for Australia. Another was a leading man-about-town in Bunyip, where a street is named after him. So, too, here in Inverloch, where the A'Becketts were leading citizens and landholders in the early twentieth century, and where the main street is named A'Beckett Street.

It's an odd thing about us Australians. Our traditions are based on the bush, yet we rush to the beach as often as we can. There are miles of beach down here. Williamson's Beach, near the Desal Plant, is the best known, though it may be a bit rough for the children. It's best on a winter's day when the westerly is whipping up the waves and the coast takes on a savage and more primitive look.

A lot of people like to look at the water rather than get into it. These are the bike-riders and walkers. Many of the cars heading for the coast have a couple of bikes attached at the back. They're heading for the Bass Coast Rail Trail most likely. I don't want this to sound like a tourist brochure, but it's hard to avoid it. You can ride right beside the sea on your bike, or even on your horse if you'd prefer. The Trail finishes at the Woolamai Racecourse, so the horse may be more appropriate. Nearly twenty kilometres of Rail Trail … and then the George Bass Coastal Walk starts at Kilcunda and takes you into San Remo. Gippsland is famous for its trestle bridges, and you'll find one of the best at Kilcunda, where the Trail takes you over Bourne Creek forty feet above the ground and right above "the crashing waves from Bass Strait" (that *is* from the tourist brochure!) The trains stopped in 1978. What a sight it must have been for the passengers as they passed over the bridge!

Cape Paterson is a few minutes' drive from Wonthaggi. Its modest population expands enormously in the summer holidays. Some locals get away for the season. You'll find them all over the place. I bumped into two Cape Paterson refugees in the middle of the bush, camped at the Hawthorn Bridge on the Latrobe River at Neerim East not long ago. Nowhere less like Cape Paterson could be found!

Cape Paterson was once a shipping point for black coal in the days before the State Coal Mine was established. Some ruins of that mining activity remain to be seen. Nowadays, it's the blue water rather than the black coal that attracts (and brings in the money). I see there's an innovative project underway to develop an 'eco-village' here at Cape Paterson that will have low-density spacing, low-carbon construction building materials, 10,000-litre rainwater tanks at each unit, solar panels, electric vehicle charging points, and a host of other environmentally-sound features. It's the way of the future, though such developments are likely to be introduced piecemeal rather than brought in intact, as with this development at Cape Paterson.

I was once having a meal in Kilcunda when I bumped into Norman Yemm. You'll remember his name and his craggy features from the TV series he starred in – Homicide, The Sullivans, Number 96, and others. You may not know that he sang with the Australian Opera Company (and in musical comedy) before taking up acting, nor that he was a gifted athlete. He won quite a few races at Stawell and played football for Port Melbourne. An all-round man! Well, the point is that he and his twin brother, Gordon, started at Warragul High School the same day as I did. Gippslanders all! Gordon, by the way, has been a notable flautist, performer and teacher.

Yarram

When the first white explorers and settlers moved into these parts they found an open, park-like country, not unlike an English pastoral scene. Just think gum trees instead of oaks. We now know, through the research of people like Bruce Pascoe, that it was because of the careful nurturing of the land by the first people, including managed burning, that gave this result.

We've got a good picture of those early days of settlement from the book, *The Pioneers*, written by Katherine Susannah Prichard, who worked in Yarram as governess to the doctor's children when she was a young woman. She writes of escaped convicts from Van Diemen's Land living here, hiding from the authorities, and also of the large volume of wool and cattle shipped out through Port Albert. *The Pioneers* won a world-wide literary competition run by Hodder and Stoughton and brought the author world-wide fame. The book was the first Australian novel to be made into a film. Katherine Susannah Prichard went on to a colourful career. She married a VC winner, Jim Throssell, and was a foundation member of the Australian Communist Party.

Yarram does not dominate the local region as most Gippsland towns do. Yarram has 2168 residents, while Alberton has 260, Port Albert 270, Robertson's Beach 360, Tarraville 360, Welshpool 331, Won Wron 192, and Devon North 478. Because of this spread of settlement, the district has kept more of a nineteenth-century character than perhaps any other part of Gippsland. The town once bore the name, Yarram Yarram, but that was officially changed in the 1920s. Collectors now look out for old envelopes bearing the 'Yarram Yarram' stamp.

The people of Yarram are very proud of their town. I visited the town again recently. The main street is very impressive, especially when you consider the size of the town. The star attractions are the stately Regent Theatre and the Old Court House, both in the main street. Nearly all the old places are in the main street! The Court House, which must be one of Gippsland's finest buildings, has become a Visitors Centre, though the Regent is still a picture theatre as well as a venue for the performing arts and all kinds of live shows. I wonder if *The Pioneers* has ever been shown here. I walked to the northern end of Commercial Street, which is a regular Church Row. Only one church door was open.

I headed out of town to renew my acquaintance with Port Albert. These are very historic pathways. Port Albert was once the undoubted 'capital' of Gippsland. Before any road or rail connection to the metropolis, Gippsland's only connection was by sea, and this was the port through which all traffic passed, human, animal, and agricultural. The port was discovered when the *Clonmel* was wrecked in 1841. The *Clonmel* was a brand-new steam-driven paddle steamer. She drove onto a sandy island off Port Albert at full speed. The passengers and crew all got safely ashore, together with supplies and material for shelter, like in *The Swiss Family Robinson*. But how to get help in that isolated place? A party of seven set out in the ship's whaleboat for help, and after surviving several near-disasters were picked up by another vessel and delivered to Melbourne. The whole party was eventually saved, and in the process the port here and the surrounding promising country were discovered. By coincidence, Angus McMillan and his exploring party arrived at Port Albert almost at the same time. Of course, the whalers and sealers had known every inch of this coastline, but they were uninterested in the hinterland.

Port Albert is very mindful of its historic past. There are many old buildings like the 1856 store, now serving fine foods, and the Bank of Victoria (1862), reincarnated as a museum. Then there's the Derwent Hotel, built in 1858, and the Old Post Office dating from 1864. We know this building well, as it's now a private home, and we used to visit friends who lived in it. Port Albert is one of our most picturesque towns. Quaint old buildings – genuinely quaint and old – nestle alongside modern suites and studios designed for holiday-makers.

There are two women I particularly associate with Port Albert, one real and the other a figment of the imagination. The real one was Agnes Buntine, who drove a bullock team on the Port Albert to Walhalla Goldfields run. She was known and feared all along the track. One old timer remembered her in these words:

> *Those days I had my own bullock team on the road. I used to meet Agnes Buntine often, yarn with her, and share each other's tobacco. She smoked an old black pipe – and plug tobacco at that. ... Anyhow, she did a man's work, so why shouldn't she smoke a man's pipe? Aye, but she could drive a team of bullocks as good as any bullock driver in Gippsland. The way the bullock wagons went from Port Albert to Walhalla must have been 80 miles or more. The journey took many days, eight at least. At night Agnes Buntine used to roll herself up in a blanket and sleep under the pole of the waggon.* (From Tom McDonald, in 'Trove')

The other woman was dubbed 'the White Woman of Gippsland'. In the 1840s people came to believe she was living with a local aboriginal tribe, perhaps against her will. The papers all over Australia were full of the tale. One story had it that she was a survivor from the wreck of the *Britannia* further along the coast. The government sent search parties to look for her. Messages were left for her in the bush:

> *WHITE WOMAN! –There are fourteen armed men in search of you. Be cautious, and rush to them when you see them near you. The white settlement is towards the setting sun.*

At one point the aborigines promised to return the woman. The appointed time came, expectation was at fever pitch, and the aborigines appeared – carrying the wooden bust of a woman, the figurehead from the *Britannia*! So much for inter-racial language understandings! There seems little doubt that the woman never existed.

Because of the early settlement of the district, there are a number of historic sites from Port Albert to the mountains and along the coast. Gippsland's first church, Christ Church Anglican, is at Tarraville. The walls are of sawn timber, two inches by nine. The uprights are slotted and the cross beams and plates are mortised, so it is built without a nail in it. The name, Tarraville, comes from the Tarra River, and that name comes from Charlie Tarra. Charlie Tarra was Strzelecki's native companion on his 1840 pioneer journey through here. Charlie is said to have saved the party from starvation by his skill in catching native animals. In the 1850s, Tarraville was the largest town in Gippsland, flourishing on the track between the coast and the goldfields at Walhalla and Omeo. Ada Crossley, the contralto, was born in Tarraville in 1871. She toured triumphantly around Australia, then in South Africa, America, and in England. Five times she sang before Queen Victoria in command performances. She also sang at the memorial concert for the sinking of the *Titanic* in 1912.

Alberton is famous for having State School No 1. In the whole of Victoria! But wait a minute! It's simply that when the schools were numbered in the 1860s, Alberton was top of the list alphabetically.

The most famous student to attend Alberton School was John Mulvaney. Mulvaney became the foremost archaeologist in the country. Indeed, he's labelled 'the Father of Australian archaeology'. It was he who established that aboriginal settlement in Australia could be dated back tens of thousands of years earlier than had been previously thought. That resulted from the finding of indigenous remains at Lake Mungo, and it's a curious coincidence that the other figure involved in the finding and identification of Mungo Lady and Mungo Man was Jim Bowler, who grew up just out of Leongatha.

Near here, in 1843, occurred the most infamous of all Gippsland's massacres. Ronald (or Ranald) McAlister, a member of the prominent pioneer family, was killed by blacks, and a reprisal party, generally known as the Highland Brigade, set out to punish them. They met up with some aborigines camped at Warrigal Creek. What happened is best described by an early anonymous writer:

> *The brigade coming up to the blacks camped around the waterhole at Warrigal Creek surrounded them and fired into them, killing a great number, some escaped into the scrub, others jumped into the waterhole, and, as fast as they put their heads up for breath, they were shot until the water was red with blood.*

Angus McMillan was a member of this and other parties engaged in killing blacks. There are eighteen memorials to McMillan scattered throughout Gippsland, and many people want them removed. Most Gippsland aborigines are remarkably generous in their feelings about the treatment of their ancestors. "I think the first thing for Gippsland is to acknowledge that it does have that history … instead of masking it," one of one of their elders, Doris Paton, has said. "And when Gippsland comes to terms with what happened, there's an opportunity to talk much better about that history."

Heading north into the hills from Yarram you come to Devon North. Curiously, there's never been a 'Devon'. Still we have 'Devon North'! Settlement here followed the old pattern – first discovery, then the squatters, followed by the selectors, then, in the 1880s and early 90s, the development of facilities like the school, the Post Office, stores and churches. Dairy-farming and timber-milling were the mainstays of the district. In the great epoch of railway building, a line was put through from Yarram to Won Wron, via Devon, in 1923, then in the great epoch of railway closures, it was dismantled thirty years later.

Won Wron itself is on the Hyland Highway, which sweeps round the eastern edge of the Strzeleckis. Most people associate Won Wron with the prison that existed here in earlier years. It was a minimum security detention centre, and we'd often hear of inmates who'd run away. No harm came of it, to my memory. The prisoners were taken to work on forestry and public works projects. Every Easter, there was a fun-run held there for children's charities. They called it 'Prisoners on the Run'! When the place closed in 2004, it became an indigenous rehabilitation facility. It helps men on community correction orders prepare to take a fuller place in society, and is properly called 'the Wulgunggo Ngalu Learning Place'.

It's a beautiful drive from Yarram through the Tarra Valley to Balook. I won't speak of the attractions here because they're so well catalogued in the tourist literature – the Grand Ridge Road, the Grand Strzelecki Track, the Tarra-Bulga National Park, and other things. Balook was once called Bulga. Like most country towns, it was once a grander place than it is now. Seventeen men who had been pupils at the School served in the First World War. I'm always amazed at how little places like this sent its men to fight for a mother-country so far away and so outside the ordinary experience of those who enlisted. The old Balook post office was a tiny building. The name, 'Balook' on the front took up almost all the width of the building.

I've dwelt quite a lot on the history of this area around Yarram. It can be argued that this is where the real history of Gippsland began. To the east, settlement was by squatters, who developed little princedoms around their holdings. But here, at Yarram and Port

Albert and the surrounding country, it was the small man – the fisherman, the farmer, the timber-cutter, the postmaster – who opened up the region, and it was this kind of development that became the continuing history of Gippsland as a whole.

Amongst the pioneers were the churchmen and their families. Take, for instance the Reverend Willoughby Bean. No, it's not the name of a coffee shop in Sydney. Willoughby Bean was the first resident minister in Gippsland, a true pioneer. Listen to his description of the voyage from Melbourne to take up his appointment in 1848, travelling in the bark, *Colina*:

> *There were 21 souls aboard and we were pressed into a space less than my family and I occupied on the voyage from England. [We spent] a dreadfully uncomfortable night, partly on deck and partly in a closely confined cabin, offensive from the smell of bilge water ... Next morning, we awakened after a sad night ... and found that we were driving before a terrific gale with such a thick mist and gusty rain that we could scarcely see from end to end of the vessel. All the passengers but myself in a sad condition of seasickness and distress. The hatches being insecure, consequently the rain poured down on the poor children ... After a dreadful experience of storm which lasted for nine days, when the anchors were lost and the vessel was almost wrecked off Port Albert, the Custom House boat put out*

> *from Port Albert (five miles distant) and after a perilous sail, the passengers were landed at Port Albert.*

Bean subsequently settled on the Tarra River between Tarraville and Alberton, but his work took him over most of South Gippsland and further afield – to Orbost, Omeo and Moe, and all the intervening country. The war historian, CEW Bean, was a great-nephew.

The churchgoers were also pioneers! Albert Clark, who wrote about the early church days of Gippsland, reminds us of this:

> *It sounds so easy to say services were held, but one needs to remember that in those days it meant a rough journey through dense bush; through beaten boggy tracks instead of over made roads, and they probably travelled on horseback or in drays or spring carts; it cost some effort to go to church in those days. Maybe because of this they received more blessing!*

In this vein, let me finish with a story. One of the early clergymen became lost looking for the place where the service was to be held – out at Lower Bulga. It was a roaring hot day, and when he eventually found the place, his tongue was sticking to the roof of his mouth. He was "drier than the Mallee in drought". He was relieved to find his host brought him a huge bowl of fresh water. He immediately drank the lot. "What," the man said, "ain't you going to baptise the baby?"